THE FICTION OF JOSEPH HELLER: AGAINST THE GRAIN

Also by David Seed

THE FICTIONAL LABYRINTHS OF THOMAS PYNCHON

The Fiction of Joseph Heller: Against the Grain

DAVID SEED

Lecturer in English
University of Liverpool

St. Martin's Press   New York

© David Seed 1989

First published in the United States of America in 1989

Printed in Hong Kong

ISBN 0-312-02795-8

Library of Congress Cataloging-in-Publication Data
Seed, David.
The fiction of Joseph Heller: against the grain/David Seed.
p.   cm.
Bibliography: p.
Includes index.
ISBN 0-312-02795-8 : $35.00 (est.)
1. Heller, Joseph–Criticism and interpretation. I. Title.
PS3558.E476Z88   1989
813'.54–dc19   88-30844
                                                     CIP

To Nana

Contents

Acknowledgements

The author and publishers wish to thank the following publishers for permission to quote from the works of Joseph Heller: Simon & Schuster Inc., A. M. Heath & Co. and Jonathan Cape Ltd. for the extracts from *Catch-22* (U.S. copyright Joseph Heller 1955, 1961); Alfred A. Knopf Inc. and Jonathan Cape Ltd. for the extracts from *Something Happened* (U.S. copyright Scapegoat Productions Inc. 1966, 1974); Jonathan Cape Ltd. for the extracts from *Good as Gold* (U.S. copyright Scapegoat Productions Inc. 1976, 1979); Transworld Publishers Ltd. and Alfred A. Knopf Inc. for the extracts from *God Knows* (U.S. copyright Scapegoat Productions Inc. 1984); the Putnam Publishing Group for the extracts from *Picture This* (U.S. copyright Putnam, 1988). The author would also like to thank the librarians of the following institutions for their assistance: Columbia University, University of Texas, Princeton University, Brandeis University and the American Academy. Thanks must also go to the following individuals for their help: John Barth, Victor A. Berch, Edward J. Bloustein, Anthony Burgess, Patricia A. Cone, Bernard R. Crystal, John Delany, Daphne Dorman, Mary-Elizabeth Gifford, Debra L. Hammond, Cathy Henderson, Kit Hume, Nancy Johnson, Tracey Jordan, Robert Merrill, Brian Nellist, Bernard Oldsey, John Pinsent, Steve Roberts, Mrs. A. Rowland, Gaynor Shutte, and Mike Woolf. The author acknowledges with gratitude the financial assistance he received from the British Academy, which greatly facilitated the completion of this study, and also the patience of Joseph Heller in answering queries and his generosity in granting access to and permission to quote from unpublished materials. Finally the author wishes to record his gratitude to his wife Joann for her unwavering help and support in writing this book, which is dedicated to her.

Introduction

One year after the publication of *Catch-22* Joseph Heller made the following statement in the course of an interview: 'There's more cant and more hypocrisy and more hollow rationalization being directed at humanity than ever before ... so that Americans can still talk of this as the land of liberty, the land of freedom and democracy, while at the same time they are trying to cope with many widespread problems arising from the exhaustion of opportunities and the severely limited freedom of each other...'.[1] Into this gap between public rhetoric and national reality Heller brought his comic methods to bear, methods which thrive on disparity and incongruity. James Nagel, the leading Heller critic, related the humour of Heller's first novel to the tradition of Juvenalian satire which mounts an 'attack on the basic principles and fundamental order of society'.[2] The notion of attack is pointedly relevant not only to *Catch-22* but to each of Heller's subsequent works where the projected images of patriotic obedience, professional and domestic success, political achievement, and pious submission become the targets of those works' ironies. As in the early works of Bruce Jay Friedman, Philip Roth, and other novelists loosely referred to as black humorists, Heller has regularly constructed adversarial fictions which are deploying caricature, parody and other tactics against the public values of contemporary American life.

Heller's creative energies were released when he discovered how Nabokov, Céline and Waugh could successfully mix the comic and the tragic together in order to gain startlingly grotesque effects. Bearing in mind that Heller has been repeatedly described as a comic novelist, it is crucial to record his declaration that 'humor doesn't represent a value in itself, but it helps in determining a set of values ... Humor can be very instrumental in helping to keep things in perspective'.[3] Heller is careful to deny that his is a vision full of metaphysical gloom. On the other hand humour in his works regularly sets up a tonal tension between a comic manner and the themes of death, abandonment and betrayal. The comic release of laughter is complicated by misgivings over the subject's accessibility to comedy. So when Yossarian acts the part of a seriously wounded airman in *Catch-22* the scene immediately

1

exposes the desire for administrative convenience, but then draws the visitors into bizarre collusion since their desire to see their wounded son 'coincides' with what is easier for the hospital authorities.

When Heller was defending *Catch-22* against an attack from Jean Shepherd, he implicitly aligned himself with Swift in rejecting the proposition that satire should be objective and impartial:

> I do not think, in fact, that it is the function of satire to present all sides of a question; that is the function of David Susskind and Section 4 of the *Sunday Times*. I'm not sure, even, that it is the *function* of satire to convey information, but, instead, to convey an attitude *about* information, and it may be that satire can only be successful in situations where both the information *and* the attitude are already shared by the satirist and his audience.[4]

By distinguishing between his own practice and the methods of journalism Heller neatly sidesteps the anxiety expressed by Nathanael West, Roth, Friedman and other American novelists that they cannot rival the bizarre actuality of the American press. And as a consequence Heller places his own satirical method at the farthest remove from reportage (he has declared again and again in interviews that he has no talent for description). Satire and satirical comedy should by his account comment on information and in his fiction he regularly establishes perspectives which will facetiously or ironically undermine the implicit solemnity of his ostensible subjects.

Authority in itself is regularly questioned in Heller's works and so any scenes containing references to the legal system take on a symbolic value. At one point in his career Heller was involved in a scheme to produce a musical about the notorious New York law firm from the turn of the century, Howe and Hummel. Heller's task was to produce the script which he duly did, although the work was never performed.[5] He did not himself choose the words, nevertheless this work does shed light on his own fiction. Howe and Hummel are blatant con-men trapping their clients in a heads-I-win tails-you-lose double bind very similar to *Catch-22*. When the lawyers are discussing their fees with a client, Hummel snatches half of their client's money to ensure that he will be found innocent and Howe the remainder to cover a possible appeal if found guilty. When the client objects that the latter might not be necessary

Hummel retorts that he should be all the more satisfied with his lawyers! The court scenes expand the ironies to include judges (who hand out absurd verdicts) and the whole legal system in a comic theatre. When Hummel is tried he confuses different roles: he is dressed as a convict, should be the defendant, and acts as his own lawyer. He even gets down on his knees to call the jurors to prayer! Such farce is exactly in keeping with the interrogation scenes of *Catch-22*, the military hearings of Heller's play *We Bombed in New Haven*, or the press briefings in *Good as Gold*. In all these cases legal and administrative processes have gone awry and lost their assumed connection with justice and truth. It is perhaps for this reason why Heller returns again and again to the notion of entrapment whereby his characters divide into opposing categories of exploiters and exploited. A prelude to entrapment might well be the unpredictability of events which Heller has indicated by weaving comic variations on the proverb 'nothing succeeds like success', rephrased as 'nothing succeeds as planned' in *Good as Gold* and 'nothing fails like success' in *God Knows*.

Heller has tended to dismiss his early stories as apprentice-work and certainly they hardly give a clue about the novels he went on to write. Nevertheless they implicitly bear on the issue of authority, this time *literary* authority, in being written as imitations of Hemingway and the realists of the 1940s. An internal sign that Heller was writing his way out of this oppressive influence comes in such stories as 'Castle of Snow' and 'McAdam's Log' where the notion of the real is examined and where Heller demonstrates a hospitality towards the fantasies of his characters.

Chapter 2 examines in detail how *Catch-22* took Heller even farther from such literary models and considers his use of circles, repetition, and flattened characterisation in his comic portrayal of the military bureaucracy. Although the action of the novel is ostensibly located in Corsica and Italy towards the end of the Second World War, many stylistic devices indicate that Heller's comedy is being directed – partly through the mouthpiece of Yossarian – against a mentality prevalent in America during the McCarthy hearings. Greater detail is essential in approaching *Catch-22* because it is Heller's most complex novel, but the intention is not to let this work overshadow the later writings. Instead it will be used as a constant point of reference in this study which will have the merit of corresponding to Heller's sense of his own career. His play *We Bombed in New Haven* has generally been neglected by the critics but in fact it represents an important extension of the themes of *Catch-22*. Alienation effects which constantly disrupt the dramatic illusion are used to ridicule national claims of military obedience and, although it refers to war in general, it is helpful to read this play (and the dramatisations of *Catch-22*) against the background of Heller's opposition to the Vietnam War.

Originally Heller had planned to make the protagonist of his next novel, *Something Happened*, a member of Yossarian's squadron but in the event he abandoned this plan. For all their outward differences Heller's first two novels stand close comparison. *Something Happened* also attacks projected public images – of success in business and of the attendant prosperity. Yossarian's opposing voice is now internalised within the protagonist's consciousness where a psychological drama is acted out between the impulse to achieve goals and Bob Slocum's sceptical questioning intelligence. Again and again in interview Heller has admitted that dialogue comes easily to him and much of his fiction is built around the clash between opposing voices. In Slocum's case the main conflict within him is represented stylistically through opposing propositions which contradict or neutralise each other.

Good as Gold develops this notion of ambivalence with reference to the political ambitions of its protagonist to penetrate the world of Washington. The opposition to this goal is voiced through Bruce Gold's father and friends who collectively point out the self-deception in his attempt to shake off his Jewish origins and to stifle his criticisms of Henry Kissinger, a precursor who simultaneously draws Gold's admiration and hatred. Heller's method in this novel is to push scenes and characters towards caricature, and to produce an ironic pastiche of Victorian novels which restore their protagonist to a lost inheritance. For all its comic surface *Good as Gold* is a bleak study of self-serving ambition which ends in failure.

God Knows is the first of Heller's novels to turn away from contemporary American subjects and presents a monologue of King David shortly before his death. Heller parodically subverts the authority of the biblical text by juxtaposing a modern colloquial speech idiom against the formal and decorous language of the King James version. In this way he 'revises' the biblical story, presenting a less than pious David who falls victim to his own sexual appetite and to the inexplicable disapproval of both Saul and God. This novel thus takes up the theme of parental betrayal which recurs in Heller's earlier works and makes it a central issue. David's characteristic reaction to this betrayal is to smother any possible responsibility on his part through a comic style which also helps him to endure the resulting isolation. The adoption of a comic style similarly helped Heller to pull through a serious illness which he describes with his friend Speed Vogel in *No Laughing Matter*. Finally, in *Picture This* Heller explores the cynical motives lying behind Athenian expansion in the Age of Pericles and the rise of Dutch merchantilism in the seventeenth century, focusing his narrative on the fates of two individuals — Socrates and Rembrandt.

1

The Road to *Catch-22*

BIOGRAPHICAL

Joseph Heller was born on May 1st 1923 to a family of Jewish immigrants living in the Coney Island section of Brooklyn. His father Isaac was a socialist refugee from Tsarist Russia who came to America in 1913. By a previous marriage he had had two children Lee and Sylvia who were reared by Joseph's mother as if they were her own. It was not until he was 15 that Heller discovered they were in fact his half-brother and half-sister. Heller's father had secured a job driving a delivery truck for Messinger's local bakery, but died when Heller was only five as a result of a botched operation. The subsequent funeral meal was more like a party than the occasion of a bereavement, and Heller's friend the journalist and biographer Barbara Gelb has argued that the true impact of this event was hidden from the young Heller, thereby causing a psychic wound which affected his whole personality. Heller himself seems to confirm this view when he admits, 'I didn't realize then how traumatized I was'.[1]

Whatever the truth of the matter Heller has repeatedly given the impression of passing a happy childhood. His father was an agnostic and his mother (who spoke little English) more concerned with observing the social forms than with religious belief. She would insist, for instance, that Heller wore his best clothes on the Sabbath. In view of the efforts made by some literary critics to force Heller's work into an ethnic category it is important to stress how secular an upbringing he received; he was not bar-mitzvahed in his teens, as were most other Jewish boys. Also the neighbourhood where he grew up had its part to play in this process. As word passed from family to family Jewish immigrants began moving out to Coney Island, so that by the 1920s the Brighton Beach district could be described as a 'miniature East Side' and Milton Klonsky remembered the tremendous spread of religions and political groupings within the Jewish community.[2] As Heller's friend the novelist George Mandel recalls, it was a Jewish neighbourhood but with no 'Jewish hangups', thereby making a strong contrast between Heller's youth and that of Philip Roth who was bemused by the disparity between his parents' tragic sense of life and the actual circumstances of growing up in Newark.[3] Two crucial physical factors in growing up during this period must have been the literal closeness of one family to another in the apartment blocks, and the use of the street and Coney Island boardwalk as a place for social meeting or where children could play. 'When the weather was nice', Heller has stated, 'there were always parents sitting out in front of the houses, talking . . . There was a lot of conversation out of the windows.' There were very few cars in that neighbourhood during the Depression and apparently an almost non-existent crime rate. Relations between the Jews and the other local ethnic group, the Italians, were good on the whole. Looking back Heller has commented nostalgically, 'I cannot imagine a better place for a child to grow up in'.[4] This general impression of security was probably confirmed when Heller attended the recently established Abraham Lincoln High School which was staffed by a high proportion of second generation Jewish college graduates. Their easy rapport with the students would have helped to avoid ethnic antagonisms.[5]

No account of Coney Island can neglect its famous fairground which Heller has admitted affected his whole attitude to life.[6] As recently as 1948 it was estimated that the fairground and beach attracted some 35 million visitors in the summer as compared with an all-the-year-round residential population of 60 000.[7] Not surprisingly Coney Island has fed the imagination of New York writers. It figures in George Mandel's 1960 novel *The Breakwater* and is used as a metaphor of imaginative playfulness in Lawrence Ferlinghetti's 1958 collection of poems *A Coney Island of the Mind*. Ferlinghetti, who lived in Bronxville in the 1920s, makes a more literal use of San Francisco as a setting but in a poem like 'We Squat upon the Beach of Love' juxtaposes images of artifice and romance with the litter left behind by day trippers. His rapid cutting to and fro between the actual and the imaginary creates a landscape of heightened images, hence his references in the series to such painters as Goya and Bosch. It is extraordinarily vivid images which also pack Norman Rosten's memoir-novel of growing up in Coney Island, *Under the Boardwalk* (1968). The boy-protagonist's imagination is dominated by the noise and bustle of summer:

Up the street ramp and onto the boardwalk: a million people! It felt like a million. The whistle of the peanut roaster stayed above the dense rattle of shoes on the boards. I walked past stores and booths of wild colors, with fake soda bottles and ice-cream, then real franks, clams, oysters, with funny old men and ladies calling out their wares. Pinwheels fluttered at my ear and kewpie dolls winked in the sunshine. I walked past entrances to both houses and outdoor pools, and along stretches of roller coaster that skirted the iron railings and roared away into dark tunnels.[8]

He cannot saunter through this scene as a casual spectator because the images and sounds are too aggressive in soliciting his attention. The real and the fake are so near to each other that the distinction between the two blurs. Rosten notes the resulting confusion ('you couldn't tell what was real in a place like this'[9]) which induces a healthy scepticism in the boy. One of the most crucial pieces of advice he receives from a neighbour is to distrust everything and rely on himself. Looking back on his childhood Heller too notes that 'there was something almost unreal' about the place, especially with its enormous seasonal fluctuations in population.[10]

Heller enthusiastically endorsed Rosten's novel as capturing 'much of the magic and mystery and excitement of growing up there'.[11] In 1962 Heller set his own recollections of Coney Island on record in an article which he wrote for the magazine *Show*. This article notes so many of the same characteristics of the place as Rosten that it virtually acts like an anticipatory gloss on the novel. Heller too notes the educative impact of the barkers' cries on the children. Where they would first learn to discriminate between good and bad frankfurters, for instance, growing up involved acquiring a necessary scepticism:

Later we came upon a different principle that trained us toward cynicism, the fact that it is often impossible to obtain fair value. We learned this from the barkers who offered to guess your weight, guess your name or occupation, the part of the country you came from or the date you were born, guess anything at all about you for a dime, a quarter, a half-dollar or a dollar, because here was a setup where the customer could never win.[12]

Here on a small scale we surely encounter the double binds which recur throughout Heller's fiction, an early form of the cynical entrapment created by an unscrupulous military bureaucracy, business corporation or political machine. Heller also stresses how the child's perceptions are dominated by the immediate to such an extent that he is insulated from an awareness of the less attractive aspects of Coney Island. On the one hand he tries in his article to recapture the moment-by-moment excitement of the child's experience, on the other he remembers with bemusement the strange sights (the beach acrobats, for instance) which the child would simply accept. Here again we can perhaps note an influence on Heller's later fiction. Once he has found his own narrative voice his novels are constantly setting up heightened comic images which verge on caricature. In Coney Island his mind was repeatedly being fed by the extraordinary sights as a matter of course.

Heller's other main emphasis in this article is on the poverty of Coney Island. He balances nostalgia for a happy childhood against a recognition that his child's-eye view of the place simply did not register certain things. As the child grows up he grows away from intensely local neighbourhoods, the blocks where he used to play. The field of experience expands wider into other areas of Brooklyn and at the same time broadens locally so that the beach becomes transformed into a sordid expanse full of litter. Whereas for Rosten's protagonist the dark area under the boardwalk is a tantalising place full of sexual promise not yet available to the young boy, Heller's article is marked by a sad recognition of the impossibility of recapturing his view of Coney Island as a child. Partly it would involve blocking out too many aspects of the area, partly changes in the fairground and new housing developments have radically changed the appearance of the place. In a programme made for British television in 1984 Heller noted that the street where he used to live had become virtually unrecognisable since all the apartment blocks had been torn down. This implicit feeling of disposession is made explicit in Heller's third novel *Good as Gold* where the disappearance of the local Italian and Jewish communities is seen as a sign of ethnic decline.

While at school Heller joined a local club called ALTEO (All Loyal To Each Other) which numbered among its members George Mandel and Daniel Rosoff. Rosoff has claimed that he filled the gap left by Heller's dead father and taught the boy how to hustle, even claiming that some of the dialogue in *Catch-22* derives directly from this club.[13] At the age of 13 Heller briefly held a job as a Western Union messenger boy, experience which he later drew on for his short story 'World Full of Great Cities'. By all accounts the young Heller was an avid reader, being well supplied with periodicals by his brother and sister, and with books by the local leading libraries. One author whose works he remembers particularly is Jerome Weidman, whose fiction deals with the Lower East Side of New York.[14] At elementary school he discovered he had a talent for writing and 'pecked out on a neighborhood boy's typewriter' his earliest story.[15] These stories were submitted to the *Daily News* and to magazines like *Liberty* and *Collier's*. Not surprisingly they were rejected.

On graduating from high school Heller worked briefly as a file clerk in a casualty insurance company, as does Bob Slocum in his second novel *Something Happened*; and then served a spell as a blacksmith's helper in Norfolk Navy Yard and as a shipping file clerk. In 1942 Heller joined the US Air Force but only served on active service abroad for about ten months which he has described as being 'like walking down Coney Island'.[16] Enlisting did not simply mean doing one's bit for a national purpose; it also offered good wages, security and glamour to Heller who suddenly saw himself as a movie character acting out adventurous roles. From May 1944 to mid-1945 he was stationed on Corsica with the 488th squadron of the 340th Bombardment Group. He flew 60 combat missions as a bombardier earning for himself the Air Medal with seven oakleaf clusters and a Presidential Unit Citation, and rising to the rank of Lieutenant. Before his discharge he served briefly as a Public Relations Officer in Texas. All apparently went well until his 37th mission over Avignon when Heller suddenly realised that his life was in danger. This particular mission, when a member of his crew was critically wounded, subsequently fed into those scenes of *Catch-22* which deal with the death of Snowden. Such episodes apart, Heller had a relatively comfortable time in Corsica. By that stage in the war there was nothing to fear from enemy air strikes so the men whiled away the time between missions playing baseball or basketball. After the fall of Rome in June 1944 Heller would go on regular four- or five-day furloughs in that city. During one of these visits Heller was sketched by the young Federico Fellini.[17] In 1966 the magazine *Holiday* commissioned Heller to retrace his wartime steps to Corsica and Italy. The difficulties he experienced in revisiting Coney Island were much more severe with this European trip. Although Heller and his family were welcomed with open arms by the Corsicans he found that all traces

of his airfield had disappeared and his subsequent visits to Poggi-
bonsi and the other Italian towns which were the targets for
bombing missions were an anti-climax.

On his discharge from the air force Heller met and married
Shirley Held by whom he subsequently had two children. Under
the GI Bill he enrolled at the University of Southern California but
then, with the help of Whit Burnett, the editor of *Story* magazine,
transferred to New York University where he graduated Phi Beta
Kappa in 1948. During the next academic year he studied for an
MA at Columbia University taking, among others, a course in
American Literature with Lionel Trilling. In 1949 Heller was
awarded a Fulbright Scholarship on the basis of 'reading for a BA
degree' and spent the next year at St Catherine's College, Oxford.
Here he followed the second year of the undergraduate course and
his reports indicate that he made 'very good progress'.[18] Looking
back on this year in 1969 Heller summed it up tersely: 'When I had
the Fulbright, I spent one term on Milton and one on Chaucer and
one on Shakespeare and I came to the conclusion that Milton is
pretty much a waste'.[19] According to Edward J. Bloustein, who
was in Oxford at the same time, Heller was impressed by the place
more than his studies and spent a considerable proportion of the
year working hard on a short story.[20]

By Heller's own account this period of his life was a time when
he read very widely in literary criticism. His reading was done
within an academic environment which perhaps led him to join the
staff of Pennsylvania State College (now University) in 1950. As a
member of the English composition department Heller had among
his colleagues Frederick Karl, the Conrad specialist, who has
remained a friend. When Heller left the college in 1952 he was
replaced by John Barth who wove his experiences teaching composition into his second novel *The End of the Road* (1958). Heller's
former colleague Bernard Oldsey has recorded that 'Joe was an
alien figure in State College in more than a linguistic sense', that is,
because of his Brooklyn accent. He missed the bustle and sophisti-
cation of New York and seems to have found the teaching rather
uncongenial.[21] Heller's attachment to New York has persisted. At
a 1974 press conference given in Sweden to celebrate the high sales
of *Something Happened* Heller declared that he could never live
anywhere else because 'he appreciated the speed with which
people communicate there', and characteristically turning his statement into a wisecrack — because the people are so unfriendly!

Hence it was no surprise that Heller left Penn State, a move which was also a complete departure from the academic world. From 1952 to 1956 he worked as an advertising copywriter for *Time*, and *Look* (1956–8), and then served as a promotion manager at *McCall's* from 1958 to 1961.

It is important to stress that all the time Heller was studying and teaching he was also writing his own work — mainly short stories. His years in business were no exception. He started work on *Catch-18*, as it was then called in 1953. Two years later his agent Candida Donadio sent a version of the opening chapter to the anthology *New World Writing* where it was published. Another two years passed and then in the summer of 1957 Robert Gottlieb of Simon and Schuster read 75 pages of the manuscript and waxed enthusiastic. The following February he read more of the novel and accepted it for publication.[22] Before the book finally appeared Heller had to cut his bulky manuscript down from some 800 to about 625 pages.[23] In 1961 *Catch-22* was published with an enterprising promotion campaign which ensured high sales for a first novel, although it never became a bestseller in the United States.[24] The composition of this novel was clearly a very slow and painstaking process, but it was not one which took place in spite of Heller's commitments to business. On the contrary Heller has gratefully noted the 'disciplines of writing advertising copy ... where the limitations involved provide a considerable spur to the imagination' and underlined this point by referring to one of T. S. Eliot's essays on the disciplines of writing — probably 'Tradition and the Individual Talent' where Eliot discusses the poet's surrender of personality to the currents of past literature.[25] What Hemingway's experiences on the Kansas City *Star* did for his career evidently his work at promotion copy did for Heller's. He would work on the novel two or three hours every evening because he was bored with television; and if his office work that day was exciting his writing would go well.[26] There seems to have been a direct, almost symbolic, relation between Heller's one area of work and his other. All of which is not to deny that Heller's ambition as a writer ultimately took precedence. Once *Catch-22* was published he took leave of absence from *McCall's* since he had by then lost interest in that job, but did not decide to leave the company for good until he had received a sizeable payment for the novel's film rights.[27] *Catch-22* was to be the major turning-point in his career.

THE EARLY STORIES

Although it was his first published novel, *Catch-22* was by no means the first fiction work by Heller to find its way into print. As early as 1950, when he went to Penn State, he had become something of a literary celebrity for the short stories he had published. Most of these stories were written while Heller was taking a creative writing course at New York University with Maurice Baudin, an expert on 17th and 18th century French drama. Heller has acknowledged the importance of the latter's advice: 'Baudin pointed out my faults to me — he'd say throw away the first three or four pages, and he was right'.[28] Looking back on the late 1940s he has stated: 'After the war, everyone who could write dialogue was copying Ernest Hemingway and John O'Hara, and everyone who couldn't was copying Irwin Shaw'.[29]

Heller had started writing short stories while still serving overseas and in 1945, when he was based in San Angelo, Texas, he submitted two to Whit Burnett, the editor of *Story* magazine. One was accepted for a servicemen's issue and was published later that same year. 'I Don't Love You Anymore' reads like a pastiche of Hemingway in centring on an argument between a returned soldier and his wife. The soldier refuses to play the role of hero (cf. 'Soldier's Home') by staying naked when they are expecting visitors, anticipating *Catch-22* in attaching a symbolic importance to the act of donning clothes, particularly a uniform. He tries to provoke his wife into admitting their relationship is finished (cf. 'The End of Something') and petulantly demands a pitcher of beer when his real desire is for something else (cf. 'Cat in the Rain'). The tension in the story emerges from the sparring between the soldier and his wife (on their first day together they had been 'feeling each other out as prize fighters do'[30]). Similarly in 'Jephthah's Daughter', another story from this period, a husband and wife meet to discuss the impending wedding of their daughter.[31] The argument rather than discussion is presented entirely in terms of tactics, of a struggle which the husband loses. As the two argue in a restaurant a young couple in the adjacent booth is introduced as a reversed version of the primary situation; this time it is a young man who is bullying his girlfriend. In 'I Don't Love You Anymore' Heller uses a physical object as a metaphor of the protagonist's ambivalence over parting with his wife. He plays with a pair of Chinese puzzle rings as if he wants to separate them but actually shows annoyance when they come apart. The story finally becomes a study in contradiction: the protagonist refuses to dress for visitors, but eventually does so; his wife refuses to bring him beer, but gives in. Heller was evidently well aware of the weaknesses of his first published story because, when *Cavalcade Magazine* approached him in 1963 about reprinting it, he refused on the grounds that it was 'decidedly inferior work'.[32]

It has generally been supposed that *Catch-22* was written in the 1950s, but the archives of *Story* show that Heller was planning a novel as early as 1945 and that he sent the first four chapters to Burnett probably at the beginning of the next year. In August 1946 Burnett wrote back to Heller confirming his own suspicion that he had fallen too much under the influence of Thomas Wolfe. The letter continues: 'I am wondering, too, if the treatment of a flier facing the end of his missions and thinking over the meaning of the war has not been pretty well done to death by people like H. E. Bates, Dan Brennan and others. If so, this book might have hard sledding'.[33] As well as giving a tantalising glimpse of the germ of *Catch-22* these lines bear witness to Burnett's helpful and supportive treatment of Heller's early writings. Heller's letters from this period suggest that Burnett played an important role in encouraging him to choose the career of writer. Once he had established himself in this career, Heller expressed his gratitude to Burnett by sending him in 1962 a statement on behalf of *Story* which he praised for being 'the best of all publications committed to the idea that fiction is not merely a diversion, but a vital form of art'.[34]

'I Don't Love You Anymore' is useful for indicating the formulaic nature of most of Heller's short stories which conform to the stereotypes then appearing in the *Atlantic*, *Collier's*, *Esquire* and *The New Yorker*. The stories usually begin in the middle of a situation and disguise the gradual release of information through apparently everyday dialogue. There is often a contrast between the ostensible subject or details of the immediate situation, and the emergence of the real subject. So in James Jones' 'Two Legs for the Two of Us' another ex-soldier visits his wife (from whom he has separated) with an army buddy and two girls. The man is drunk and different possibilities are raised about why he has made the visit. Is it to go back to the wife, or to insult her, or to use her as a sounding board for his own bitterness? The source of the latter (and the significance of the title) becomes evident when we realise that the husband is an amputee and the wife's invitation represents an impossible attempt to put the clock back. Concealment is crucial in this story where gradual revelation becomes a means of indicating emotional depth. Once again the model is Hemingway. In retrospect Jones (whose first published story appeared with one of Heller's in the March 1948 *Atlantic*) has commented, 'at the time I believed with Hemingway that one should not point one's story points up'.[35] Evidently Heller agreed because he too made his techniques implicit, concealed within the realism of his narratives. 'Girl from Greenwich' (1948) begins at a literary reception and sets up a series of ironic digs at the gap between literary success and quality, the actual opinions of Duke, the point-of-view character and the hypocritical social routines he has to perform at the party.[36] The girl of the title seems to be safely categorised as a naïve provincial who has got her first break but the story reveals *Duke's* naïveté in forming this opinion. Pursued by a man who seems to be a rival for her attention, the girl finally discloses that he is her husband. The narrative hinges on this key information ('all the pieces fell together in a horrible pattern') which triggers a pious wave of revulsion in Duke.

A final ironic twist also figures in 'Nothing to be Done' (1948), a story which derives directly from Hemingway's 'The Killers' in exploiting threat and suspense.[37] Heller uses a pool-room setting where Hemingway has a lunch-room; and presents the potential victim instead of the potential killers. In Hemingway's story Ole Andreson is only seen towards the end lying in his room. Nick Adams tries to persuade him to leave town but the answer is 'There ain't anything to do now'. Heller extends this scene to fill virtually the whole story and revises Andreson's answer into a refrain which echoes fatalistically throughout his story. Where Hemingway leaves vague the exact reason for the killing Heller ꜰᴘᴏᴄᴊꜰᴏᴏ ᴀ ꜰᴏᴏꜰ ᴏꜰꜰ ᴘꜰᴀᴄᴏᴏꜰ ᴏ̯ꜰ ᴀ ᴊᴀꜰᴋᴊᴏꜰᴀꜰ, ꜰꜰᴇ ꜰᴇꜰᴀꜰꜰꜰᴏ ꜰꜰᴇꜰꜰᴊꜰᴊꜰᴡᴀꜰ'ꜰ static dialogue between an older man (Carl) and a boy (Nat). While it seems that Nat has been responsible for losing the bet the story actually ends with Carl furtively destroying the betting slip which he had all the time. This twist sheds a different retrospective light on the details of his movements and on the sadistic way in which he tells Nat of the syndicate's cruelty. 'A Man Named Flute' (published the same year) is also an ironic study of courage, juxtaposing scenes which deflate the protagonist's self-image.[38] Dave Murdock runs a bookmaker's business behind a stationery store and is forced to close temporarily while the police clean up the town. He discovers that his son has been buying marijuana from a dealer called Flute, confronts and hits his boy, and tries the same thing on Flute, with humiliating results. Heller uses the device of parallelism in this story to compare the exercise of police authority on Murdock with his less impressive exercise of paternal authority on his son. Since he too is an illegal dealer like Flute (who uses a pool-room as a hang-out), his authority is undermined morally and then undermined physically since Flute is a stronger man. Concealment from his wife becomes more and more crucial in Murdock's efforts to preserve his self-respect. Heller seems to have planned a series of stories with overlapping themes and settings (in 1945 he actually suggested to Whit Burnett the possibility of bringing out a book of stories), since 'A Day in the Country' (in the Brandeis University collection) also opens in a pool-room and describes a young addict's desperate attempts to get hard drugs.

Heller has repeatedly admitted that the stories he wrote from 1945 onwards were frankly imitative. He has stated, for instance, 'I would read a story in a magazine like *Good Housekeeping* or *Woman's Home Companion*, and I would then try to write a story for them . . . I wasn't even writing out of my own experiences as much as writing out of my experience of reading other people's work'.[39] When a humorous theme he had written as a freshman at the University of Southern California was returned with an *A* he even erased the grade and submitted it to *Esquire*. The piece, which converts his childhood friend Marvin Winkler into a fictitious character, was accepted and published in 1947 under the title 'Bookies, Beware!' − a fantasy-article about a student who uses pure science to predict winners at the races. (Winkler also figures in an unpublished essay about American conversation habits, 'The Art of Keeping Your Mouth Shut', this time as an academic.)[40] Imitative or not, these numerous early stories (the Heller collection at Brandeis University includes 23 stories in manuscript as well as texts of the seven which were subsequently published) probably gave Heller valuable formal practice in managing dialogue, creating situation and controlling the dynamics of narrative.

One of the stories from these early years which does not seem derivative is 'Castle of Snow' which was selected by Martha Foley for *The Best American Short Stories of 1949*.[41] The time is the Depression. The boy-narrator remembers the apparent serenity in the relationship between his uncle and aunt in spite of the contrast between the sensitive idealism of the one and the hard worldliness of the other. His uncle loses his job, the family endures increasing hardship until their misfortune seems to lift when he secures a new job with a bakery. When the boy returns from school that day, however, he finds his uncle playing with other boys in the street building a snow fort. Heller skilfully and movingly uses the concrete imagery of possessions to convey the spiritual cost of poverty. The sight of furniture piled on the sidewalk during an eviction establishes the street as a place of public humiliation, at first only applicable to others. Then the boy's family starts selling off their own furniture little by little until his uncle makes the supreme sacrifice in parting with his cherished books. The season plays its part in this process as poverty coincides with the onset of winter (it is a nice irony that the uncle misreads the snow as a good omen).

So far it may seem as if the story is a naturalistic study in poverty but the ultimate subject is a clash between rival attitudes to experience. For instance the aunt offers to find work as a waitress forgetting that she has lost her looks. Under the final strain of the bakery job not materialising Uncle David regresses into childhood, finding relief from an unbearable present in playing with the boys. The result is rejuvenating for him and also play becomes a means of access to favourite memories (specifically when he built her a castle of snow in Russia when she was only 15). When Aunt Sarah confronts him in the street there is a brief struggle between the voice of memory ('Do you remember the time?') and the aunt's authoritative voice of realism ('come upstairs'). The latter wins out and Uncle David seems to collapse and age instantly. Heller brilliantly manages the perspective so that the uncle avoids absurdity and the aunt never seems gratuitously cruel, the imperatives forcing each to behave as they do being implied retrospectively by the narrator. This exercise of memory enacts an understanding of his uncle which was simply not available to him at the time of the events. Then he could only feel shame and embarrassment. Now he perceives the Depression as the last in a series of betrayals in his uncle's life (romantic hopes never quite realised, revolutionary idealism disappointed by subsequent events in Russia) where his imagination is brought into a head-on collision with the actuality of American life. The nephew's retrospective sympathy for his uncle as demonstrated in his tolerantly uncritical narrative voice contrasts very strongly with his Aunt Sarah who is established as a harshly critical vocal presence from the very beginning of the story. 'Castle of Snow' admits a far more complex range of feelings than the buttoned-up ironies of Heller's other early stories.

Around 1950, sensing that the stories he was writing were too imitative and were anyway going out of fashion, Heller stopped writing and began casting around for the subject for a novel. Two stories which were published much later in fact date from this early period. The one, 'World Full of Great Cities' (written in 1947 and influenced to a certain extent by William Saroyan) is a situational study of how startling the intersection between two lives can be in an urban context. It is narrated from the point of view of a messenger boy who is asked to make love to a beautiful actress but instead of realising a dream it confuses him and jolts him out of the security of his role as messenger. The story was included by Nelson Algren in his anthology *Nelson Algren's Own Book of Lonesome Monsters* (1962) presumably on the strength of his enthusiasm for *Catch-22* which he had declared was 'the strongest repudiation of our civilisation, in fiction, to come out of World War II'.[42]

'McAdam's Log' (written in 1950, published in 1959) is the other story which stands on its own merits and which is thematically similar to 'Castle of Snow' in exploring the tension between imagination and actuality. Its protagonist is a retired hardware dealer referred to throughout the story as 'the Captain' who seeks refuge from monotony in imaginary voyages. The Captain's fantasies are morally related to his kindness towards his grandchildren and are contrasted with the brutal voice of reality expressed by his son-in-law and daughter. Heller uses an apparently realistic matter-of-fact narration to set up a perspective on the Captain which is more tolerant than his treatment at the hands of his family. Partly this is a matter of small verbal details ('vision', 'miraculously', etc.) which hint at a dimension to experience other than the literal; partly it is a matter of separating indicators of place (he is both 'in a deckchair on his porch' *and* 'at sea') so that the imagined and the actual do not collide. The voices which cut through this finely balanced ambiguity are cruel and destructive. Neil (the Captain's son-in-law) both spoils his children's games and literally beats his son. Even the Captain's daughter Cynthia turns against him, forcing an admission that his voyages are 'lies'. In effect she forces together the two dimensions to experience which Heller has been scrupulously keeping apart, and which are articulated spatially through images of openness and of enclosure. The trope of voyaging is a traditional enough metaphor of the opening out of the imagination towards far horizons and distant lands which might bear no relation to actual countries. The Captain's travelling is no exception since it transforms geographical places into exclusively exotic images:

> Italy became a land of festivals and mandolins in which the sole means of conveyance was the gondola. There were no coal mines in Spain; groves of citrus trees covered the countryside, and the women were as fertile as the land and had dark hair and dark eyes and were all lovely and vibrant with a wholesome, passionate, and incorrigibly pagan wantonness.[43]

At issue is not the truth or falsity of these images but rather their indication of a purpose in the Captain's inner life. Where he goes on a directed voyage, his son-in-law 'drifts' helplessly when Cynthia almost dies from an abortion. The Captain's 'voyages' reflect his ability to negotiate nightmare and terror at the closeness of death which unnerve the other members of his family. But, again as in 'Castle of Snow' (even the title implies a fragile structure), actuality ultimately destroys the Captain's imaginings in two scenes. The one is Cynthia's insistence that they are lies; the other is a betrayal through a sailor called Simpson who seems amazingly tolerant of the Captain but who is arrested for smuggling. The Captain too is put through an interrogation which probes deep into the most private areas of his self. Once again Heller distinguishes his narrative from the actions of his characters by presenting this scene through a summary which reverses the transformations of the Captain's imagination, reducing his voyages to a 'bleak odyssey'. In both these scenes imaginary space contracts down to the confines of the Captain's bedroom and of the cabin where the interrogation takes place. Once his 'illusions' have been destroyed he has no life left and the story ends with him composing a final fiction preparatory to his death.

Most of these stories are only important as apprentice-work in Heller's career. They show his technical skills at realism, although in a rather derivative way. Interestingly, in view of the novels which he went on to write, the best of these stories — 'Castle of Snow' and 'McAdam's Log' — demonstrate Heller's escape from the straightjacket of tightly structured, ironically realistic short stories. Without sacrificing realism 'Castle of Snow' sets up a conflict between hope and actuality which looks forward to *Catch-22* and *Good as Gold*. The snow castle itself becomes a symptom of regression to childhood and in its fragility a metaphor of the uncle's failed hopes. It is characteristic of this story and 'McAdam's Log' that actuality should be expressed in harsh, even brutal, ways. The cruelty of the Captain's daughter and her husband shades predictably into his interrogation by the authorities. As we shall see a similar pathos grows out of the chaplain's interrogation in *Catch-22* with the complication that he is at the mercy of an officialdom gone mad.

2

Catch-22

By Heller's own account he began making notes for *Catch-22* in 1953, but it was not until almost a decade later in 1961 that it was finally published.[1] Initially it was greeted with mixed reactions in America. On the one hand it drew enthusiastic admiration from writers like Nelson Algren and Thomas Pynchon; on the other it was savaged by Whitney Balliett in the *New Yorker* who complained: 'It doesn't even seem to have been written; instead it gives the impression of having been shouted onto paper'.[2] Fortunately there were plenty of readers who disagreed with Balliett and American sales of the novel rose steadily (in contrast with Britain where it became an immediate bestseller), suddenly accelerating towards the ends of the decade when *Catch-22* became the chosen text of the anti-Vietnam War protest movement. By the 25th anniversary of its publication Heller estimated that some ten million copies had been sold.[3] One result of this staggering success is that Heller's title has been paid the supreme compliment of gaining acceptance into the language and is now listed in the dictionary. The other result is more problematic. Although some critics now argue that *Something Happened* is his most important novel, for the vast majority of his readers Heller will remain the man who wrote *Catch-22*. This novel has remained the major point of reference in his career, the work against which he measures his subsequent work. Although at one point he considered writing a novel about Dunbar (a character who disappears in the novel), Heller never progressed beyond the opening line and when questioned in 1985 about bringing his novel up to date he answered: 'I initially went into it because I dread the idea of a sequel;' and yet only two years later Heller had sold the rights for just such a sequel, due out by 1990.[4] Although *Catch-22* has attracted far more critical commentary than any of Heller's other works, there is still no general agreement about such basic issues as its structure and it is still essential to demonstrate that novel's complexities and also its calculated provocations which challenge many assumptions of literary decorum. For the sake of convenience I have broken down

22

my discussion into sub-sections which should help to highlight particular aspects of its organisation without damaging its unity.

YOSSARIAN AND AMERICAN WAR FICTION

Two preliminary sketches made while Heller was working on *Catch-22* give us important hints of how he originally conceived his protagonist Yossarian. The first begins as follows: 'Now they had just about everything to make a perfect plot for a best-selling war novel. They had a fairy, they had a Slav named Florik from the slums, an Irishman, a thinker with a PhD . . .'.[5] The only character missing from the set is the 'sensitive Jew'. Instead Heller has another Jewish character named Yossarian 'who didn't want to make anything out of anything'. Heller makes the fictional pattern an explicit part of his own narrative, thereby drawing attention to its own fictiveness. On the one hand the sketches make it clear that he was taking his point of departure from the two most famous American novels to deal with the Second World War — *From Here to Eternity* (1951) and *The Naked and the Dead* (1948); on the other it is equally obvious that Heller is not setting out to rival their realism so much as parody many of their procedures. These novels which, according to Heller, delayed the composition of *Catch-22* by years shed light on the nature of his own eventual work.

James Jones treats the army as a microcosm of American society (*From Here to Eternity* is essentially a peacetime novel), stratified and class-ridden. Its two narratives represent failed or abortive attempts to cross divides. Prewitt, like Yossarian, develops a reputation as a trouble-maker and almost wilfully destroys his own army career. The romantic counterpart to this lack of co-operation is his love for a prostitute which comes to an end with the general evacuation of the islands after Pearl Harbor. The second narrative is of Sergeant Warden who falls in love with his company commander's wife. This relationship is not so much doomed as dependent on Warden's willingness to take a commission which, at the last moment, he refuses. Jones's main concern in the novel is to reveal the conservatism and rigidity of the American army which restricts at the same time as it attacks its members. Prewitt both loves the discipline of the army and always finds it askew of his personal values. Accordingly his narrative is one of descent through demotion to the stockade. In the sections dealing with the stockade the class significance of Jones's narrative becomes absolutely explicit as Prewitt meets a motley collection of dissidents and social dropouts.

Heller clearly approaches the army in a different way. It is used, he states in a 1976 interview, 'symbolically for the whole government structure.'[6] Given this shift of emphasis from society to administration and his avoidance of the mode of realism which he only sees as a specific limited phase in American fiction from the late 19th century to World War II, we could hardly expect to find a trace of Jones's novel in *Catch-22*.[7] In fact Heller has divided Prewitt's nonconformism and romantic idealism between Yossarian and Nately who falls in love with an Italian prostitute. Vance Ramsey has noted the latter similarity between Nately and Prewitt but without pointing out the huge social differences in their origins — Nately from the New England aristocracy, Prewitt from Harlan County mining area in Kentucky.[8] Warden's affair is repeated briefly by Yossarian with Lieutenant Scheisskopf's wife at training camp, rendered so briefly and ludicrously as to be a parody of *From Here To Eternity*:

> 'Darling, we're going to have a baby again', she would say to Yossarian every month.
> 'You're out of your goddam head', he would reply.[9]

Heller here excludes a possible source of pathos from his own novel. Although the general situation is reminiscent of *From Here To Eternity* the announcement of pregnancy goes even further back to Hemingway's *A Farewell To Arms* and forms a virtual quotation from Chapter 21. Scheisskopf's wife (never named) repeats her monthly phrase to Yossarian *and* to her husband only to be greeted by the latter's own catch phrase. 'Don't you know there's a parade going on?' In both Hemingway's and Jones's novels love functions as a refuge from war or the military, but as a possibility which fails. In *A Farewell To Arms* the notion of a separate peace is ruled out by the interweaving of the two narrative lines. By accelerating tempo Heller increases his parody, contrasting the frenetic pace of *Catch-22* with the futile efforts of Hemingway's characters to slow down the passage of time. Other revisions of *From Here To Eternity* have taken place in *Catch-22*. Jones's Amerindian character Chief Choate becomes Chief Half Whiteoat; and the issue of who runs the mess is blown up into staggering proportions through Heller's mess sergeant Milo Minderbinder.

A similar process seems to have taken place in Heller's assimilation of *The Naked and the Dead*. His second sketch for his novel now contains an acceptable Jewish character who is distinguished this time from Yossarian. Again ironically Heller notes that he is stronger than the antisemite in the group and not a graduate of City College, as if these were drawbacks, a clear allusion to Mailer's Roth who has attended CCNY. The opening chapter of *Catch-22* contains traces of an initial intention on Heller's part implied in these sketches to burlesque Mailer's gathering of ethnic types in *The Naked and the Dead*. Types are converted into stereotypes in Heller. Mailer's Texan hunter Sam Croft becomes the nameless Texan patriot with his 'indestructible smile cracked forever across the front of his face like the brim of a black ten-gallon hat' (16). It doesn't really matter that the analogy is slightly forced and not quite easy to visualise. The point is that the Texan has become a clichéd image. Other elements from Mailer's novel (the importance of the mail, the forging of patrol reports, etc.) are incorporated into Heller's comedy, in one case into his characterisation of Yossarian. In Chapter 12 of Mailer's novel a character named Minetta is sent to hospital after being wounded in the thigh (cf. Yossarian). Determined to be sent home, he fakes madness, screaming at spurious hallucinations until a genuine case of shell-shock almost breaks him down. He then pretends to come out of his mania although the doctors know that he has been faking his symptoms. This malingering becomes one of Yossarian's 'routines' in Chapter 18 of *Catch-22* where he simply mimics the screams of a patient (particularly 'I see everything twice!'). Heller exploits repetition, duplication and echo-effects to the full, turning the satirical perspective against the hospital administration and then against Yossarian. Like Minetta, his acting has been understood by a doctor. In *The Naked and the Dead* Minetta's scheme is related to issues of courage and responses to combat. In *Catch-22* malingering is woven into the general theme of theatre. Heller's 'rewriting' of Mailer is this time non-parodic, extending the theatricality of malingering and cutting out passages which might give us access to the malingerer's mind. The comedy of this episode depends partly on Heller's keeping events external. Heller has described the impact Mailer's novel ('the masterwork') had on him when it first appeared as a daunting one: 'In reading Mailer's work I saw for myself years and years of arduous application, requiring more education than I felt I had. So it had a very prohibiting effect

on me'.[10] Partly this was a response to Mailer's craftsmanship,
partly an anxiety over the brevity of his own military service.

These reactions help to explain how, years later, Heller as it were
purged himself of the oppressive influences of Jones and Mailer,
partly by parody and partly by incorporating revised episodes from
both novels into his own work. The effect of these revisions is to
create an impression of a palimpsest as if Heller were writing over
a previous familiar text, exploiting the reader's sense of familiarity
so that he can disrupt it in startling ways. The comic treatment of
Yossarian's brief affair with Scheisskopf's wife and the intermittent
description of his relationship with Nurse Duckett (whose friend
Nurse Cramer is as disapproving as Catherine Barkley's companion) distance Heller's own narrative from the novels of Jones and
Hemingway; and at the same time they question the possibility of
romantic withdrawal from war as a possibility. And Heller's
absurd evocation through Orr's 'voyage' to Sweden of the journey
up Lake Garda to freedom in *A Farewell To Arms* deals comically
(though not dismissively) with the question of escape. The burden
of these earlier novels on Heller exactly demonstrates what Harold
Bloom has called the 'anxiety of influence' and parodic allusion in
Catch-22 becomes a means of resisting the authority of these
prototexts. Parody and for that matter the whole range of non-
realistic techniques used in this novel faced the reader of 1961 with
a problem. As John W. Aldridge states, 'most reviewers were
locked into a conventional and − as shortly became evident − an
outmoded assumption about what war fiction should be. They
had, after all, been conditioned by the important novels of World
War I and reconditioned by the World War II novels of Norman
Mailer, Irwin Shaw, [etc.] . . . to expect that the authentic technique
for treating war experience is harshly documentary realism.'[11] On
every page *Catch-22* thwarts these expectations and yet, although it
does not work within the realistic mode, it does nevertheless insist
on the actuality of war and the constant nearness of death.
Romance is generally treated as another case of self-delusion;
Nately, for instance, is presented as the fool of his own naïveté in
falling in love with a whore. When Nelson Algren stated in his
review of Heller's novel that the works of Jones and Mailer were
'lost within' it, he was right to pinpoint the influence but wrong to
imply that it is concealed.

Heller's original plan to depict Yossarian as a Jewish character in
spite of his Armenian name can be explained by the influence of

Joyce's *Ulysses*. Heller subsequently explained his purposes as follows: 'I wanted somebody who would seem to be *out*side the culture in every way — ethnically as well as others . . . I wanted to get an extinct culture, somebody who could not be identified either geographically, or culturally, or sociologically — somebody who has a capability of ultimately divorcing himself completely from all emotional and psychological ties'.[12]

Hemingway's location of his American protagonist in an Italian context was too specific to be followed by Heller. Where Joyce's Bloom supplied one model, Bloom's Jewishness evidently created problems for Heller because he would be moving too near to the stereotypes of recent American war fiction. William Saroyan's story 'Twenty Thousand Assyrians' alerted him to an ethnic alternative because it defined Yossarian so little. Partly from his reading of Nelson Algren's *The Man with the Golden Arm* Heller has declared that he wanted an 'open hero' with a fluid identity, the sort of identity Yossarian prematurely boasts about to Clevinger: 'They couldn't touch him because he was Tarzan, Mandrake, Flash Gordon. He was Bill Shakespeare. He was Cain, *Ulysses*, the Flying Dutchman . . .' (19: my emphasis). Like the protagonist of Richard Farina's novel *Been Down So Long It Looks Like Up To Me* (1966) Yossarian claims immunity from his environment by appealing to a medley of comic book, operatic and literary figures. Farina's Gnossos Pappadopoulis like Yossarian adopts varied comic roles to manoeuvre through situations of emotional and physical danger with the least risk to his self. Ultimately his immunity breaks down biologically when he catches gonorrhea and politically when his draft papers catch up with him. It remains to be seen how immune Yossarian really is.

Initially Yossarian emerges as an anti-hero, comically (but sensibly) devoted to survival: 'his only mission . . . was to come down alive' (29). His tricks and stratagems to avoid danger (breaking his intercom, checking into the hospital with fake symptoms, etc.) relate his actions to the general direction of the novel's ironies. Tony Tanner has rightly commented on the symbolic importance of Yossarian's flying style which physically increases his crew's chances of surviving the flak and which reflects Yossarian's attitude towards the army: 'He is forced to remain within the system, but by his way of moving [ducking and weaving] he can refuse to be of the system, ignoring or negating its rigid patterns'.[13] By defining himself against the system through what he won't do

Yossarian becomes a voice of sanity amid the prevailing mania. He
is one of the few characters who actually remembers that there is a
war going on and who clings on to a residual rationality in spite of
the fact that such terms as 'crazy' or 'goofy' are used so often that
they almost lose their meaning.

Yossarian maintains his sanity through facetious 'routines'
which reduce his opponents to fury. The early chapters, for
instance, contain important arguments between himself and
Clevinger which play their part in mocking patriotic pieties. The
following exchange is typical:

> 'They're trying to kill me', Yossarian told him calmly.
> 'No-one's trying to kill you', Clevinger cried.
> 'Then why are they shooting at me?' Yossarian asked.
> 'They're shooting at *everyone*', Clevinger answered.
> 'They're trying to kill everyone'.
> 'And what difference does that make?' (16)

Yossarian's logic represents an effort to detach himself from mass
purposes and to rationalise his own individual survival. It makes
no difference whether he is shot at by the Germans or by other
Americans, or whether he is poisoned by food in the mess.
'Enemy' becomes an umbrella term for all forces trying to kill him,
forces which are summarised externally and internally: 'There was
Hitler, Mussolini and Tojo, for example, and they were all out to kill
him . . . There were lymph glands that might do him in' (170).
Yossarian imagines himself at the focus of a massive conspiracy in
a comically exaggerated form of paranoia which might seem ludicrous but which is repeatedly being confirmed by the facts. Towards the end of the novel Nately's whore seems to hold Yossarian
guilty for Nately's death and is constantly trying to kill him,
moving from place to place with incredible speed and adopting an
unlikely variety of disguises. She realises Yossarian's verbal
antics revolve around the most serious topic of all – death. Joking
becomes a tactic for recognising death and staving it off briefly by
defusing a situation of its sinister implications. The 'death' of the
soldier in white becomes an occasion for facetiously accusing the
Texan of being a murderer; Yossarian's joke about the German
Lepage gun which glues whole formations of plans together temporarily injects comedy into the general fear of bombing Bologna;
and so on.

The sort of logic Yossarian uses in the exchange quoted owes a debt to *Alice in Wonderland*, specifically to the dialogue-games with the caterpillar and the Cheshire Cat, and to the why? — why not? question and answer sequence at the mad hatter's tea-party.[14] Yossarian has no monopoly over this kind of argument but uses his skills to telling effect. His arguments question assumptions of patriotic purpose and his joking could be seen as a protective device, an insulating series of performances which buffer him against hostile situations. He performs as the wise fool of the novel, the buffoon whose horseplay conceals a steady resistance to authority for the sanest of reasons — self-preservation. He is particularly quick to identify the roles required of him, as when he is visited by the hospital psychiatrist and starts feeding him the expected lines about his ambivalence, sexual repression, etc. Major Sanderson's refusal to accept his answers (when Yossarian says he dislikes fish because they are too bland he comments 'we'll soon discover the true reason') links the psychiatrist with the administration's general inability to recognise the explicit and obvious — the whole novel is in that respect a sustained assault on common sense — and also discards a possible way of reading the novel through psychological decoding. Yossarian's verbal games then express covert or open defiance of his military superiors and of the administrative procedures to which he is subjected. To a certain extent his sentiments and tactics are endorsed by the narrator who repeatedly injects facetious lines to undermine the decorum of what is being described. When Lieutenant Scheisskopf triumphs in a military parade by training his men not to move their arms, we are told that he won the parade 'hands down'. This appalling joke ties consistently in with Yossarian's hostility towards the pennant prizes for the parades. Heller uses him to set up a Swiftian perspective on them (cf. the ribbons in the Lilliputian court) as empty, meaningless objects. By refusing their symbolism Yossarian is making one of a series of gestures of withdrawal from army values. The most startling example of silent protest is of course his appearance naked to collect a medal after the mission to Avignon. Nakedness has traditional connotations of disengagement from society in American literature. During Huckleberry Finn's journey down the Mississippi, for instance, Huck and Jim briefly enact their separation from the society of the shore by travelling naked. If clothes carry with them suggestions of society's corruption, the act of stripping them off and swimming (Huck in the Mississippi,

Hemingway's Jake Barnes in the Atlantic, Yossarian in the Mediterranean) becomes a token cleansing of the self. When Yossarian returns early from the first Bologna mission even the vegetation of Pianosa becomes diseased. On his way to the beach he sees thousands of new mushrooms 'poking their nodular fingers up through the clammy earth like lifeless stalks of flesh', a grotesque image combining life (fingers, phalli?) and death. The stream has a 'bloated gurgle', the very waves make an 'apathetic moaning'. It is only when he has performed a ritual immersion that this projective imagery can recede: 'He submerged himself head first into the green water several times until he felt clean and wide-awake...' (142). Nakedness can be both cleansing and subversive of military rank. Without their uniforms all men are reduced to the same level of humanity. Yossarian's decision to parade without his uniform asserts his individual existence just as he attends Snowden's funeral again naked and by climbing up what he only half-facetiously calls his 'tree of life'. Like the protagonist of Heller's first published story Yossarian's refusal to don his uniform represents a refusal to play a role. Heller has commented on his refusal to buy a dinner jacket in relevant terms: 'I hate uniforms. I hate uniformity. A tuxedo is worse than a soldier's uniform. A soldier has no choice. Wearing a dinner jacket is *voluntarily* dressing in a uniform, and that is an attempt to dignify a social occasion, to create a sense of pomp'.[15] Yossarian preserves a limited autonomous identity for himself by choosing even though it is a negative action, and thereby contrasts himself with that embodiment of military decorum Lieutenant Scheisskopf who welcomed the outbreak of war 'since it gave him an opportunity to wear an officer's uniform every day'! (69)

Yossarian's actions confirm Heller's assertion that he is 'innocent and good' by constantly asserting the simple truisms which a manic bureaucracy obscures – the horror of death, the need to live as long as possible, and so on. His comically extreme reactions to women (instant drooling frenzy) have brought prim comments from the critics but without recognition that most of Yossarian's sexual activity takes place in his imagination. Under the stress of combat missions where death is always at hand women became converted into tantalising images of vitality. This description of an Italian countess and her beautiful daughter-in-law is typical: 'He could picture ... the kind of underclothing they wore against their svelte feminine parts, filmy, smooth, clinging garments of deepest

black or of opalescent pastel radiance with flowering lace bor-
ders . . .' (155). Yossarian slows down the image to relish it, but it is
an image of absence. Women are constantly eluding him, denying
him the sexual comfort he craves. One exception is Nurse Duckett
who offers Yossarian affectionate company — to blow the relationship up into a love-affair would risk repeating Hemingway. Chapter 30 oscillates between life and death, making Nurse Duckett's
importance as emotional refuge clear. In spite of her presence
Yossarian's thoughts turn to death by water and particularly to the
first corpse he ever saw. In recoil he turns for Nurse Duckett:
'Yossarian had once stood on a jetty at dawn and watched a tufted
round log that was drifting toward him on the tide turn unex-
pectedly into the bloated face of a drowned man . . . He thirsted for
life and reached out ravenously to grasp and hold Nurse Duckett's
flesh' (331). The action of reaching out imaginatively or physically
is characteristic of Yossarian's dealings with women. As often as
not they slip through his fingers. Even here the deceptive calm of
the beach is suddenly shattered by the grotesque death of Kid
Sampson.

Yossarian's main problem is how to avoid an early death and
Heller has suggested that a development takes place in him towards the 'birth of Yossarian's consciousness of himself as a moral
being'.[16] Heller locates the sign of this new awareness as an
explicit sense of responsibility to himself. By the end of the novel
three options are presented to Yossarian in order to set up his final
decision. He could simply stay in hospital, but that would be
inconsistent with our sense of Yossarian as a character in motion.
Hospital would reduce him to inertia, to a state of passivity
associated ultimately with the soldier in white; and anyway hospital does not provide a refuge from death, it simply makes death
seem quieter. Yossarian's second option is to accept the deal
offered him by Colonels Korn and Cathcart to become a war hero,
in effect a PR man for the American army. He accepts this deal and
prematurely experiences a surge of exhilaration ('He was home
free; he had pulled it off; his act of rebellion had succeeded
. . .'(419). Here again Heller orders events so that Yossarian's
confidence is undercut. The final details of Snowden's death
follow this decision which he takes back. Here we come to the third
option — to desert. The news of Orr's arrival in Sweden introduces
a crucial note of hope into Yossarian's considerations even though
the possibility of rowing so far is ludicrous. Throughout the novel

Yossarian has been yearning to get to a sanctuary (Majorca, Switzerland and Sweden are mentioned), a symbolic point outside the cycle of corruption and death. The fact that Sweden is so remote and the fact that Yossarian apparently cannot row are irrelevantly realistic considerations to an ambiguous token act. When Yossarian declares that he will 'catch' a ride to Rome and that 'they'll have to try like hell to catch me this time'; and when he 'takes off' in the last line of the novel Heller has revised two of the book's key terms so as to suggest liberation from the entrapment which has beset Yossarian throughout. But his escape remains a matter of nuance and ambiguous suggestion. Almost any discussion of the ending makes it sound more positive than the text would warrant.

An important issue arises here over Yossarian's status in the novel. Heller has compared *Catch-22* to *On the Road* and *The Ginger Man* as all being works where the author's ideas are the same as the main character's. We have seen examples of a close correlation between Yossarian's sentiments and those of Heller outside the novel. Faced with such correlations and with some rudimentary autobiographical parallels between Yossarian and Heller himself (Heller did fly bombing missions in the Mediterranean and did have a horrifying experience during a raid on Avignon), the reader might be tempted to see Yossarian as a stable and reliable figure amid the grotesque characters and events which surround him. The unusually complex and disconcerting structure of the novel tempts the reader to make an uncritical identification with Yossarian. Is he in fact as immune as he claims? Let us take first of all the circular logic games which Yossarian plays with Clevinger. Behind these games lurks an issue of power − who wins? Clearly Yossarian triumphs over Clevinger (which is important for undermining patriotic certainties) but then just as thoroughly Orr defeats Yossarian in the half-mile questions and answers over why he used to carry apples in his cheeks, thereby forcing Yossarian into the ultimate refuge of silence. The circular games Yossarian plays resemble the circular procedures of the administration too closely to be dismissed as mere horseplay and in fact many of Yossarian's 'games' rebound on him. His forgery of signatures while censoring letters leads, via a travesty of causality, to the interrogation of the chaplain. His malingering in the hospital leads to him being forced by a doctor who claims that 'we're all in this business of illusion together' to act out the role of a dying Italian airman. The latter episode, where farce tugs against pathos, actually reduces Yossarian to tears. Similarly his joke about the Lepage gun is taken up by others with the result that even he later imagines it is true; the reappearance of the soldier in white in Chapter 34 leads to repeated jokes (?) about his bandages being stretched over a void. In these cases Yossarian's identity blurs into the collective hysteria. Since he is not alone in indulging in verbal routines it is impossible to separate Yossarian rhetorically from the other characters. His imagination of conspiracy, his apparent readiness to believe even his own facetious jokes implicate him in the general madness of the novel. Walter Nash's comment on the characters certainly includes him: they are trapped 'within a closed system of argument which envelops all, and from which they cannot escape because they have recourse only to propositions generated within the system'.[17] For all his scepticism towards the war Yossarian becomes involved in the collective guilt (by causing the death of Kraft when he makes two approaches during the raid on Ferrara). He is primarily important as a *voice* opposing with administrative processes, repeatedly and futilely insisting on their arbitrary nature. His gradual isolation as his friends disappear (Orr and Clevinger), die (Nately) or turn into murderers (Aarfy) enacts the gradual diminution of rationality in the world of the novel.

THE CHAPLAIN AND 'CHARACTER'

The first page of *Catch-22* links Yossarian with the group chaplain R.O. (originally R.C.) Shipman. Only an intermittent presence in the first half of the novel, the chaplain later develops into as important a character as Yossarian because he too is an outsider, haunted more and more by thoughts of his own marginality. His religion (Anabaptist) was chosen for the same reason as Yossarian's ethnic identity: to suggest familiarity *and* strangeness.[18] Heller develops the chaplain for several reasons. Whereas we are only given brief access to Yossarian's memories and nightmares the chaplain's inner thoughts become all the more prominent as his professional role becomes irrelevant. While the men only see the latter, only see the uniform as it were, Heller counteracts this external view in order to explore the pathos of the chaplain's loss of faith. His uncertainty is not confined to himself but given a broader representative significance in connection with his belief in God. The various religious allusions in the novel thus converge on the chaplain. Kraft goes down in flames on the seventh day 'while God was resting' in an ironic allusion to the Genesis creation-story.[19] Prayers are considered by Colonel Cathcart, but only as an exercise in publicity so that he can get his picture in the *Saturday Evening Post*. And Yossarian attacks the comfortable illusions of Scheisskopf's wife until she collapses in tears, insisting that 'the God I don't believe in is a good God, a just God, a merciful God'. Yossarian's attack hammers home the negative implications of the novel's inverted religious allusions, specifically mocking out of existence the twin notions of God as a source of justice and as a causal principle. When Yossarian plays God in tinkering with letters it is significantly in a destructive form 'obliterating whole homes and streets' and Major Major's father uses his so-called Calvinism to change his son's name. Predestination turns into a practical joke.

The disappearance of faith does not represent a specifically religious problem in the novel but is part and parcel of its undermining of a stable objective reality. The chaplain's role then is to register the epistemological doubts which beset many of the other characters. He is literally and figuratively an outsider, beyond the military hierarchy, living apart from the other men in a 'passive, half-voluntary exile'. His 'aide' Corporal Whitcomb is actually his tormenter, alternatively threatening and probing in spite of his lower rank. In fact the chaplain experiences severe problems and is himself a problem for others because it is so difficult to place him in the military hierarchy. He is subjected to abuse from lower ranks as well as from superior officers. If authority is seen as essentially *placing* the self, the chaplain's doubts about God then become the internalised form of his difficulties over rank. The chaplain's naïve faith in truth is shown by his simple direct statements to Whitcomb and the other officers which are universally greeted with distrust or derision. One image which unsettles the chaplain is that of the naked man up the tree at Snowden's funeral. This is mentioned before we see it because it is important for raising questions in the chaplain's mind — is it a hallucination or a revelation of absolute truth? He cannot decide and falls victim to spirals of uncertainty: 'There was no way of really knowing anything, he knew, not even that there was no way of really knowing anything' (262). The chaplain's own particular version of catch-22 is a logical circularity where intellect tugs against feeling and where the narrative syntax repeatedly forms balancing pairs ('he was either blessed or losing his mind'). The symmetry of these alternatives is a trap in itself because it rules out a third possibility: that the chaplain really *did* see a naked man up a tree. But the chaplain's personal isolation encourages him to direct all doubt inwards at his own expense. Figures seen in the distance are assumed to be talking about him and he constantly imagines that he is the victim of some kind of irony or joke. Not even his memory of his family is exempt from this process so that his imagination leads him to construct fantasies of violence which he can never bring himself to entrust to his letters. A brilliant hallucinatory sequence in Chapter 25 enacts this process. The chaplain sets out to see Major Major but rushes into hiding when he sees an officer approaching (who turns out to be Major Major!). In Major Major's office he actually mimics the former's actions by jumping out of the window and then unconsciously avoids Major Major for a *second* time. When he realises this he returns yet again to Major Major's empty office. The frantic motion in this episode converts the chaplain's uncertainty into gesture; is it movement towards a goal, or the avoidance of it? Characteristically the impetus of the chapter sweeps the chaplain on to fresh visions, description being geared very closely to his perspective. So when Flume (another exile, this time from fancied murder) suddenly appears, it is as the 'mad hermit in the woods', then he is humanised into a pathetic victim and reconverted into a spectre when he vanishes back into the undergrowth. Pace and tempo are crucial here for causing the chaplain's bewilderment. He literally does not have time to digest all the things he sees so that they become (like the naked man up the tree) images detached from a meaningful context, teasing him towards a significance that stays beyond his reach.

Ironically the only liberation the chaplain can experience is through lying. It is only when he learns to detach language from truth and learn the 'handy technique of protective rationalization' that he can gain any physical relief. This process involves semantic revision 'to turn vice into virtue and slander into truth' (356). As usual there is a twist. Shortly after the chaplain has learned these new tactics he is arrested and interrogated. The chaplain's experiences dramatise the fate of belief before circumstances which will not support that belief. His initial assumptions resemble those of Clevinger, Nately and more minor characters, and stand at the opposite extreme of the moral spectrum to the old man whom Nately meets in Rome. The latter functions as a pagan oracle voicing an amoral creed of survival which shocks Nately with its cynicism but which is at least overt and free from the prevailing hypocrisy. Heller attaches condemnatory adjectives to him ('sordid', 'intuitous', etc.) which collapse as he constantly wins his argument. It is impossible to take at face value the description of him as fiendlike because his destructive logic is arguing in favour of life and anyway closely resembles Yossarian's exchanges with Clevinger. The old man participates importantly in the novel's general erosion of patriotic platitudes before he too succumbs to death.

In a novel where individuality is constantly under threat from the administration it is not surprising that Heller avoids a realistic depiction of character. As many critics have noted, most of the characters are attenuated down to the two dimensions of a comic strip and are only given sufficient identity to articulate or embody a point of view. They are what Heller himself has called 'cartoon eccentrics' designed to represent the 'caricatures produced by war'.[20] They are defined simply through four main devices: a verbal mannerism (Doc Daneeka's stock response to any complaint is 'You think you've got problems. What about me?'), personal obsessions (Orr with fixing a valve, Corporal Whitcomb with censoring letters), through association with items of dress or physical objects (Aarfy with his pipe, McWatt with his red pyjamas), and finally as physical caricatures. Milo, for instance, 'had a long thin nose with sniffing, damp nostrils heading sharply off to the right, always pointing away from where the rest of him was looking' (63). The point here is division, to give a physical rendering of his theoretical appeal to principle and legality which masks the blatant cynicism of his commercial dealings.

The characters' names obviously play a crucial part in defining their type-qualities. On the simplest level Colonel Korn delivers corny addresses to his men. 'Aarfy' is taken from the stylised bark of a friendly dog in a comic strip (in the stage adaptation of the novel he is introduced by the sound of barking) and even sees himself as 'good old Aarfy' after he has committed murder. Orr is described by Heller as the 'most intelligent person in the book' because 'he is advancing a false self' to conceal his plans for survival.[21] If he represents an alternative ('or') to compliance it is ironically appropriate that it should be through total disguise. Major Major's name reduplicates a word which is not a name and draws attention to military rank. It is exactly rank which he tries to evade through his disguises but paradoxically it is disguise and resemblance which most define him, the comparison with Henry Fonda contrasting sadly with his own lack of self-confidence. Names then can raise possibilities about a character's role. Is Milo a 'minder' (which might fit his ostensible post as mess sergeant) or a 'minderbinder', a creator of 'binds' patterned on catch-22 itself? The reader's general tendency to look for connotations in names here becomes an analogue of how the characters read each other. The typographical blank in Major − de Coverley represents spatially his enigmatic quality to his own men and to the Germans. By the same token Nately suggests an inherent (in*nate*) character, the product by birth of a transmitted set of values which no longer apply. Nately is usually seen in relating to two characters: his whore who supplies him with a substitute family, and the old man in the brothel who becomes a rival father. When Heller was revising Chapter 23 of the novel, substantial passages relating to Nately's background were edited out, revised and published separately under the title 'Love, Dad'.[22] This sketch is a satirical portrait of a family with aristocratic pretensions, satirical because Nately's mother constantly betrays her own ignorance and because his father is simultaneously ironic and credulous towards their own status. The series of letters from his father to Nately, far from being 'eloquent' and 'brilliant' as the latter supposes, mix together an odd jumble of patriotism, slogans and quotations (from Polonius among others), and sexual nudges. 'Love, Dad' sharpens an irony which is subdued in the novel, namely that an emphasis on birth is irrelevant when death is so close.

If names play their part in representation we also need to ask how stable they are since *Catch-22* obviously gains many of its complicating effects through confusion. The loss of a name is a crucial event in modern literature because it brings identity under a special pressure. When Bloom is interrogated in the Nighttown section of *Ulysses* the fact that he can't remember his name coincides with the dispersal of his self into separate fantasy figures. Similarly in Ralph Ellison's *Invisible Man* the protagonist's lack of name reflects his vulnerability to a society which will force readymade identities on him. In the fiction of Joyce, Ellison and Kafka (the latter's works, as Heller admits, influenced *Catch-22*) attenuation or loss of name goes hand in hand with interrogation, implying a primal guilt in the character and an overt hostility between the individual and his surrounding social institutions.

This pattern is repeated in Heller's chaplain whose name is suppressed in favour of his role and who is then charged with forging signatures. In *Catch-22* names are reassuring to the authorities because they offer a means of control. Forging a signature thus becomes an act of subversion because the forger is playfully borrowing multiple identities, thereby undermining the stability of official records. During the chaplain's interrogation in the cellar he is asked to sign his name 'in his own handwriting'. When he does so he is told to his astonishment that it is not his handwriting. As usual in the novel the interrogators reject the obvious in favour of the hidden and mysterious, denying the chaplain's 'character' in a double sense. Denying one means of self-representation here confirms the chaplain's own doubts about his identity ('perhaps he really was Washington Irving') and ironically increases the general confusion. The administration's inefficiency actually defeats its own object, proliferating names and identities beyond their control. Names become detached entities generating their own power. It is Yossarian's *name* specifically which fills Colonel Cathcart with a panic which he tries to purge by converting the name into a message: *'Yossarian!!!(?)!'*. Having written down the name he tries to decode it in a farcically right-wing manner: 'there were so many esses in it. It just had to be subversive' (207). This sort of reading grotesquely resembles the way in which a name is read in a literary text and perhaps for that reason Heller takes famous literary names (T. S. Eliot, Washington Irving, John Milton — the latter two reversible) as forgeries or names without referents within the novel. Cathcart is superstitiously falling into the logical fallacy of Humpty Dumpty who tells Alice: 'It's a stupid name enough! . . . What does it mean?'[23] The answer for Cathcart lies in his own paranoia. He interprets 'Yossarian' (even fantasising multiple Yossarians!) as a principle of conspiracy focused on himself. Instead of carrying a fixed relation to a character, names prove to be rhetorically vulnerable and relative to role (Yossarian becomes Giuseppe when playing the dying Indian airman) and context (Yossarian becomes A. Fortiori by occupying the hospital bed with the latter name on it and therefore all the more obviously — *a fortiori* — the other man). The name explicitly draws attention to the manic logic involved in this identification and helps to explain why characters have to insist on their own names in a desperate effort to cling onto a vestigial identity. Here, as elsewhere in the novel, common sense is no help at all.

The fact that most chapters are named after characters gives a misleading impression of an orderly progression through a gallery of grotesques and comic figures; and the titles are anyway of ambiguous importance since they were added at the last minute just as the novel was going to press.[24] In fact the chapters which devote their main contents to their title characters (such as Major Major in Chapter 9) are the exception rather than the rule. The chapter 'McWatt' devotes far more attention to Milo and 'Nurse Duckett' concentrates more on Yossarian's questioning by the psychiatrist. Chapters are not structured around characters because character is so unstable. They overlap with each other: the chaplain unconsciously imitates Major Major's furtive escapes from his office, Major Major imitates Yossarian's forgeries and so on. Not even their status is fixed. Because the novel avoids linear chronology and sets up a variety of limited perspectives, one character is repeatedly attenuating into a memory-image or a fantasy figure in the consciousness of another character. Given this shifting status in characters and the frequently deceptive nature of the novel's chapter titles, we now need to ask: does it have a kind of structure? Is there an order which is not accessible to the characters but plain for the reader to see?

STRUCTURE AND CHRONOLOGY

When *Catch-22* first appeared it was attacked by the *New Yorker* for being a 'manic travesty' of war fiction which is exactly right, although the evaluative conclusion drawn by the reviewer was very conservative. The travesty of ordered realism starts in the opening lines of the novel with a romantic cliché, a startling application of it and an apparently unrelated paragraph giving details of the military hospital (although it is not until the second page that we discover the setting is military). Even allowing for Heller's compositional mannerism of starting his novels with an eye-catching phrase, he has given the opening of *Catch-22* a typographical arrangement which stresses the discontinuity between each item, and sure enough *dis*continuity not continuity becomes the norm throughout the novel. There is a constant undermining of expectations: drama, narrative, even the stability of the text itself are all denied.

Not long after the publication of the novel a lengthy review by

Roger H. Smith appeared in the journal *Daedalus*. The review was unusual in that Smith avoided superficial expressions of hostility or enthusiasm by going into considerable detail over the book's rhetorical strategies. Smith's conclusion is negative and misguided about the absence of structure ('Heller's book reads as if the pages of the manuscript had been scrambled on the way to the printer') but useful for identifying the target of Heller's ironies: '*Catch-22* is immoral in the way of so much contemporary fiction and drama in being inclusively, almost absent-mindedly, anti-institutional'.[25] Smith is right about the anti-institutionalism but says nothing about the novel's mockery of an institutionalised literary solemnity which Heller had encountered at university shortly after the war and which he feeds into the character of Clevinger, 'a very serious, very earnest and very conscientious dope' who 'knew everything about literature except how to enjoy it' (68). His verbal defeats at the hands of Yossarian and his subsequent disappearance hint at the irrelevance of a certain kind of reading. Heller has always denied that his novel has a 'message' and has explained his particular kind of humour as a means of avoiding didactic earnestness: 'I use flippant humor as a way of expressing certain attitudes without being pontifical or moralistic'.[26] One sign of this light humour is Heller's use of passing allusions to Arnold, Shakespeare and Dostoievsky among other writers. In the film shows, for instance, 'for the daily amusement of the dying, ignorant armies clashed by night on a collapsible screen' (26). Here Heller throws out a grim aside which combines references to death, confusion, nightmare and illusion. One of the operative conventions in *Catch-22* is that it should understate its own seriousness, repeatedly converting death, terror and tragedy into bizarre comedy. More sportive and light-hearted is Heller's exploitation of literary cliché to introduce Milo's chapter:

> April had been the best month of all for Milo. Lilacs bloomed in April and fruit ripened on the vine. Heartbeats quickened and old appetites were renewed. In April a livelier iris gleamed upon the burnished dove. April was spring, and in the spring Milo Minderbinder's fancy had lightly turned to thoughts of tangerines. 'Tangerines?' (246)

This mock-formulaic opening moves from general to specific allusion. First Heller pairs phrases symmetrically in the second and third sentences to articulate the traditional resurgence of life in spring. Then he gives a virtual quotation of the tenth couplet from 'Locksley Hall', the second line of which has become proverbial. All these references converge on the one crucial tem missing from the quotation - love. By replacing the expected with the unexpected Heller sets up a question, notionally from a character, but really an anticipatory expression of the reader's surprise. This tactic is of course a very literary one — Byron introduces the love-scene with Julia in Canto I of *Don Juan* with a similar combination of facetious romantic formulae and self-conscious gestures towards the reader — and strengthens two closely related themes in the novel. The first is love which is either indicated as an absence, a comically instantaneous physical response, or self-deception (Nately with his 'whore', where the retention of the latter term brings Nately's romanticising under critical pressure). Secondly the traditional associations of spring are usually expressed through metaphors which render love concrete and link it to the natural processes of the season. But in the case of Milo the metaphors are again blocked off. The ripening fruit is literally that, fruit which Milo will convert into a saleable commodity.

Briefly playing on metaphorical and literal levels of signification this passage relates to the general direction of Milo's deals which reduce objects to items, and also draws the reader's attention to a series of puns culminating in the quotation from *King Lear* which is Snowden's 'message' — 'ripeness is all'.[27] Where Edgar uses 'ripeness' to try to induce a philosophical acceptance of impending death in Gloucester, Heller blocks off this area of meaning, reducing the term to physical reference. One important metaphysical theme in *Catch-22* is the physical vulnerability of man which the purposes of the war or the military bureaucracy exploit to the full. Death in this novel is presented as a conversion process whereby human beings become mere matter and are assimilated into the non-human: Kraft becomes a 'bleeding cinder', Kid Sampson is sliced in half and quite literally becomes a 'poor, bare, forked animal'. Snowden similarly spills his guts which happen to be full of ripe tomatoes, and so Heller implies that man may become no more than the fruit, vegetables and meat he consumes. Where Edgar pleads for acquiescence, however, Heller sets up Yossarian as a voice of refusal, of resistance to the inevitability of death; and ironically juxtaposes ripeness with death to link Milo's dealings with the more obviously destructive processes of military combat.

When Heller acknowledges that his novel 'intentionally reverses the conventions of storytelling' he is giving a usefully general indication of its frequent tactic of inversion.[28] Again and again he pursues a method of depressing the tragic and inflating the ludicrous. This reversal of expected priorities was learnt partly from the fiction of Evelyn Waugh which Heller read while at Penn State College. When reviewing *The End of the Battle* (the last volume in the *Sword of Honour* trilogy) Heller argued that Waugh's capacity to treat the important as if it were unimportant had become a boring liability because his protagonist is so wooden.[29] In contrast Heller praises the scene in *A Handful of Dust* (Chapter 3.vi) where Brenda Last is informed of the death of John. Horrified at the thought that it is her lover she sighs with relief that it is only her son. The reaction comically reveals her priorities just as Heller's emphases appear to collude with the values of an officialdom he is actually satirising. The closest direct equivalent to the scene from *A Handful of Dust* is probably the encounter which takes place between Milo and Yossarian up the tree during Snowden's funeral. Milo's attention keeps sliding off the ceremony back on to the problems of his commercial deals constantly rendering ambiguous his expressions of regret. Similarly the death of Kid Sampson is played down in favour of Doc Daneeka's official 'death' and Yossarian is arrested for being in Rome without a pass instead of Aarfy who has just committed murder. In these cases the commercial and the official are given a spurious priority over their alternatives.

In another writer, this time Nabokov, Heller encountered the 'flippant approach to situations which were filled with anguish and grief and tragedy'.[30] The specific text which suggested this possibility was *Laughter in the Dark* where the protagonist Albinus' idealistic love is expressed in terms of light and darkness of what is seen and what is not. When Albinus is blinded in a car accident the physical injury confirms his blindness of feeling and renders him all the more vulnerable to tricks at the hands of his mistress and her lover. Heller similarly sets up a tension between narrative tone and subject as, for instance, in the chapter dealing with Doc Daneeka's wife. Her reactions to his 'death' are summarised in a prose which distances the reader — not unsympathetically — from her so as to concentrate attention on the rival communications she receives from the Doc and from the War Department. Potentially these letters could double her grief (since she seems to be bereaved twice) but the summary conveys a rapid sequence of events which sweeps Mrs Daneeka ironically on to prosperity and happiness. Distancing the reader from this potential tragedy does not simply understate emotional impact. It raises ironic questions about who is the true victim, here the Doc himself who disappears out of the text into limbo.

The examples above suggest a text which delights in disconcerting the reader, which sets up a context of profanity apparently hostile to conventional literary effects but pursues literary strategies, and which constantly pretends to underwrite the official values of the military administration through its perspective. In fact the text of *Catch-22* is far less stable than these examples suggest. Events are repeated, names are fluid, situations are not quite fixed so that dialogue may jump to a character not physically present. Heller has explained that he 'tried to give it [the novel] a structure that would complement the content of the book itself, which really derives from our present atmosphere of chaos, disorganization, absurdity, cruelty . . .' and saw a similarity between his own experiments and those of Kerouac and Donleavy because they were all responding to 'conditions of breakdown of form'.[31] On the most superficial level then the chaotic appearance of *Catch-22* is mimetic of a perceived disorder. This begs the main critical question, one which has occupied a lot of critical attention: does the novel have a structure? Jesse Ritter sees Heller as using a modified stream of consciousness method but any account of *Catch-22* in terms of psychological time must either hypothesise a consciousness which embraces the whole of the novel or collapse before the self-evident fact that Heller grants us access to a number of minds (so no *one* consciousness is privileged) and anyway carefully specifies that events are external and actual.[32] This marks a huge difference between the novel and its film version. The latter begins at the end with Yossarian striking his deal with Korn and Cathcart and then being attacked by Nately's whore. As Yossarian collapses into unconsciousness the film dissolves into the past, performing an extended loop before we return to the opening scene. This means that the film is framed within Yossarian's consciousness making a dismissal of scenes as fantasy or hallucination all the easier. The novel presents scenes which might be physical possibilities without giving the reader the time to decide one way or another.

The critical arguments over the structure of *Catch-22* revolve around Heller's treatment of time and his use of repetition. A

danger involved in the former was exposed in an exchange between Jan Solomon and Doug Gaukroger.[33] Solomon argued that
there were two time schemes working together — one moving
backwards and forwards in Yossarian's consciousness, and the
other following Milo's linear series of successes. Gaukroger took
issue with this account on the grounds that the factual details did
not fit, and then proceeded to demonstrate that the events in the
novel could be rearranged into a perfectly consistent linear time
scheme. It does credit to Gaukroger's patience in unravelling this
chronology but it also does a radical disservice to the novel which
uses perceptions of time to disorient the reader. The possibility
that all events fit together is something which the reader only
suspects and it is a combination of suspicion and uncertainty
which gives the novel so much of its power. To overnaturalise or
oversystematise its time-sequences would undermine this power.
The other main explanations of the novel's structure have concen-
trated on repetition, variously locating an expanding static image,
'an interplay between present narrative and the cumulative repetition and gradual clarification of past actions', a 'cyclical pattern of
continually repeated motifs', the advancement of five standard
routines, and a progression 'by epicycles within larger cycles'.[34]

Before considering repetition let us see how time figures in the
novel and particularly whether it is accessible to orderly explanation. The standard syntactic form in *Catch-22* is the simple declaratory statement. Only occasionally do we get longer sentences like
the following which begins in the simple narrative past tense: 'The
system worked just fine for everybody, especially for Doc Deneeka
who *found* himself with all the *time* he needed to watch old Major –
de Coverley *pitching* horseshoes in his private horseshoe pitching
pit, *still wearing* the transparent eye patch Doc Daneeka *had
fashioned* for him from the strip of celluloid *stolen* from Major
Major's orderly room window *months before* when Major - de
Coverley *had returned* from Rome with an injured cornea *after
renting two* apartments there for the officers and enlisted men to
use on their rest leaves' (emphasis added) (33). The only source of
difficulty in following this sentence is in keeping track of the time
indicators. Every episode contains references to other episodes so
that the reader is constantly invited to make connections but these
connections multiply and extend too far for the connections ever to
be finally made. The reader is thus in a position similar to that of
one of the characters in being haunted by a sense of connectedness

which can never be adequately substantiated. In constituting the text of *Catch-22* then we must be on our guard against assembling the various episodes into an overtly neat sequence which does not correspond to the experience of reading the novel. The linear rise in the number of required combat missions tantalises us with the possibility of an order lying behind events but this order is so well hidden that, as one critic has shown, it even led Heller himself into some factual errors.[35] Our difficulties with chronology are further compounded by Heller's evocation of different aspects of time. On the lowest level there is the singular occurrence like Orr's fight with a prostitute which resists being fitted into a context and therefore resists meaning. As Paul Ricoeur states, 'to be historical, an event must be more than a singular occurrence, a unique happening. It receives its definition from its contribution to the development of a plot'.[36] An event like Orr's fight implies an inchoate or hidden plot which helps to explain why for so many characters plots turn into conspiracies. Yossarian is used often as a structural convenience linking one section to another simply by being present (at the beginning of Chapter 5, for instance, both Doc Daneeka and Chief White Halfoat tell their stories to him); hence it is quite consistent formally for officers to suspect him of being involved in everything. Time is also crucial in *Catch-22* as series (the opening chapter shows Yossarian in hospital *once again*), as continuity (the war *goes on* as a permanent state without any end in sight), as repetition (the act of flying missions) and as linear sequence (the inevitable raising of the number of required missions is a premise to the novel). Much of the novel's complexity grows out of intersections between these different perceptions of time which divides our attention. In the first chapter we are torn between Yossarian's activities as a beginning, a primal event which will be repeated later, and the suggestion of earlier recurrences. What did he do the previous times? One of the significances of the novel's title is similarly to indicate a series: if catch-22 is so bad, what are the other ones like? One effect of this complexity is to blur our sense of origins and to locate characters within processes which repeat and repeat over and over again. As with most important issues in the novel, time becomes an explicit topic of conversation at the end of Chapter 4 where Dunbar startles Clevinger and Yossarian by proposing a notion of time as acceleration against which the individual struggles helplessly. Time's speed is inseparable from the nearness of death ('You're inches away from death every time you go on a mission. How much older can you be at your age?' (38). Dunbar makes it clear that all the combat officers in the novel are in a race against time specifically to be sent home before the missions are raised, and generally in an effort to slow down transition and maximise duration. This is expressed in contrasts between periods of calm and rapid activity as in Chapter 28 where the lazy beach scene is suddenly transformed by Kid Sampson's death into one of frenzied movement. Linear chronology in the novel becomes associated with official versions of reality and as such becomes discredited. The fragmentation of time-sequences could thus be seen as a structural analogue of Yossarian's flying patterns. By fracturing the continuity of his narrative Heller forces the reader to examine the nature of its connections, 'to *experience* the book rather than simply read it'.[37] Unpredictability at once guarantees the reader's interest and insecurity. And if we begin to suspect that we are the victims of a practical joke aren't we essentially repeating the characters' suspicions of a joking and indifferent God?

The structure of most individual chapters grows directly out of the time-shifts which take place within them. For instance, Chapter 13 takes as its present the immediate aftermath of moving the Bologna bombing line. Major – de Coverley has disappeared so the main character reference in this chapter is to the absence hinted at in his very name. We move backwards to an unspecified, generalised time to get a summary of his character, then back again to his establishment of military accommodation in Rome, back slightly to his entry into Rome, and back yet again to a point where Milo begins one of his commercial deals in eggs. The chapter moves backwards and forwards in narrative requirements which present information and imagery to be taken up at other points in the novel. The backward jumps can only partly be naturalised as memory and at any given point the narrative details can only be partially understood.[38] Heller seems to have borrowed from *Ulysses* the simple device of releasing information before a context makes it comprehensible. The point of a particular chapter may have nothing to do with its character title. Chapter 5, for instance, assembles two stories of characters' pasts, those of Doc Daneeka and Chief White Halfoat, who tell them to Yossarian rather than each other. The juxtaposition invites comparison and comparison shows that both characters are victims, the implication being that they should be depending on each other instead of hating each other. This irony is brought to bear in the last part of the chapter on the combat missions. The second importance of the chapter is the Doc's exposition of catch-22 which is revised into a joke about whether Appleby has flies in his eyes transmitted from Orr to Yossarian, Appleby and Havermeyer, and thereby actually demonstrating its own tendency towards reduplication.

In interview Heller has stated that his main model for disrupting a time scheme was Faulkner, particularly the two novels *Absalom, Absalom!* and *The Sound and the Fury*. In the former Quentin Compson is probing into the past to learn more about Thomas Sutpen, the founder of a Virginia plantation which subsequently failed. It is a narrative of Quentin's efforts to constitute a story where he adopts the roles variously of listener, viewer and investigator. He is haunted by the gaps in his knowledge; his subject repeatedly vanishes back into the void of lost time or attenuates into a spectral figure incapable of stabilisation.[39] Heller's characters similarly vanish or become ghosts as a result of death's sudden erasure or of characters' epistemological doubts about the existence of others. *The Sound and the Fury* is also a narrative of absences where the different members of the Compson household try to relate themselves to a missing structure – the family. Heller wanted 'the effect of something being chaotic and anarchistic and yet have the pieces come together' which is not really what happens in Faulkner nor, as I hope to show, in his own text.[40] Both Faulkner novels enact efforts to assemble a narrative through characters' struggles with their own limited knowledge and perspective. In that sense they do anticipate the limitations of Heller's own characters as investigators of their own predicament. Comedy constantly grows out of the clash between rival versions of reality as paranoid meets paranoid.

The primary narrative unit of *Catch-22* is the episode or image which comments metonymically on the novel's action. When Yossarian goes to break up a fight in Hungry Joe's tent 'the jumbled black shadows kept swirling and bobbing chaotically, so that the entire tent seemed to be reeling' (128). Here a perfectly plausible visual impression becomes a visual emblem of disorder with far broader connotations than the local scene. Similarly the soldier in white, surely the most famous image in the book, becomes a physical embodiment of circularity and evidently (this qualification has to grow stronger) a casualty with only the broad shape and displaced traces of humanity – it has 'zippered lips' inside its elbows. It is the ultimate representation of passivity but always seen from outside, unlike the protagonist of Dalton Trumbo's *Johnny Got His Gun* (1939; reissued in 1959 when it was read by Heller). In this novel the perspective is from within. The protagonist has lost limbs and his nose, and is blind and deaf — but can still think. The problem is how to break out of the prison of self and communicate, which is managed eventually by tapping out morse. The soldier offers himself as an educational exhibit but is told by the authorities that it is against regulations. At the end he lapses back into semiconsciousness. Where Trumbo has created a minimal physical existence Heller has devised an image which challenges characters' assumptions about reality: is the shape a shell? Is the soldier ever 'really' seen? The figure recurs twice even more dehumanised into gauze and bandages, and finally perhaps a little shorter. This suggestion of difference is important for implying a kind of recurrence rather than a simple time-loop and also draws our attention to one way in which Heller uses repetition. By far the best explanation of how Heller uses repetition has been given by Robert Merrill, who sensibly declares that 'the real point to be made about the chronology is that Heller chose not to unravel it'. For Merrill repetition is built into the tripartite structure of the book where Chapters 1–16 give us initial information in a broadly comic tone, Chapters 17–33 suspend time sequence to repeat the earlier information in a bleaker way, and the last chapters turn to a more linear time-scheme building up to the climax. Repetition is a tactic forcing us to revise our initial impressions away from simple comedy and each section of the novel is introduced by the appearance of the soldier in white.[41] Merrill's explanation is lucid and convincing, and he rightly implies that the meaning of episodes and images builds up gradually.

Thus by a principle of incremental repetition expands the significance of specific scenes, the most crucial examples of this process being the wounding of Yossarian and the death in his plane of the new gunner Snowden. Snowden is first mentioned in a joking context of death during a briefing. As Heller has admitted, the main missions in the novel are used as reference points, particularly the one to Avignon.[42] The episode is first filled out at the end of Chapter 5 where the dislocation between spoken and silent speech is established. On the first mission to Bologna Yossarian tears his intercom out of its socket as a pretext for turning back, but the nightmarish possibilities in this action are soon developed in the next chapter (and next mission) where a further important contrast is established between Yossarian's panic and Aarfy's grotesque delight. Each time the twin scene (Bologna-Avignon) is repeated new dimensions are added. Yossarian's momentary illusion that it is snowing helps to substantiate one of the lines of association established between whiteness, Snowden and death. White becomes one of the three colour-codes of the novel, the others elaborating the orange of bomb-bursts and the blue of the sea into chromatic versions of death. As Yossarian shouts into a void his sense of unreality mounts: 'Wind whistling up through the jagged gash in the floor [a piece of flak has shredded Aarfy's maps] kept the myriad bits of paper circulating like alabaster particles in a paperweight' (148). Every detail adds to the significance of this passage. The wind whistles, joining the general hubbub; the gash anticipates the wounds of Yossarian and Snowden. The paper fragments relate to the administration of the novel predictably going round in circles. This sequence of repetitions becomes a means of retarding the revelation of meaning, a means too of gradually realising the experience of dying. Panic (Yossarian) is added to frenzy (Dobbs), physical detail to physical detail until the final revelation scene at the end of Chapter 41 where Snowden's entrails become an ironic omen, a grotesque demonstration that, 'the spirit gone, man is garbage' (430). This final scene functions as a predictable culmination to the sequence discussed above and is also the only major disruption to the simplified time-scheme in the last sections of the book. Positioned immediately after Yossarian's agreement to a 'deal' with his superiors, it functions as an implicit turning-point where Yossarian recoils from death, reneges on his agreement, and decides — symbolically at least — to run towards life.

To a certain extent his decision has been made earlier during his visit to Rome while AWOL. This chapter (39) originally entitled 'Night of Horrors' forms the imagistic climax of the book, combining traces of Dante, Dostoievsky and the Nighttown section of *Ulysses*.[43] Heller has explained: 'it was a trip to the underworld, a purgation from which Yossarian emerges . . . He is guilty, and that is the dark beginning of his moral consciousness'.[44] The best critical account of this chapter has been given by Minna Doskow who argues that the street scene distorts appearance and sound to bring about a change in Yossarian from observer to participator in a common human suffering.[45] A cinematic sequence makes visually

explicit what the novel has been implying all along: that the bizarre
has become the norm. Rome is described as a city of ruins whose
inhabitants are now defined through disease, deformity and physical vulnerability. Heller is running a considerable risk in comparing
Yossarian with Christ. When he reflects on human suffering in a
series of questions he almost becomes a scapegoat figure as if
wanting to take all suffering upon himself. This is inconsistently
lucid and altruistic for Yossarian. His authentic responses in this
scene are of bewilderment and dislocation, to function almost as a
camera registering more and more surreal sights. It is true that
Yossarian cries out against the things he sees but it is equally true
that he experiences a series of recoils. Appropriately Heller incorporates Raskolnikov's horse-beating dream into this sequence because Yossarian like Raskolnikov is alienated from the forces of law
and order. It is a vision of legalised brutality ('mobs with clubs
were in control everywhere') followed by a stylised procession of
the deformed. Yossarian is forced into an ultimate state of isolation
without even the sexual refuge of the one girl who remains, since
Aarfy has murdered her that same evening. It is crucial here not to
exaggerate Yossarian's decisiveness. Doskow's explanation of the
chapter (and even to an extent Heller's own) suggests that Yossarian has become less passive. While he is certainly less *acquiescent*,
he is just as much at the mercy of circumstances as he has been
throughout the novel. Heller arranges crucial paragraphs dealing
with Aarfy's murder and Yossarian's arrest so that the main information is given rhetorical prominence, almost like the punch line
of a joke. Yossarian's arrest *is* a kind of joke because of its distorted
priorities, but is too familiar to be any longer funny.

The visit to Rome takes place within a comparatively straightforward line-sequence in the last chapters of the book. This too Heller
has explained with reference to a decision by Yossarian: 'The narrative line in *Catch-22* assumes a forward motion only towards the
end of the book when Yossarian decides to desert'.[46] Once again
there is a danger in exaggerating Yossarian's capacity for independent action. The simplifying of chronology takes place much earlier
in at least Chapter 28 where Sergeant Knight's description of Orr's
survival establishes his credentials and where later in the same
chapter Orr's cryptic remarks suggest a plan. At the end of the
chapter Orr has disappeared. Then follows a series of deaths
(disappearance usually suggesting death anyway) including that of
Nately which brings about Yossarian's decision not to fly any more

missions. A second series, this time of farewells, suggests that Yossarian is about to leave but he does not decide to do so until much later, until his options have diminished further.

The ending of the book does not tie together loose ends or ambiguities in the earlier chapters. Nor does it express a decisive assertive act on Yossarian's part, although it has been approached in such a spirit by several critics. Josh Greenfeld, for one, finds it 'flat and unconvincing' because 'it is the result of process rather than an expression of character'.[47] But Yossarian's entanglement in the manic administrative processes he witnesses implies that the dynamic for his escape can not come from himself. Indeed Heller has implied something on these lines when he states: 'Yossarian finds that the moral of the life of action is to desert from it, and with my sanction'.[48] Heller's sanction amounts to the cumulative impact of his ironies and disruptions of chronology. By deserting Yossarian is acting out the implications of the whole novel's rhetoric. The simplification of the time-scheme rather is a trajectory out of rhetorical and narrative circularity which articulates characters' collective desire for release and which guarantees no final resolution or closure. Unlike Bellow's Herzog whose silence does suggest a resolution of sorts, a period of calm after his efforts to constitute a self through private gestures of communication, Yossarian simply 'takes off'. Like Benny Profane in Pynchon's *V.* he runs off the edge of the page, escaping final definition. As Heller has stated, structure defines character: 'The human lies in the way human beings — the victims of the structure — seek to manipulate it or circumvent it by employing the institution's rules and regulations'.[49] Paradoxically these rules both restrict and define their victims. In revising Chapter 1 of the novel Heller cut out a detail relating to a girl Yossarian loved in America so as to maximise his dependence on the present not past for an identity; 'Yossarian has no past', he has declared.[50] Therefore his 'escape' at the end is a leap into a void beyond the underlying structure which creates his identity through his opposition to it. Structure is imposed by the military bureaucracy in such a way that it is repeatedly discredited. It is here that the full meaning of the novel's title emerges.

CIRCLES

While the syntax of *Catch-22* is straightforward for the most part, the novel does make extensive use of two main kinds of utterance which bear directly on its central themes. On the one hand Heller uses inverted ('it took months of hard work and careful mis-planning') or self-cancelling propositions ('Yossarian had stopped playing chess with him because the games were so interesting they were foolish'); on the other he exploits echolalia. Inversion will commonly take the form of positive expectations being negated, implying a ludicrous redirection of energy. Self-cancellation repre-sents a more complex device because rival versions of an action, character, etc. clash with each other. Take the case of Mudd. 'The dead man in Yossarian's tent was a pest, and Yossarian didn't like him, even though he had never seen him' (22). Proposition B only follows plausibly from proposition A if the adjective 'dead' is reversed. How can a dead man be disliked? And further, how can he be in Yossarian's tent if Yossarian has never seen him? Such apparent paradoxes suggest that the soldier is dead and not dead. They affront our sense of reality by juxtaposing logically conflicting propositions which the reader struggles to reconcile.[51] The military administration almost usurps the place normally occupied by objective truth when we learn that this soldier was killed on a mission before he had officially signed in, and so has no existence as such. The fact that his kit is still in Yossarian's tent proves nothing because the novel repeatedly undermines characters' capacity for empirical verification. The real and the illusory blur together. Flume dreams that he is awake and Hungry Joe dreams that a cat is on his face, finally being smothered to death by that same cat. Paradox induces a state of uncertainty in the reader comparable to that of many characters, denying an overview of actions.

Paradox is also related to one of the novel's most striking characteristics — its discontinuity. This begins on the first page where the typographical separation of a title and out-ceeding statement which thwarts the expectations of that cliché gives us a foretaste of the jumps the narrative will take from character to character and from one point in time to another. Within individual sentences paradox throws us back to the be-ginning of a proposition to locate the source of its contradiction. Self-cancellation obliterates the proposition as it is being made. And echo once again throws us back to the first proposition to see what is being echoed. In all these cases an effect rather like chiasmus is obtained where sequence is thwarted and individual rhetorical units round themselves off. Gary W. Davis has given an excellent account of how such devices work in the novel, arguing that discontinuity operates in all forms of exchange, prominently but not exclusively in language. He concludes that the novel 'exposes the meaninglessness of our conventional understanding of discourse and its processes', seeing it as a critique of language which engrosses the characters themselves: 'abandoned to a labyrinth of words and appearances, they are elements of a discourse which, referring only to itself, neither comprehends nor controls some "world" beyond'.[52] Davis usefully identifies the fate of language as one of the main themes in the novel, showing that it becomes more and more self-referential. In that sense he sees *Catch-22* as a metafictional work, comparable to the fiction of Nabokov, Borges and Barth.

Catch-22, however, does not entirely lose sight of the real. It becomes obscured, attenuated almost out of existence, but never disappears entirely. Partly this is a question of Yossarian's role in the novel as a voice to articulate horror and incredulity. It is crucial that he has to shout louder and louder and that his shouts fall on deaf ears. The repeated scene with Aarfy when Yossarian is wounded is locally nightmarish and also makes a sinister general comment on the fate of common sense. As Davis points out, even such notions as 'death' are transformed by language. The most ludicrous example would be the death of Doc Daneeka, officially deceased because his name had appeared on McWatt's manifest. This is one of the cases where a character's name (i.e. a written or bureaucratised version of that character) determines his or her existence. The way Heller describes the sequel to Doc Daneeka's 'death' is to report on individual reactions without any narrative comment at all:

> Sergeant Towser's heart was heavy; now he had *two* dead men on his hands — Mudd, the dead man in Yossarian's tent who wasn't even there, and Doc Daneeka, the new dead man in the squadron, who most certainly was there and gave every indication of proving a still thornier administrative problem for him. (334).

It should be remembered that two deaths (those of Kid Sampson and McWatt) are ignored in favour of the Doc's as if by common consent among the authorities. Towser supplies a parodic version of grief here (similar to Milo's reactions during Snowden's funeral)

which symmetrically balances two paradoxical figures in a sen
tence ostensibly reporting deep emotions but which suddenly
reveals Towser's true priorities through the all-important adjective
'administrative'. This sort of rhetoric uses a deadpan tone to play
off the expectations aroused by one part of the sentence against the
implications of its conclusion. In other words it is anything but
noncommittal, exploiting tonal irony to mock the absolute priority
given to administrative convenience. This is typical of the perspective which Heller adopts throughout the book. Apparently neutral
narrative masks a constant irony, implying an alternative to the
values of the novel's characters. When an enlisted man tells Doc
Daneeka 'you're dead, sir' he is simply voicing the collective
reliance on administrative accounts of the truth, making a statement which is initially just ludicrous but which then becomes
sinister as the authorities 'realize' his death. After Chapter 31 Doc
Daneeka does indeed become dead, virtually disappearing from
the novel. If official language conceals death or distorts it, Heller's
use of expanding references to Snowden's wounding could be seen
as an attempt to counteract this process. The repeated image builds
up to a climactic revelation of the physical horror of death. Its
effects are mainly visual and the novel has played throughout on
what can be seen and what cannot in both optical and perceptual
senses.

Doc Daneeka's death is 'confirmed' by accumulating official
documentation and Heller repeatedly draws attention to the ways
in which documents and messages either cause confusion or create
spurious information. Yossarian's game with the letters he is
censoring is actually a playful exercise of power which has all sorts
of unforeseen consequences later in the novel. Letters become a
means of manipulation, of exercising official control, and more and
more characters take over his initial idea. Partly Heller uses such
details to demonstrate the unpredictability of a manic world. A
gesture of friendly co-operation such as getting Doc Daneeka's
name entered on McWatt's flight lists, for instance, can have the
opposite effect to that intended and actually lead to Doc's death.
As messages proliferate so do paper identities (Washington Irving,
Irving Washington) and the number of minor officials needed to
verify them. Bureaucracy is demonstrated to have an entropic tilt
in creating more and more work for itself. As Heller stated in his
Realist interview, 'any organized effort must contain the germ of
continuing disorganization'.[53] Yossarian himself becomes such a

'germ', repeatedly identified by his superiors as a source of dis-order. Heller introduces the theme of communication in the open-ing chapter of the novel though a nameless colonel who receives 'glutinous messages from the interior'. The colonel is seen first as a means of transmission and then as an enigma in himself to be 'investigated' by a ludicrous array of specialists who combine pathology, politics and communication theory. The colonels' so-called 'messages' (signs of illness or of a wound?) look forward to Snowden's revelatory entrails. Since Heller relates communicated messages to the hidden meanings of literary texts (Clevinger knows Aristotle but is incapable of 'reading' Scheisskopf's words; the chaplain worries that the Bible may just be another book like *Bleak House* and *Treasure Island*), it is appropriate that the main sender of messages, General Peckem, should be a literary stylist. Peckem sends miniature homilies rather than messages, and quib-bles scholastically over the niceties of phrasing. It is a crowning irony that he should think of himself as a realist since he has an aesthetic relish for words in themselves and since he is responsible for inventing the phrase 'bomb pattern'. As he explains, 'it means nothing, but you'd be surprised at how rapidly it's caught on' (318). Peckem's Wildean style cannot be taken just as an individual idiosyncracy because his verbal invention has military conse-quences. It is no surprise that his idea catches on but it *is* a surprise to hear such an open admission of what an empty fiction it is.

The only validation of a tight bombing pattern is a document – an aerial photograph – and documents progressively become the referents of other documents. If an officer cannot realise his desire to have parades he finds a compromise in publishing an order postponing them. This detachment of official documents from any observable reality reflects the general fate of language at the hands of the administration, whose inventions become more and more blatant matters of expediency. Nately's whore is melodramatically transformed into a Nazi assassin for public consumption, and Milo becomes a juggler of the terms 'profit' and 'loss' so that no other character can pin them down to observable realities. It is an ironic consequence of Heller's analogy between the army and big busi-ness that two characters of low rank, Corporal Whitcomb and ex-PFC Wintergreen, should become two of the most powerful characters in the novel precisely because of their clerical roles as purveyors of messages. Wintergreen even possesses a mimeo-graph machine! If paper is the prime means of transmitting the messages which give the military administration its raison d'etre then paper as a substance takes on connotations of death. On the second mission to Bologna Yossarian's plane is filled with scraps of paper like snow when flak shreds the navigation maps, while another plane undergoes a transformation into a 'shred of colored tissue paper' as it plunges to the ground in flames. Paper can even become fatal as M & M Enterprises slips replace the morphine of the medical kits.

More astonishing than the replacement of actuality by representation is characters' acquiescence in the process. Only a small minority (Yossarian and the chaplain most notably) protest against the way things are. Their presumptions of commonsense order, like the reader's, are outraged at every turn. Several critics have noted a similarity between Yossarian and Alice in this respect. Caroline Gordon and Jeanne Richardson, for instance, have argued that *Catch-22* and *Alice in Wonderland* use essentially the same methods: 'over and over the absurdities of life are contrasted with the way things ought to be or would be if the universe were governed by the principles of formal logic'.[54] Alice's wonderment finds its analogue in Yossarian's constant complaints about the way things are. In so far as each novel presents a world controlled by mysterious and ludicrous principles the comparison holds so well that Heller has named one of his characters Snark. But there is also a crucial difference between them. The basic rhythm of the Alice books is of an alternation between the familiar and the strange. Strangeness is the result of transforming a familiar object into a living creature or a gigantic form. For instance an egg becomes Humpty Dumpty who aggressively promotes a power politics of discourse ('the question is ... which is to be master') and then lapses into silence before he can become too threatening a figure. Similarly in the trial scene Alice can reject reversed justice (verdict first, trial afterwards) by reducing all the characters to cards. Both a line house and with a gesture of rejection by Alice which reasserts her control over dream or imagined fiction. For the chaplain and Yossarian there is no comparable release available. The chaplain's interrogation suddenly ends with his punishment pending. It is a release which is not a release at all since it leaves his imagination to run riot. Similarly when characters run from one point to another in the novel their search for refuge is always met with fresh horrors. Like Alice they are confronted with an unstable and bewildering world whose verbal explanations increase its mystification, but there is no release from its processes, as rendered metonymically in the remorseless rise in required missions.

The characters are trapped and the rhetorical expression of this entrapment is found in the circle, and specifically in catch-22. The latter title-phrase is introduced unobtrusively in the first chapter as a regulation governing censorship. Heller has subsequently stated that the idea grew out of the idiomatic expression 'catch' which he then institutionalised by giving it a number.[55] The number was originally 18 but had to be changed at very short notice because the title would have clashed with that of Leon Uris' *Mila 18* (due for publication the same year). Accordingly Heller's editor Bob Gottlieb came up with 22 which, while arbitrary in one sense, also received Heller's approval. It had a 'relevance to the novel because so many things do repeat themselves'.[56] As the phrase is repeated through the novel is becomes the shorthand expression of a bureaucratic principle. Before the circularity of the catch is spelled out Heller gives us a physical embodiment of its characteristic in the soldier in white. In the original form of this chapter (published in 1955 as 'Catch-18') the soldier's symbolism is made explicit. The Surgeon Major explains that the reversible drips represent a process: 'It's a cycle ... Everything moves in cycles'.[57] Heller subsequently deleted this comment from the text but the symbolism remains. The soldier in white is caught in a circular process which somehow makes him so irrelevant that the suggestion of 'eliminating the middle man' and simply linking the jars together is not at all a facetious irrelevance; it is more a wry glance at human dispensibility. When Doc Daneeka explains catch-22 to Yossarian it is important to note that we have already encountered at least one example of its application in Colonel Korn's rule that 'the only people permitted to ask questions were those who never did' (135). This is a 'stroke of genius' because its circularity preserves the decorum of the military educational sessions intact. When it is explained to him Yossarian reifies it into an artefact − a mobile: 'There was an elliptical precision about its perfect pairs of parts that was graceful and shocking, like good modern art, and at times Yossarian wasn't quite sure that he saw it at all . . .' (46).

As the application of catch-22 expands it becomes established as a principle rather than an individual rule, a justification for any official action. One of its latest occurrences is its most chilling when the old woman in the Rome brothel tells Yossarian that the

authorities took the girls away for 'no reason'. Yossarian asks if
they showed her catch-22:

> 'They don't have to show us Catch-22', the old woman
> answered. 'The law says they don't have to'.
> 'What law says they don't have to?'
> 'Catch-22'.
> 'Oh, God damn!' Yossarian exclaimed bitterly.
> 'I bet it wasn't even really there.' (398–9).

This passage shows catch-22 to be a replacement for rationality
itself, all-justifying and self-concealing. Initially it represents a
double bind of mutually exclusive propositions which trap its victims whichever way they turn. Now it is further revealed as a
bureaucratic principle which protects itself by appealing to a ludicrous legality which in turn can never be verified. Yossarian can
never dismiss it as a collective illusion because it can never be
verified one way or the other, and so what should function as an
explanation ironically turns out to induce and promote uncertainty.
While catch-22 refers mainly to military logic it also includes
capitalist trading and an exchange between Yossarian and Luciana
on Italian marriage conventions. Luciana laughs at Yossarian's
light-heartedness and perhaps the reader laughs too but we also
recognise that his word games implicate him in the very circularity
he is trying to escape. Virtually every detail in the novel in some
way or other draws our attention to this circularity. The fact that
Yossarian went round over Ferrara twice on a bombing mission
is explicitly duplicated in his subsequent conversation with his
superior officers about that mission. Repetition and circularity
constantly draw our attention to the operative conventions of
discourse which are being parodied – addressing a superior officer
as 'sir', for instance, or making routine enquiries about health in
hospital visits. Heller thus manages ingeniously to extract significance from decreasing verbal efficiency. Officers' repetition of
other officers' words makes their utterances redundant but their
very redundancy makes an oblique point about their sycophancy
and inability to take a decision. These characteristics identify an
inert administration which is more typical of postwar America than
the situation of 1944.

CATCH-22 AND THE MCCARTHY ERA

Whatever the exact nature of the novel he began around 1945 Heller clearly made a fresh start in 1953. Again and again in interviews he has insisted that the true subject of *Catch-22* was contemporary and that it was only obliquely about the last World War: 'I regard this essentially as a peacetime book. What distresses me very much is that the ethic often dictated by a wartime emergency has a certain justification, but when this thing is carried *over* into areas of peace; where the same demands are made upon the individual in the cause of national interest ... this wartime emergency ideology transplanted to peacetime, leads not only to absurd situations, but to very tragic situations'[58] One of the most striking indications of transposed emphasis in the novel is how little attention is paid to the Germans. As Heller later explained, 'it's essentially a conflict between people — American officers and their own government. They are the antagonists of *Catch-22* — much more so than the Germans and Hitler, who are scarcely mentioned'.[59] The vocabulary of battle is transferred to the American air force exclusively, thereby forcing the reader to revise his sense of sides and to locate characters within the American power structures. Quasi-military manoeuvres become utterly self-serving (Colonel Cathcart is an 'industrious, intense, dedicated military tactician who calculated day and night in the service of himself') or a reflex to opposition from fellow-officers. General Peckem redefines strategic objectives to Lieutenant Scheisskopf as an effort to take over every other bomber group and the one enemy he indicates on his map board is General Dreedle. Threat is internalised into one's own army and then internalised again into private fears and uncertainties; Cathcart, for instance, wavers between extremes of confidence and terror.

An all-pervading atmosphere of paranoia spreads through the novel, a suspicion of potential anonymous enemies referred to collectively as 'them'. Here Heller anticipates reactions to the Vietnam War. Philip Roth has recorded that during this period 'one even began to use the word "America" as though it was the name ... of a foreign invader that had conquered the country and with whom one refused, to the best of one's strength and ability, to collaborate. Suddenly America had turned into "them" '.[60] The alienation Roth describes finds its equivalent in Heller's use of anachronisms which, as we shall see in a moment, make it impossible to read the novel as a realistic account of events towards the end of World War II. The reader can neither naturalise the setting nor the period of its action since it incorporates material from two very different eras. In that sense Heller's revision of the name of the novel's island setting from Corsica to Pianosa is a symptomatic shift away from realistic description.

Heller creates ludicrous comedy out of the surveillance practised by the CID officers whose disguises are transparently obvious, and who even start investigating each other. As usual in the novel comic possibilities develop a more sinister edge where the forces represented by these officers are no longer out in the open. Nurse Duckett warns Yossarian of a conversation she overheard behind a closed door, that 'they' are going to 'disappear' his friend Dunbar, and sure enough Dunbar vanishes. The constant references to conspiracy relate the novel to postwar America. As Heller has stated, 'it was the America of the Cold War I wrote about, the Rosenberg trials, the McCarthy hearings, the loyalty oaths'.[61] Captain Black, the group intelligence officer, has an important role to play in this context. Heller neatly parodies the chauvinist and illiterate suspicions of the McCarthy era through Black's response to a corporal: 'Captain Black knew he was a subversive because he wore eyeglasses and used words like *panacea* and *utopia*, and because he disapproved of Adolf Hitler, who had done such a great job of combating un-American activities in Germany' (34). In this throwaway line Heller reduces Hitler to a minor appendage of the American right and begins to establish a set of terms ('subversive', 'Communist', and so on) which revolve around the fear of internal conspiracy. Ludicrous as it sounds, Heller is drawing on Cold War revisions of recent history for in 1951 McCarthy levelled an attack against the American military leadership arguing that they were responsible for the worldwide spread of Communism through their conduct of World War II.[62] Heller disperses different facets of this mentality among his characters. High-ranking officers suspect conspiracy; Chief Half Whiteoat rejects as immigrants and aliens all European settlers in America; and Major Sanderson the psychiatrist attacks Yossarian for having 'no respect for excessive authority or obsolete traditions', pronouncing him an 'enemy of the people'. Every example makes a different satirical point against the irony of one immigrant group's hostility to another (hence the attention to Anglo-Saxon names as against Yossarian's) and against an irrational conservation which masks itself with populist slogans.

Captain Black's Glorious Loyalty Oath Crusade is one of the many parodic references in the novel to topical events. In 1949 as part of a growing anti-Communist hysteria the authorities of the University of California amended their routine loyalty oath to exclude from office members of organisations dedicated to the overthrow of the United States government. The oath issue spread to other universities, even catching up with Heller himself – who was subscribed to one while teaching at Pennsylvania State College. In the novel Black's actions are fuelled by personal bitterness at not becoming squadron commander. Once he has the idea of the oath, the procedure mushrooms, based on a naïve equation between loyalty and the number of oaths taken. The rise of the 'crusade' burlesques in miniature a wave of political nationalism where opponents' timidity keeps them silent and the process even generates a spurious doctrine ('Continual Reaffirmation') of its own. One of the many examples of administration run mad, the loyalty oath crusade fizzles out as suddenly as it began when a major simply ignores it.

In the preceding quotation from a 1975 interview Heller makes it clear that his sense of the McCarthy period is of one dominated by trials and hearings, and the interrogation scenes of *Catch-22* clearly reflect this political introversion. The first important interrogation takes place in cadet school in California when Clevinger is charged with conspiracy to overthrow the cadet officers. The scene starts out as a burlesque of military authoritarianism, the presiding officer being an anonymous 'bloated colonel' who undermines the possibility of meaningful utterance by turning every answer against Clevinger. In that sense he embodies the double bind which allocates the same defending *and* prosecuting officer to the hearing. The culmination of the scene is the ultimate in rhetorical circularity:

[the colonel speaks] 'Read me back the last line'
" 'Read me back the last line,"' read back the corporal who could take shorthand.
'Not *my* last line, stupid!' the colonel shouted. 'Somebody else's.'
" 'Read me back the last line,"' read back the corporal.
'That's *my* last line again!' shrieked the colonel, turning purple with anger. (77)

Heller takes to an extreme a closed system of thought (ironically the very fact that records are taken accurately in shorthand helps to undermine the process) which makes a mockery out of the investigation ('Clevinger was guilty, of course, or he would not have been accused'). The episode functions as a revelation to Clevinger of how intensely the superior officers hate him. Coming so early in the novel (Chapter 8), it helps to identify the enemies. In 1969, when asked by Whit Burnett to contribute to a volume of short prose pieces, Heller selected this very scene and put the following gloss on its significance:

> This chapter was written in the early 1950's, when we were at war in Korea, on the brink of war with Russia, and city, state, Congressional, and Senate committees were browbeating and interrogating everybody they could about everything they could think of — really just for the hell of it. I tried very hard to capture this ludicrous and grotesque activity in a funny, frightening trial scene set in World War II. Actually, there are three interrogation scenes in the novel, each successively less humorous and more directly savage; I choose this one, 'Lieutenant Scheisskopf,' because it is most fully descriptive of the native dangers we faced in those days and contains my sharpest mockery of the people responsible for them. I choose it also because it warns of those same dangers today — militarism, coercion, slander, inquisition, brute force, and outright legal tyranny.[63]

The main interrogation in the novel, however, is that of the chaplain in Chapter 36 when he is taken by a colonel (the same one?) into a cellar which contains a collection of melodramatic torture implements (brass knuckles, rubber hose, etc.), which may glance at the famous array of equipment McCarthy had in his basement office on Capitol Hill.[64] This time the burlesque touches at several points on contemporary events, particularly on the 1949 trial of Alger Hiss for perjury. Just as that case revolved around such details as his possible pseudonym, his use of a Woodstock typewriter and the fact that some of the relevant microfilm was hidden in a pumpkin, so the chaplain is accused of stealing a tomato (compare also Alice's trial — who stole the tarts?) and of forging his signature on documents. Heller excludes issues which might act as a justification of the enquiry (national security, etc.) to concentrate our attention on the same circular logic to the investigating officers' questions. In answer to the chaplain's insistence that he is not guilty he is asked: 'then why would we be questioning you if you weren't guilty?' Not even the chaplain's crimes are specified, the presumption of guilt is so strong. The cruelest cut of all is that the chaplain is suddenly released so that his accusers can devise his punishment.

Some of the central documents in this interrogation are the letters signed by 'Washington Irving' and Heller repeatedly points out how the atmosphere of paranoia blinds characters to obvious, accidental or playful meanings. Yossarian signs letters with pseudonyms to vary the monotony of the hospital. Wintergreen answers Colonel Cargill with another name — T. S. Eliot — which is divorced from its context and transformed into a 'cryptic message' which puzzles the officers. An administrative preoccupation with mystery and secrecy surcharges apparently incidental messages with a significance all the more tantalising because it stays out of reach. Writing on the Red Scare of 1919, but in terms directly relevant to the 1950s, Murray B. Levin states: 'secrets, because they are a mark of exclusiveness and the unknowable, can evoke envy, anger, and a sense of fascination and mystery. The very mystery and unknowability of the secret make the secret conspiracy a good target for the projection of fantasy'.[65] In *Catch-22* Heller creates comedy out of the very fact that the military can function at all in the face of such widespread suspicion. Officers see Yossarian as a conspirator, and Yossarian — true to the novel's symmetrical reversals — sees the military administration at work against himself. One of the points about catch-22 is that it is hidden and that the administration thereby has an implement of power in that it can never be checked. As such it becomes the typical secret according to Levin in that it is contentless, suggesting rather a means of provoking uncertainty.

The interrogation scenes of *Catch-22* — to Heller's disappointment omitted from the film — raise a general question of justice. The vast majority of Heller's characters divide themselves into two broad categories — the victims and the victimisers — usually including themselves in the first. Apart from the incidental irony that the two categories are constantly blurring together, this means that the characters are partly defined through a common sense of injustice. The chaplain embodies this sense particularly strongly, hence the importance of his interrogation. In 1969 Heller explained the topicality of this scene and its debt to Kafka in the following terms:

Kafka's *The Trial* was very much present. It's the idea of being charged with something and not knowing what it is, and being judged guilty and they'll tell him what he's guilty of once they find out what crime he's done and they're sure he must have committed some crime because everybody's committed some crime. The thing that inspired that was the congressional hearings that were going on then — this was the period of McCarthy and the House Un-American Activities Committee.[66]

When Joseph K. is arrested he is worried by the fact that he cannot identify the rank of the officials. Similarly the most sinister of the chaplain's interrogators wears a uniform without insignia. There are, however, quite important differences between *The Trial* and *Catch-22*. Kafka demonstrates the inadequacy of Joseph K.'s bourgeois confidence that if he continues doing his work well he will be freed. *The Trial* narrates a series of discoveries made by Joseph K. that the legal bureaucracy (the 'Court') owns property and has officials in all the areas of his home city. This process of learning is counterpointed against the legal proceedings which have little to do with information but which enact the slow laborious movements of a hypertrophied administration. Kafka reveals the bureaucracy as an enormous hierarchy spreading upwards beyond any individual's comprehension. Heller, on the other hand, presents the military administration as atomised, riven by personal rivalry and ludicrous in its individual actions. His comedy is thus *de*mystifying, although he skilfully manages to suggest qualities of threat as well as absurdity. We can laugh at Clevinger's interrogation because the officials are caricatures, even at Major Major's questioning by the CID officer because the latter's surveillance has been so inept. The interrogation of the chaplain, however, is far less comic because the torture implements lead us to expect physical cruelty and the echoes of *The Trial* to expect the death of the subject under investigation. In fact neither of these occurs. It is the threat of violence, the sinister innuendo which carries force here and throughout the novel.

Kafka comments on the distortion of justice through a visual emblem, a painting commissioned by a High Court official which transforms the figure of Justice into a 'goddess of the Hunt in full cry'.[67] Heller makes justice an explicit issue in his characters' speech. The colonel in charge of Clevinger's hearing defines justice to him as 'a knee in the gut from the floor on the chin at night sneaky with a knife brought up down on the magazine of a battle-ship sandbagged underhanded in the dark without a word of warning' (79). The calculated incoherence of this definition through confused images of physical attack contrasts with Clevinger's own rationalisation of events as a punishment for sexual immorality. This extrapolation from Euripides' *Hippolytus* collapses, like all orderly explanations in the novel.

While Heller was writing *Catch-22* he came across a review of Richard Condon's *The Manchurian Candidate* (1959), read the novel, and had the following reactions: '. . . I think there's a great deal of similarity, first of all in the concern, or the use of political and social materials – or products of the political and social conflicts – as the basis for his book, and there's a great similarity in the attitude toward them, so that they are at once serious and at the same time it's almost like watching a kind of burlesque. . .'.[68] Given these comments, it is important to insist on the differences between Condon and Heller in their treatment of Cold War themes. Condon does indeed burlesque the rise of McCarthy through his protagonist's step-father who is blatantly manipulated by his wife. The central character in this novel is Raymond Shaw, apparently a hero from the Korean War, in fact an ex-prisoner of war who has been programmed to kill through two reflex-triggers. Condon blurs together political and psychological manipulation in focusing the action on Shaw's mother, and in exploring her son's sexual ambivalence. Because Shaw cannot reconcile his simultaneous feelings of hatred and sexual attraction towards his mother his psyche is made all the more vulnerable to brainwashing at the hands of the Chinese. Shaw's mother combines political manoeuvring with sexual predation, reducing her second husband to impotence while pushing him on his anti-Communist crusade, and forcing Robert to continue acting out his role as war hero. The novel develops two simultaneous lines of plot: what is Robert's ultimate task (actually to assassinate the next presidential candidate) and how will his past be revealed? The gradual investigation of the latter transposes psychotherapy into espionage as it brings Robert's murders to light. Condon's melodrama grows out of the incapacity of surface realism to deal with the conspiracy spreading through American society. Accordingly scenes are constantly disrupted by nightmare or violent death building up to a predictable dénouement where Robert is re-programmed at the last minute to kill his step-father. Melodrama becomes an indication of the psychic and political forces at work behind social appearances. In fact appearances prove to be malleable and vulnerable to exploitation. Robert's military 'record' has been fabricated to create the desired image just as his step-father adopts the rhetoric of McCarthy to lead his public by the nose. Robert's mother becomes an embodiment of power for him, glamorous, frightening and invulnerable. He figures her through images from consumerism: 'There she sits like a mail-order goddess, serene as the star on a Christmas tree, as calm as a jury, preening the teeth of her power with the floss of my joy, soiling it, shredding it, and just about ready to throw it away, and she is getting to look more and more like those two-dimensional women who pose for nail polish advertisements...'[69]

Where Condon reveals conspiracy through the melodrama of espionage Heller uses burlesque and caricature, turning conspiracy into comic theatre. Major Major adopts the absurdly obvious disguise of a false moustache and a pair of dark glasses in a futile effort to stand outside the military hierarchy but his men exploit the transparency of his disguise to beat him. The sudden appearances of characters through windows sets a pace of farce which contrasts very strongly with Condon's stress on efficiency; Communist agents can penetrate American society effortlessly whereas Heller's marionettes are driven by personal obsession or purely administrative impetus.

Through the figure of Milo Minderbinder Heller parodies the postwar profiteering impulse which swept through America on its new wave of prosperity. In 1975 he explained that he had drawn Milo from at least one specific figure: '... when Milo Minderbinder says, "what's good for Milo Minderbinder is good for the country", he's paraphrasing Charles E. Wilson, the former head of General Motors, who told a Senate committee, "what is good for the country is good for General Motors, and vice versa" '.[70] Although Milo is a parodic figure Heller took care to avoid a 'blinkered plutocrat stereotype' and created instead a personification of commercial activity. It is crucial that Milo speaks in slogans — sometimes his own, sometimes borrowed from Benjamin Franklin (on the value of thrift) or from Calvin Coolidge ('the business of government is business'). These slogans are self-promoting and also identify Milo with a tradition of national enterprise. Within himself he encapsulates the history of capitalism from its early stage of individual production (one of Milo's first deals produces a quarter of a bed-sheet as 'profit'!) to its modern extension into international cartels. When Yossarian accompanies him on a mission to Malta, Oman and Cairo his exhausted bewilderment is the physical result of trying to keep track of Milo's deals. The long circular journey is a physical correlative of the circularity in Milo's explanations which are constantly reversing the predictable relation between buying and selling. Milo in effect extends into a huge self-contained system. As he states to Yossarian, 'I'm the people I buy . . . from'. (227) He develops Pavlovian reflexes to any commodity which might bring profit and exclaims in horror when Yossarian *gives* something away. 'M & M Enterprises' duplicates his name (Milo & Minderbinder) and engrosses abstract values, transforming them into the arbitrary names of the planes he uses to transport his goods (Courage, Justice, etc.). The fact that he can effortlessly assimilate the Germans into his syndicate implies that the capitalist ideology binds together two countries more closely than their notional hostility, against the real enemy, Russia. In the hands of Milo warfare becomes a commercial transaction where considerations of national or military purpose are obliterated by the pursuit of profit. Significantly Milo realises this profit by 'doing nothing more than signing his name twice.' For Milo, however, signing his name is a Pilatic gesture, shrugging off responsibility for any specific casualties that might happen. Even after the Americans bomb and strafe their own men Milo 'opens his books' and deflects public criticism by showing a huge profit. The sections of *Catch-22* revolving around Milo constitute an extended parable on the reduction of man to passive commercial roles whether as consumer (it is important that Milo deals in foodstuffs because consumption becomes a physical necessity, even a drug numbing the consumer's scruples), or as middleman whom Milo would like to 'eliminate'. Heller transposes the language of military heroism into commercial deals ('He had flown fearlessly into danger and criticism by selling petroleum and ball bearings to Germany at good prices'), appearing to endorse the official double-think which is going on, and then spells out the blatant contradiction: 'Milo had been caught red-handed in the act of plundering his countrymen, and, as a result, his stock had never been higher' (362). The long exchange between Milo and Colonel Cathcart in Chapter 35 demonstrates that Heller's ironies work not only against Milo's split values but also against an officialdom ridiculously eager to placate him and preserve appearances behind the circular pseudoslogan 'what's fair is fair'.

Initially Milo is presented as a comic wheeler-dealer. As his deals extend and grow more outrageous they are revealed in all their cynicism as dealing in death and as being part of a system in which others enthusiastically participate. The main characters of *Catch-22* embody specific aspects of a common predicament and Milo's single-minded drive for profit, success and fame is only a ludicrously extreme version of a motive recurring in other characters. The group is volunteered for a mission so that an officer can get his photograph in the *Saturday Evening Post*. Even the deal offered Yossarian at the end of the novel – act the hero in return for avoiding punishment – could be seen as an attempt to use publicity as a camouflage. When Nately's whore tries to kill Yossarian she is immediately converted into a 'Nazi assassin' because this would be more flattering to the group publicity machine. Milo's so-called 'shares' are the metonymic representation of a collective involvement in his system.

Milo's enterprises represent the sort of commercial enterprises associated with peacetime accelerated, expanded and transposed on to the theatre of war.[71] War heightens the cynicism and hypocrisy involved in the deals. Like *Gravity's Rainbow*, *Catch-22* exploits historical retrospection to show a continuity between the novel's ostensible subject (the last stages of World War II) and its investigation of contemporary America. Both Pynchon and Heller insert anachronisms into their texts to break open their fictitious time. Pynchon puts in references to contemporary figures; Heller inserts references to IBM machines, helicopters and the political developments in America of the 1950s. Heller even planned originally to have a number of 'supernatural things' occurring in the novel, again presumably to disrupt the fictional illusion.[72] The other strategy which Heller uses to indicate to the reader that his subject is not exclusively Mediterranean warfare in 1944 is an international one. In *Catch-22* the narrative information is divided between present and past. The present includes the layout of the planes, details of missions, the description of Rome, and so on. The past includes such history of the characters as usefully establishes a continuity between peacetime and war. Clevinger, for instance, is the academic of the novel, the star debater whose skills collapse before Yossarian's verbal assaults. Aarfy is a 'fraternity man', a case of arrested development who tries to apply college principles to war and commits murder. Doc Daneeka's prosperity from the outbreak of war is rudely snatched away from him once he is conscripted; and so the list could continue. Heller is not attempting to repeat Mailer's use of Time Machine sections from *The Naked and the Dead* where a combination of biography and flashback establishes a context for the individual's reaction to combat. Heller only supplies enough information about his characters to keep their type-quality intact and their relevance to national issues and stereotypes clear. Chief White Halfoat has lived through a parodic version of his race's dispossession since he has become a human divining rod for oil. This account of his past does not give him a psychological 'substance' but raises the issue of ethnic divisions within America, a theme subsequently developed through the references to alien names.

Alienation is in fact the crucial cumulative effect of Heller's anachronisms and parodies. In chronological terms he forces the reader to superimpose one period (the 1950s) on another (1944) as if in mimicry of Joseph McCarthy's paranoid re-reading of American military history. A continuity is thus implied between a period of warfare and one of peace — at least one of *ostensible* peace since the Cold War could be seen as a time of latent warfare. By burlesquing the key trials of the postwar period Heller uses absurdist techniques to bring to the surface the hidden ideological assumptions of the McCarthy era: its paranoia, xenophobia, racism and general preoccupation with secrecy. The novel repeatedly converts conspiracy into comic theatre as if Heller's characters were performing in an endless farce, where the momentum of their own activities acts as the justification of those activities and obscures the most obvious realities of their situation. In the course of an excellent discussion of nonsense literature Elizabeth Sewell offers the following summary:

> I am going to describe something — a system, call it a political system. . . These are some of its traits: (1) it is ruled by an obsessive logic, starting from principles that may be inhuman or absurd but are to be rigidly followed; (2) those within the system are compelled to work with it not by external force so much as by the sheer compulsion of logic on the human mind; (3) the system is totally insulated from all that we agree to regard as normal life; (4) it requires nonsensical tasks to be performed; (5) each individual within it is isolated from every other, by a policy of propaganda, control, and terror.[73]

It would be difficult to imagine a more concise summary of the political nature of the system in *Catch-22*. In almost every respect Sewell's description matches the self-perpetuating, insulated logic which guides the military bureaucracy and, as if that wasn't enough, Sewell draws parallels between such a system and the McCarthy hearings as well as other developments in postwar America. By showing such absurdities Heller's humour performs a political function, since it brings to the surface the implicit assumptions of a right-wing, Cold War mentality and in that respect *Catch-22* looks forward to Heller's subsequent writings of the 1960s.

3
The Plays and Other Writings of the 1960s

WE BOMBED IN NEW HAVEN

At the end of Chapter 13 of *Catch-22* Yossarian reaches an agreement with Colonels Cathcart and Korn that his 'punishment' for going over the bridge at Ferrara twice during a bombing mission should be to receive a medal. Korn ushers him out of the office commenting 'exit smiling'. It is only a passing joke but the phrase indicates a characteristic of the novel: that its scenes are often organised like those in a play. This is no mere detail because Heller has admitted in several interviews that his original ambition was to become a playwright. At high school he wanted to write farces like those of Moss Hart and George S. Kaufman.[1] Hart and Kaufman collaborated in a series of works from 1934 to 1940 which would have been produced in New York during Heller's teens. It is possible that he developed a feel for tempo and understood their skill at playing off characters' obsessive purposes against each other. Hart and Kaufman also convert potentially serious themes (marriage as a means of escape from one's class, fulfillment of ambition in Hollywood, etc.) into comedy. Heller follows similar strategies in *Catch-22*, creating absurd effects through the entrances and exits via Major Major's window, setting up a narrative tempo from scene to scene which maximises the ludicrous impact of individual scenes, and masking the ultimate seriousness of the novel's subject (what could be more serious than death?) by jokes and burlesque.

On his return from military service Heller's dramatic ideal had shifted to Clifford Odets and when his first story appeared in print he was quoted as being 'busy trying to get a play produced'.[2] Evidently his efforts were unsuccessful and much later he admitted that he found Odets' most famous play *Waiting for Lefty* very dated. Where Odets was 'converting the theatre into a union hall' Heller declared that he was converting the theatre into a theatre.[3] This

71

sounds like a tautology but, as we shall see, he uses a series of devices in his own play *We Bombed in New Haven* to remind the audience that they are watching a play. Heller's interest in the theatre continued to develop. In 1949 his chosen subject for his master's essay at Columbia University was 'The Pulitzer Prize Plays from 1918 to 1935'. While teaching at Penn State he collaborated with his colleague Robert Mason on an abortive play and in about 1952 wrote a three-act play with his friend George Mandel called 'The Bird in the Fevverbloom Suit'. The latter was never produced and is among the Heller papers deposited at Brandeis University. If we add to these writings Heller's enthusiasm for drama criticism, his liking for some classical drama (especially Aristophanes and *King Lear*) and the fact that he was appointed to Yale Drama Faculty along with over 20 other writers for a period from September 1967 to January 1968 (when he gave classes on Aristotelian theory among other topics), then *We Bombed in New Haven* can be seen as the logical outcome of a long-held interest. In a 1970 interview Heller admitted: 'I can write plays very quickly because . . . dialogue comes easy to me' and it was apparently this same facility which led Heller to become involved in scripts for the cinema and television.[4]

Heller's interest in the theatre provides one context for *We Bombed in New Haven*. The Vietnam War provides the other. In fact there is a clear continuity between his first novel and the play. Soon after *Catch-22* was published Heller was invited by Paul Newman to consider working with the members of the Actors Studio on adaptations of sections of the novel. Heller subsequently gave a series of public readings from *Catch-22* when 'he conceived of having four actors and actresses do readings from the book plus readings from Shakespeare'.[5] As the plan developed he decided to give the play a separate identity. Visiting Yale in December 1966 to speak to classes, Heller mentioned his idea to his friend Robert Brustein, the Dean of the Yale Drama School. Brustein was enthusiastic and by the following Spring Heller had produced a draft called 'Bomber in New Haven', apparently written as a 'manuscript to be read like a novel'.[6] Brustein (who was also instrumental in getting Heller his temporary teaching appointment) suggested that the play should be produced at Yale. Heller agreed and after unsuccessfully approaching Mike Nichols (who subsequently directed the film of *Catch-22*), Larry Arrick was taken on as director. The play opened at the Yale Repertory Theatre on December 4,

1967; then ran for a period on Broadway, finally touring the country, being performed mainly in campus and community theatres. The circumstances of the play's production are important because Brustein was particularly active in making the Yale Drama School a centre for a theatre of protest against the Vietnam War. The first dramatic comment on that war (Megan Terry's *Viet Rock*, 1966) opened there and other productions included Barbara Garson's *MacBird* and the Living Theatre's *Paradise Now*. The Yale Draft Refusal Committee had purchased a block of seats for the opening night of Heller's play and planned to disrupt the production because, as Brustein recalls, 'Heller's ending signified to them an acceptance of induction'.[7] In the event they were dissuaded by Brustein and Jules Feiffer and the play went on without a hitch.

We Bombed in New Haven is a play which protests against war in general. It was mainly the occasion of its production which gave it a specific relevance to the Vietnam War. During the rehearsals the leading officer developed a Southern accent which Heller objected to on the grounds that it suggested L. B. Johnson too specifically. 'By projection the play is about the Viet Nam war', Heller explained. 'Specifically, it's about a very unspecific war'.[8] For this reason Heller included allusions to the previous world wars and also to the wars of antiquity so as to avoid an overtly specific reference. In this respect *We Bombed* contrasts strongly, say, with David Rabe's *The Basic Training of Pablo Hummel* which grew directly out of Rabe's experiences in Vietnam. When the curtain rises 'prematurely' Heller makes his first use of a tactic which is employed throughout the play, namely to remind the audience that a play is being produced. The assembling and dismantling of the scenery is only one way of breaking the theatrical illusion and of drawing out attention to the play's central subject − that of role-playing. In the first act the Major carries a manuscript which doubles as military orders and as the script of the play itself. Heller has commented on this manuscript as follows: 'In my play the audience gets to realize that in the script the major carried around everything is written down so that the question is: Do the actors have free will? Can they break away from the script?'[9] By leaving gaps in his text which could be filled according to the personal details of the particular actor or according to audience reaction, Heller avoids an impression of total textual closure and encourages us to expect choices from his characters, but as the play moves towards its close our sense of the script as destiny becomes

stronger and stronger. The repeated references to time running out
build up a suggestion of impending doom especially after two
gestures of defiance fail.

Before we consider those gestures we should note that *We
Bombed in New Haven* revises certain aspects of *Catch-22* and so can
hardly be considered independently of the novel. There is also an
external reason for comparing the two works. During the late 1960s
Catch-22 reached its maximum annual sales in America and became
closely associated with the anti-Vietnam War movement. Probably
the novel's popularity had to do with a growing frustration at
America's imperceptible slide into a massive military commitment
without public examination of the issues. The novel's presentation
of the conduct of war as an absurd, self-perpetuating administrative process justifies Heller's claim that it was 'far more factually
descriptive of Vietnam than of World War Two', and more and
more writers found literal confirmation of the novel's absurdities in
official accounts of military events in Vietnam.[10] Indeed the Vietnam War induced a crisis of confidence in the official media.
Harrison Salisbury's eye-witness reports on the bombing of Hanoi
gave the American public an alternative source to that of the
government and exposed glaring credibility gaps. *We Bombed*
touches obliquely on these themes by opening with a briefing
session which revises the equivalent scene in Chapter 21 of
Catch-22. In the novel the briefing is disrupted by the presence of
General Dreedle's nurse who fills the men with frenzy and General
Dreedle himself who fills the briefing officers with panic. In *We
Bombed* the briefing is used differently to establish the arbitrary
nature of military objectives. The first bombing mission of the play
is to attack Constantinople — not Istanbul. In this way Heller
detaches the place name from a referent as he does in the novel.
An ambiguity thus arises about the nature of the mission just as an
ambiguity persists right through the play as to whether the action
is working on an illusionistic or anti-illusionistic level. One scene
brings this ambiguity out pointedly. Sergeant Henderson (the
nearest figure in the play to Yossarian) points to a globe and says
he wants to smash it, only to be nonplussed when his superior
officer gives it him. The play on names and representations taking
precedence over their referents is far less substantial than in
Catch-22, but a significant theme nonetheless.

Heller avoids any
The defiance of military protocol, common to play and novel,
anticipates actors' defiance of realistic acting conventions in *We*

Bombed which amount to political gestures of non-compliance. Henderson and others are constantly stepping out of roles, shifting tones and verbal register before one role can be firmly established. Ruth, for instance, comes on stage declaiming melodramatic lines which contrast absurdly with her actual role in the play as cook. When characters comment on her coffee she retorts: 'I know – it stinks, doesn't it? So what? I'm an actress, not a cook'.[11] This is not a casual aside but part of a running complaint against her role. A crucial tonal difference between *Catch-22* and *We Bombed* is that in the play characters are far less acquiescent and rail against their situation but Henderson, like Yossarian, falls victim to collective illusions. He actually starts believing the fictions he has been attacking. The test case for this gullibility in Act One is the death of an airman called Sinclair (a new version of Snowden). His disappearance gives a new urgency to the discussions of reality and illusion as can be seen in the following exchange between Henderson and Captain Starkey:

STARKEY

There *was* no Sinclair. He never lived. He didn't die.

HENDERSON

Then who did we just bury?

STARKEY

Sinclair. But he wasn't real. It didn't happen.

HENDERSON

Why did we bury him?

STARKEY

Because he was killed.

HENDERSON

Where is the boy who was playing the soldier who was killed by accident just now –

STARKEY

Not by accident. There are no accidents.

HENDERSON

By accident. He was killed in my plane when one of his own bombs exploded, wasn't he? That's an accident. He used to be an actor about my own age. He was here a little while ago. He isn't here now.

STARKEY

He isn't supposed to be here. We don't need him any more. That's why we killed him.

HENDERSON
I'm going to look for him. (76)

This dialogue resembles passages in *Catch-22* which deal with
death in terms of an absence, which in turn contradicts a character's physical presence or vice versa; but now shifts the terms of
opposition on to stage illusion. In spite of the fact that Henderson
has been constantly stepping out of his role, his expression of
concern for Sinclair is complicated by its naïve illusionism and then
rendered absurdly tortuous when he tries to rephrase his question.
Whereas in *Catch-22* the military authorities promote a certain
version of reality for the sake of administrative convenience, the
authority figures in *We Bombed* are presented as sinister play-
wrights, engineering the script for purposes of expediency. But
because Starkey also makes statements which belong to a context
of political totalitarianism ('that's why we killed him') the audience
is forced to juggle two different levels of reality which support each
other.

The interweaving of theatre and reality, and specifically the
analogy between destiny and dramatic role, is made the subject of
explicit comment in Act Two. Starkey quotes two passages from
Epictetus' *Encheiridion* and Suetonius' *Lives of the Caesars* which in
their new context become attempts at coercing the men into acceptance. The passage from Epictetus begins and concludes: 'Remember that you are an actor in a play, the character of which is
determined by the Playwright . . . For this is your business, to play
admirably the role assigned you; but the selection of that role is
Another's'.[12] In his text Heller does not capitalise the final word
which is an important detail since a gloss in the Loeb translation,
which was Heller's source, explains that 'another's' refers to the
deity. Where Epictetus is trying to induce humility before God's
mysterious purposes, Starkey secularises the reference to try to
force obedience to military authority. In this respect the passage is
not just another example of Starkey's posturing, but makes an
important comment on the central themes of the play. He tries to
impress his audience (his subordinates) with the dignity of classical
texts and by referring to the emperor Augustus Caesar who,
according to Suetonius, used the same analogy on his death-bed,
but Starkey's quotation is interrupted by sarcastic comments from
the other men which reduce the analogy to cliché (Bailey sneers
'the great playwright in the sky') or a means of supporting status.

By rejecting Starkey's quotation they are at once rejecting military *and* literary authority. Only the idiots on stage applaud. Henderson 'distinguishes' the analogy in the legal sense by asking questions which erode its value as general truth and thereby rejects exactly the same fatalistic submission to authority as Clevinger unsuccessfully tries to induce in Yossarian.

By stepping in and out of their roles Heller's characters do not destroy them but rather multiply these roles. In one of the best discussions of Heller's plays Linda Micheli offers the following explanation: 'First, Heller's characters and actors are superimposed, not clearly distinguished. Each figure on the stage has a double role . . . Second, as a result the action does not take place in clearly defined worlds of the "play" and the "real world"; rather the characters often seem to inhabit an ambiguous middle ground'.[13]

Heller uses stage illusion as a constant target for attack and reference so that almost every line in the play becomes a self-reflexive pun. The Major tells Henderson: 'Start acting your age. There's nothing really funny about this, you know' (102) in Act Two where the tone of the action begins to change. Even the title of the play is a pun which straddles theatre and military action. Although Heller has professed to dislike the title because it is 'cute' the pun is actually woven into the play's dialogue in Act One.[14] As the local emphasis shifts from one area of meaning or experience to the other, the terms 'bomb' and 'kill' supply means of showing military action as theatre and theatrical action as aggression (the Major says of a hostile audience that he will 'blast them off the map'). This punning is one aspect of Heller's use of metaphor in the play. When Captain Starkey first appears on stage the directions describe his movements as showing 'much the same self-assured manner of any well-placed civilian executive reporting for his day's or evening's work' (15) which immediately draws an analogy between the military and business. The parallel is extended when Heller introduces two parodic stereotypes – the Golfer and the Huntsman – as backers. They are incorporated into the action as MPs whose presence veers between the ludicrous and the brutal. One of them finally shoots down Henderson by which time their 'sporting' implements (shotgun and golf-club) have become the arms of a brutal police force. The identity of these figures literally *is* their role. That is why they are never given names. Their first appearance suggests the analogy between warfare and sport similar to Mailer's description of a hunting trip in *Why Are We in Vietnam?* (as Larry Arrick has commented, 'war is a metaphor here for a game these people are playing') which is filled out when Starkey starts distributing toys and sports equipment to the men.[15] Their Pavlovian eagerness to start playing ball then shifts the analogy to a comparison between their cultural conditioning and their military training – when they march they move like automata. One purpose of Act One then is to set up various metaphors whose implications are developed in Act Two. The presence of the Sportsmen, for instance, implies that the play is briefly representing the military-industrial complex in miniature where money feeds the military and exerts ultimate power.

Heller expands a minor theme in *Catch-22* to develop the political implications of playing out a role in this play. Yossarian's gesture of not wearing clothes after Snowden's death was, as we saw, an act of personal purgation, of shunning the polluted garments of officialdom. In *We Bombed* uniforms, whether for combat or sports, carry similar predictable connotations of conformity. But when Henderson appears with his uniform stained with blood, his appearance is assimilated into the general argument over Sinclair's death. The Sportsmen wear MPs uniforms only from the waist up, and sports gear from the waist down, rendering visual their function as links between the military and business. Henderson never appears naked but he does decide not to play his role any longer and confirms the decision by donning civilian clothes. Ironically it is the uniformed Starkey who persuades Henderson to continue, and then himself tries unsuccessfully to get out of his military role. Uniforms are costume and in a sense that is all there is to characters. So when Sinclair's clothes are brought in at the beginning of Act Two the suggestion is that his role will continue while it should like else would them. If roles trap the performers, this implies that Heller is creating a fiction within a fiction where the play enacts the production of a play. Production becomes an analogue for the exercise of military authority and the recital of lines from other plays becomes an indication of the sort of roles not available in the 1960s. Stephen W. Potts has rather hastily decided that the literary allusions are 'ineffective and of dubious artistic purpose' but they point to the alternative great roles which the characters yearn for.[16] When Starkey recites from T. S. Eliot it occasions an argument between himself and Henderson about their respective acting abilities which do not match their military rank. When Henderson recites Henry V's speech from the Battle of Agincourt, lines from Shakespeare alternate with lines in an ordinary speaking voice reminding us that the former are just lines without any applicability to the present. Henderson raises the issue of heroism in battle through his quotations which imply the very absence of heroism and diminished scope of his present role.[17] His death confirms these implications.

Allusions to two other plays introduce an important theme which is mainly developed in the second act: the conflict between generations. Ruth claims that she would make a very good Cordelia in spite of Starkey's mocking claim that she would not be able to hold her tongue. The allusion is more relevant than to fill out the various references to acting, however. In *King Lear* a father's paradoxical decision to yield up the territory which creates paternal authority, while clinging to the respect which that authority carries, sets sister against sister and child against father. In domestic miniature it creates a civil war. When Heller claims, 'I can relate *We Bombed* . . . to much of *Lear*, in structure and philosophy' he undoubtedly has in mind the emphasis on the youthfulness of the victims of war (Ruth harangues the audience over the death of Sinclair − 'another young boy').[18] At the beginning of Act Two Fisher's kid brother appears as a raw recruit to replace Sinclair. Up to this point there has hardly been a mention of parents but then Starkey persuades Henderson to continue in his role by speaking to him 'like a father to a son'. The claim to parental concern is dismissed as histrionics and then demonstrated to be a betrayal because Starkey has actually been asking Henderson to acquiesce in his own death. Most of the dialogue in Act Two identifies duty with virtual suicide. Although Henderson makes one gesture of resistance it is Starkey who is faced with two crucial points of decision: whether to help Henderson (and fulfill his claimed 'paternity') or his son. In the event Starkey fails on both counts. The tug between paternal obligation and military duty proves to be an unequal one. Henderson is shot because Starkey will not intervene with the Major and his son is sent to his death because Starkey's efforts to help him escape come too late. The following exchange between Starkey and his son enacts an estrangement brought about by the former's military compliance. As characters they recede into their respective roles as 'the captain' and 'son', thereby giving this scene an entirely different kind of pathos from the reunion between Lear and Cordelia at the end of Act IV. There it is

the solicitous daughter who invites identification ('Sir, do you
know me?'). Here it is the father who claims forgiveness as a salve
to his conscience:

(Starkey turns from the Major and looks at the boy closely)
                    STARKEY
Do you know who I am?
                    STARKEY'S SON
Yes, Sir. You're the captain.
                    STARKEY
Do you know why you're here?
                    STARKEY'S SON
They want me to go into an airplane and be killed. You're the
one that's going to send me.
                    STARKEY
And you'll go?
                    STARKEY'S SON
If I have to.
                    STARKEY
What's your name, son?
                    STARKEY'S SON
(With a trace of bitterness)
Son. (191)

Where Shakespeare's scene culminates in a loving recognition *We
Bombed* ends with an exclamation of disgust ('Bastard!'), a rejection
by Starkey's son of his father and even of the very notion of
paternity.

Stephen W. Potts has commented that the closing lines 'reflect
the widely held contention, tied to the anti war sentiments of the
period, that sons were paying with their lives for the sins of their
fathers'.[19] Potts may well be right about the topicality of this
emphasis (it also appears briefly in Mailer's *The Armies of the Night*)
but Heller varies his allusions to universalise the theme of youthful
sacrifice. At one point in Act Two the actor/character Henderson
remarks that he was 'killed once' in R. C. Sherriff's *Journey's End*
(1929). This play, set in the trenches, revolves around three main
characters: Stanhope, an officer and former head of rugger at his
school; Osborne, a teacher and a member of the England rugger
team; and Raleigh, the ironically named, naïve youth who looks up
to both Stanhope and Osborne. The sporting details are crucial

because Sherriff dramatises the inadequacy of public school values, where sport systematises honour and bravery, to deal with the facts of modern warfare. Raleigh's one mentor is killed and the other, Stanhope, survives as a shattered wreck. When Raleigh himself dies at the end of the play his death signals the demise of an idealistic attitude. Henderson's laconic comment ('the whole war was all in fun') seems to dismiss the play from relevance but Sherriff's attention to youth relates to similar areas of indignation in *We Bombed* and the fact that Heller makes extended use of the sporting analogy perhaps implies that a lesson should have been learnt from *Journey's End* which was not. Where Sherriff erodes sport as a system of values, Heller uses athletic equipment to raise questions about the man's instinct towards conformity. If they are playing a game, who has set the rules.

Several important shifts take place as we move from the first act to the second. Firstly, the references to America are tightened up as part of a broad strategy of bringing war home to the audience. The first bombing mission is to Constantinople; the second is to Minnesota. One name mentioned towards the end of the play is Brandwine, a throw-away reference to the Battle of Brandywine (1777) which was an American defeat on American soil. Secondly, comedy is phased out of play. Heller has steadily insisted that it is a tragedy. Thirdly, characters' roles become much more rigid. There is comparatively less movement in and out of realistic illusion and a growing realisation that roles are a means of entrapment. This is demonstrated particularly poignantly in the case of Starkey who quits. The Major retorts:

No, you won't quit. You're a captain, and captains don't quit. Captains obey. You're conditioned to agree and you're trained to do as you're told. You like the pay and the prestige, and you do enjoy your job here, remember? So you'll stay right where you are, do just what you're supposed to, and continue reciting your lines exactly on cue − just as you're doing right now. (144)

Heller exploits the ambiguity of future tenses here so that we cannot be sure whether the Major is making predictions or giving orders. In a sense it doesn't matter because Starkey's capitulation (the use of this verb in the stage directions glances relevantly at the vocabulary of battle) confirms the Major's generalisations which even extend outwards to cover the whole play. Performing roles actually prevents the characters from forming any concerted resistance to their fate. As Heller has commented, 'the crucial things were the aspirations of the people, the absence of any feeling of responsibility toward each other, the very pettiness of their ambitions'.[20] Bailey, for instance, wants to be promoted at the expense of Henderson. Accordingly the scene where Starkey discovers Henderson hiding in a closet takes on a symbolic significance. The ritualistically repeated three knocks on the door by the Sportsmen (echoes from *Macbeth* and other works) sets up a suggestion of inevitable discovery but in the urgency of the moment Ruth urges Starkey to help Henderson. This is one of the many points where an allusion to *Catch-22* supports the local dramatic effect. The repetition of 'help him. ... help him' echoes the most famous scene in the novel, of Snowden's wounding, and implies that Starkey's assistance is just as much a matter of life and death. However it fails partly because of Act Two's greater emphasis on violence, especially on violence between the American characters. The Major's promise to kill Henderson is fulfilled (unlike Starkey's promise) in a carefully orchestrated scene where dialogue and movement support each other, ironically undermining Starkey's confident lie 'It's a free country isn't it?' (166). The golfer's actions with his club reverse the analogy beween sport and war, and enact a physically immediate threat. Henderson's naïve, childlike astonishment confirms a whole series of associations Heller has built up between youth, victimisation, home, baby's *pacifiers*, etc., before he is shot down. He clings to Starkey for support repeating his appeal for help and smears blood down the latter's shirt-front, symbolically marking him as a murderer. The scene's sequel returns to the play on illusion and reality when Henderson's corpse is referred to as 'junk', a half-repetition of an earlier line which identifies the dead body with the scenery. Horror at the death swings round to relief when Starkey applauds Henderson's performance, and then back to horror when it is discovered he really is dead.

In a scene like this Heller is obviously playing with the audience's reactions and in fact he makes a general effort throughout the play to exploit the space of the stage and at the same time to break down the proscenium arch as a comfortable barrier between audience and actors. During the rehearsals of the play Heller added a passage of direction which insisted that, however much the setting might change, 'there is always the sense ... that the space is really very firmly enclosed, and that the people inside it are enclosed with it'.[21] The stage functions then as a spatial metaphor of the actors' confined roles but Heller carefully undermines any theatrical illusion so that the confinement actually comes to include the members of the audience. This process starts early when Henderson takes the audience into his confidence about his acting abilities (*we* know that he has star quality, don't we?). The aside convention quickly slides into direct accusation when Ruth harangues the audience over Sinclair's death. The use of direct address, the positioning of actors so that they include the audience's fate in that of the characters, and devices such as that which closes Act One when a time bomb (real or toy?) is thrown into the audience, all undermine a spectatorial passitivity. Starkey's self-justifying speech ('I am a man' . .: 17–18) implicitly puts the audience into the role of accusers and actively involves them in the moral issues of war. One problem here, however, is that of rhetoric. Starkey excuses himself inadequately by claiming that he yearns for a bigger role and his final bland summing-up ('there is no war taking place here now!', and so on) reads like an official whitewash, a cover-up rendered absurd by an explosion off-stage. In both these cases Starkey demonstrates that he is the gull of his own rhetoric, but when his son refers to King David the result is awkward and declamatory. His son's appeal for an authentic emotional response by Starkey is smothered by the play's general emphasis on histrionics. *All* utterance becomes suspect and emotional impact has to be sought through action (killing) or through new youthful characters who are exempt from the prevailing theatricality (Fisher's brother convincingly so; Starkey's son slightly less successfully). Ironically Heller subsequently decided that the lack of relief at the end of the play and the involvement of the audience in the actions of his characters made the play a failure, 'because it made people feel guilty, made them accessories to murder'.[22]

The latter phrase has resonances from the law courts and this is no accident because the skewed relation of legality to justice is a dominant theme in both *Catch-22* and *We Bombed*. The all-justifying regulation of the novel's title traps the men who try to evade it, whereas in the play injustice is rendered directly and concretely in Starkey's son being brought back on to the stage after he has tried to escape by climbing out through a window. Injustice is a constant topic of argument in *Catch-22* and the play. *We Bombed* replaces the principle of a self-serving self-protecting bureaucracy with the

'script' which becomes a short-hand term for a fatalistic acquiescence to authority. As Robert Merrill comments: 'The notion that
everything is determined is a convenient fiction, intended to dis-
courage argument or even inquiry'.[23] Heller establishes a set of
identifications between obedience, following the script, donning
uniforms, and destiny which the techniques of his play work
against. Linda Micheli's identification of the play's central subject
as being 'not war *per se* but the individual's capitulation to nameless, bureaucratic authority' rightly implies a similarity of theme
with *Catch-22* and also helps to explain the various dimensions to
the characters' 'disobedience'.[24] When Heller wrote a foreword to
his dramatisation of *Catch-22* in 1972 he went to considerable
lengths to stress the importance of 'due process gone awry' in his
works, relating it to notorious current cases having to do with the
Vietnam War: the Harrison 6 (charged with conspiring to kidnap
Kissinger), the Catonsville 9 (who poured animal blood over draft
records in Maryland), the case of the Pentagon Papers, and
others.[25] For Heller these prosecutions brought the American legal
system into total disrepute because 'the true motives behind these
court proceedings were not lofty but selectively spiteful: to inflict
severe, disabling punishments upon these individuals more for
their irreverent opposition to official policy than for actions
seriously criminal'.[26] 'Irreverent' too sums up the tone of the
attacks Heller levels against officialdom in his novel and its adaptations, and in *We Bombed*.

Heller has consistently denied writing polemical works but he
did not deny the relevance of *We Bombed* to the Vietnam War. In
interviews given around the time of the play's production he was
vociferous in opposing the war which he saw as a betrayal of the
American people by its own government. Between 1967 and 1971
Heller was regularly interviewed for his opinions on the Vietnam
War as well as on literature and in those interviews he made it clear
that he opposed the war on a whole variety of grounds. It was
firstly an irrational war since the USA had slid imperceptibly into
involvement under the impetus of its Cold War attitudes: 'The
belief in stopping communism wherever it threatens to advance
simply carried over into another culture long after the *reason* for the
belief disappeared.'[27] Heller's argument that America's public
ideology was drifting under its own momentum perhaps helps to
explain the popularity of *Catch-22* in these years. The novel burlesques the chauvinism, racism and paranoia hidden behind official

purposes and thereby foregrounds the sort of ideology Heller refers to in his interview. In effect *Catch-22* uses absurdism to challenge American readers to justify their cherished national slogans
and in doing so put a halt to this culture lag. Similarly he explained
that *We Bombed* hoped to counter a kind of brainwashing: 'We
accept the fact that when our sons grow up they will be called to
war. We accept the inevitability of our male children dying in a war
... This is true totalitarian thinking'.[28] His play questions this
inevitability through individual characters' protests and also by
representing fatality as theatre. The official justification for anything in *We Bombed* is an irrational appeal to 'the script', to prede-
termined hidden purposes, and the play's true impact lies in its
bringing to the surface a set of conditioned attitudes and revealing
them as both brutal and arbitrary.

Heller has been absolutely consistent in seeing Vietnam as a
domestic issue. As early as 1965 Heller had written a piece (published in 1975 under the title 'This is called National Defence')
against the FBI's bugging of telephones under a catch-all justification ('national defence' is the favourite slogan of Captain Black in
Catch-22).[29] The Vietnam issue exacerbated this abuse of civil rights
and in 1967 Heller wrote an indignant letter to the *New York Times
Magazine* commenting sarcastically on the acceptance by Bertrand
Russell and 'other British intellectuals' of official accounts of the
war, and complaining about investigating agencies interfering in
the universities.[30] Civil rights were abused again by the enforce-
ment of a possibly illegal form of conscription (since war had not
formally been declared) into the army where the conscripts auto-
matically forfeited their constitutional freedoms. Heller's statements about the war are partly pleas on behalf of these conscripts
whom he saw as cannon fodder, the victims of a cynical government policy. In 1967 he insisted: 'The American government is
making war on the American people – not on Ho [Chi Minh]' and
the next year repeated the charge.[31] Minnesota was chosen as the
second target in *We Bombed* because it was the home state of pacifist
Senator Eugene McCarthy; and Heller attacked the deceit of
Hubert Humphrey 'who was going around defending the Vietnam
War with the most bombastic and pompous and fanatic lies and
deceits'. Lying was also the speciality of L. B. Johnson who, for
Heller, had presided over a steady corruption of national ideals
which had created such severe internal divisions that civil war
could not be ruled out.[32] In 1967 Cecil Woolf and John Bagguley

drew up a questionnaire on the Vietnam War designed to resemble that circulated in 1937 on the Spanish Civil War by Auden and others. Among those who answered the overwhelming majority were opposed to the war (respondents included Mailer, Burroughs, James Jones and Irwin Shaw). Heller's reply was forthright: 'I *am* against the military intervention of the US in Vietnam. It was a ghastly choice, and thousands die each month because of it ... we ought to stop murdering Asians. We ought to stop sending young American boys, against their will, ten thousand miles away to be killed and mutilated in battle against people that do not threaten us and did us no harm'.[33]

It should be remembered that such statements were being made in 1967 and 1968, the latter year when race riots rocked major American cities and when Johnson tacitly admitted failure by withdrawing from the presidency. That year the Tet offensive gave the lie to any official statement that the USA was winning the Vietnam War, led to a demand by General Westmoreland for yet more American troops to be committed, and also signalled a huge decline in public support for Johnson. It was events such as these which made Heller state that *We Bombed* had become more relevant the year after its first production. Heller's most specific political commitment this year was the result of meeting McCarthy in a New York restaurant. McCarthy was running for the Democratic presidential nomination on a peace ticket and early in 1968 began to attract huge support among American students. Heller explained that 'the issues were so stark that in good conscience I had to get involved'.[34] Accordingly he agreed to run as an anti-Johnson delegate to the Democratic Party's national convention, and contributed to the McCarthy campaign as well as making speeches on his behalf on different campuses.[35] Symbolically McCarthy was invited to the Broadway premier of *We Bombed* No Iah as 1941 Vietnam was still an important issue in Heller's interviews. This time he saw Nixon as a liar and Agnew as a totalitarian demagogue inciting violence. Frustrated by the persistence of the War, Heller stated: 'I am in total sympathy with the students. I think indifferences and stupidity of the government administration has made it necessary to move from peaceful dissent to acts of violence'.[36] Frustration over Vietnam heightened Heller's disgust over government in general, a disgust which feeds directly into his third novel, *Good as Gold*.

THE DRAMATISATIONS

When Heller started on *We Bombed in New Haven* he knew next to nothing about the process of drama production so that although he wrote his first draft very quickly, he subsequently had to revise it again and again. He changed the mimeographed script after preliminary meetings with Brustein and Arrick, and added further changes during rehearsals and between the Yale and Broadway premieres, partly because of a critical review by Clive Barnes of the *New York Times*. Yet more revisions were made of the Broadway script for productions elsewhere, and also for the published versions of the play.[37] Apart from this constant revision Heller admitted that the production came to him as a shock, since he realised that the director and actors had a positive creative role to play ('They've seen things in it, psychological things, I never thought of'). Since Heller had confidence in Arrick and the group of actors this was reassuring but it also created a tension between himself and the director which, Heller felt, threatened his literary personality. When he declared 'I don't want Joseph Heller distorted' he clearly had in mind the sum total of effects which make up his authentic individual voice.[38] His readiness to dismiss most of his early stories springs from exactly the same impulse because he sees them as *in*authentic, just exercises in imitation. Apart from such a fundamental reservation Heller also apparently found the rehearsals nerve-racking (chewing an orange Stim-u-dent stick to shreds in the process!), the selection of actors tedious and, above all, the necessity of working in a team an unwelcome change from his essentially solitary methods of composition. Add to these problems of performing status (the professional actors for the Broadway production were self-conscious whereas amateur campus groups threw themselves into the play whole-heartedly) and it becomes easy to understand why Heller saw the stage adaptation of *Catch-22* as a specific chore to be done and then forgotten. In 1970, while he was working on this adaptation he insisted: 'I never want to be personally involved in the production of a play again'.[39] As soon as the script was finished he sold it to the theatre publishers Samuel French.

The original idea of converting the novel into theatre had come to Heller as early as 1962 when he began experimenting with adaptation, revising the three interrogation scenes, a love scene between Yossarian and Nurse Duckett on the beach, and the scene where Doc Daneeka tries to establish that he is still alive.[40] The project was then shelved until 1971 when Heller met up again with Larry Arrick (the director of *We Bombed*), who said he would be interested in mounting a production. Heller finished the adaptation and it was first performed on 13 July 1971 in the John Drew Theatre of Heller's present home town of East Hampton, New York.

Catch-22: A Dramatization (1971) is obviously not a dramatic work in its own right but is worth a brief consideration to see how Heller modified his emphases. Heller had an enormous problem of sheer length in trying to condense the novel into two acts and for the first production had 12 actors playing 41 roles. By doing this Heller ingeniously kept repetition — it would be a positive advantage for actors to be recognised in different roles — without sacrificing economy. The reduplication of roles does not adequately substitute for the use of expansive repetition in the novel, at least as far as Snowden is concerned, because his death on the stage does not culminate in meaning. Through the dramatisation Snowden is attenuated to a point of reference and his death, since it is too gruesome to be shown directly, has to be made an exposition by Yossarian. The cinema, and perhaps specifically the filming of Heller's novel, plays its part in determining the theatrical techniques used. Thus the direction note reads: 'A conscious attempt is made to focus the attention of the audience upon characters only when they are active, in much the same way that a camera guides the attention of an audience in a movie theatre'.[41] Partly this involves cutting out group scenes, partly shifting the dialogue backwards and forwards between different areas of the stage.

The structure of the dramatisation is of a series of cameos whose significance is heightened by using the chaplain and Yossarian as expository figures. Adopting the convention of reading aloud, Heller has the chaplain comment obliquely on scenes through letters he is writing to his wife. This function increases the chaplain's authoritative status in the play (as distinct from the military hierarchy) whereas in the novel it is crucial for his insights to contrast ironically with his lack of official status. The letters also mark another important difference from the novel. There the chaplain censors his own mail so that his wife never really gets a glimpse of his private agonies. Here his private thoughts are converted into explicit comment through the epistolary device. Indeed one general problem with the adaptation is that it makes so

many things awkwardly explicit. Yossarian's 'assault' on Nurse
Duckett becomes a matter for discussion and their dialogue about
their own feelings too straight in spite of a seasoning of theatricality
which draws on the Ruth–Starkey relationship in *We Bombed*.
Worst of all is the physical appearance of Colonel Cathcart who is
loaded down with props. He wears a black eye, an Indian head-
dress (feathers in his cap), carries a cigarette holder, a box of
tomatoes (to set up the chaplain's 'crime') and a bell for summoning
others. Such a strong visual impression draws his teeth as a
character making him seem simply ludicrous, not ludicrous *and*
dangerous. *Catch-22* disperses its comments on the action among a
large number of characters and the novel's complicating humour
grows from the clash between rival versions of events. In *We
Bombed* Heller introduced a Jacobean chorus of silent idiots to make
an obvious enough comment on the soldiers' acquiescence in their
roles. For the dramatisation of the novel Heller makes Captain Black
into a sinister choric voice, rubbing his hands with glee at every
new mission, and implying that the men are the Promethean
victims of cosmic punishment ('Eat your liver', he exclaims again
and again). In spite of his presence the general exclusion of the
bleaker aspects of the novel has been seen by critics as a serious
weakness in the adaptation since it smothers our sense of antagonists and shifts the overall tone towards light comedy.[42]

Three other changes are prominent in the adaptation. Firstly the
role of Wintergreen as a controller of information is given much
greater prominence. In his 1975 *Playboy* interview Heller explained
that 'Wintergreen came out of both my military and my corporate
experience' in being an apparently minor clerk who really exercises
considerable power.[43] So we now see him exerting that power by
tearing up letters ('sorting' them, as he puts it) and Heller introduced a new line which makes his position absolutely clear: 'I was
going to cancel the Normandy invasion, until Eisenhower committed more armor' (p. 20). Wintergreen's power grows out of his
capacity to manipulate the means of transmitting information but
his role in the novel is rather too subdued to reflect this. The
second emphasis which Heller changes is the metaphysical theme
of cold which is articulated by Snowden in the novel. Having
diminished his role Heller still makes considerable play on the
connotations of 'cold' (suggesting 'uncaring') and on contracts
between the internal warmth of the hospital as against the cold
outside. Feeling cold becomes a physical register of approaching

death and so clearly an important support to the play's subject.
Finally Heller sometimes makes very effective use of different
characters being on the stage simultaneously. One of the best
examples is the scene where Doc Daneeka's wife is informed of her
husband's death. Appropriately enough as the personification of
military bureaucracy, Wintergreen crosses the stage to hand over
the news of the death. The scene loses the bureaucratic proliferation or documents from the novel but exploits the Doc's physical
presence to highlight the absurdity of the official procedures. In
the novel Mrs Daneeka only functions as a passive recipient for her
mail. In the dramatisation she is given lines like the following
which naïvely appreciate the conspiracy to dispose of the Doc: 'I
think it's just wonderful the way so many people are doing so
much to help us bury him' (p. 69). Much of the dramatisation
consists of passages of dialogue transferred almost verbatim from
the novel. Around these passages Heller had the task of converting
sequences of narrative comment into linking or expository dialogue.

From this same period dates *Clevinger's Trial* (1973), a stage
adaptation of Chapter 8 of *Catch-22* into a flashback scene which
was too long to be retained in the dramatisation of the novel. As
with the previous adaptation reactions are made explicit. It is not
enough for a character to enact hatred; he must *state* it. For the
most part qualities in the original scene are made stronger:
Clevinger's idealism, the play on Scheisskopf's name, the reversal
of verdict and trial, etc. There are self-reflexive references to
Chapter 8 of the novel ('*That*'s when it began') and Heller draws
again on *We Bombed* to stress the theatricality of Scheisskopf's
address to the trainees.[44] He is carrying a sheet of paper which
functions like a prompting script. His address becomes an ironic
dialogue with Yossarian who answers back *sotto voce*. Here we note
another change under the influence of the intermediary play.
Clevinger, who was originally a rather passive and bewildered
figure at his hearing, now answers back much more; in other
words he speaks out more vociferously against the injustice he
experiences. One difficulty in converting this scene to stage use
becomes evident when the Colonel asks whose foot he is stepping
on. Being a printed text the novel can concentrate our attention
exclusively on a rapid sequence of words where gesture, expression, etc. are temporarily irrelevant. On the stage, however,
the audience's eyes would immediately turn to the characters'

postures to verify for themselves what is happening so that appearance would actually work against a primarily *verbal* confusion. *Clevinger's Trial* is the last in a series of five closely related works: *Catch-22*, *We Bombed in New Haven*, the film of the novel (1970), and its dramatisation. Although Heller only played a very minor role in the novel's filming, discussion of that work is best placed among Heller's other writings in the 1960s for the cinema and television.

OTHER WRITINGS FROM THE 1960S

Heller's earliest professional contact with the cinema seems to have come while he was teaching at Penn State College (1950–52) when Twentieth Century Fox asked if he would like to work on movie scripts. One result was a collaboration with his then colleague Bernard Oldsey on a work called 'The Trieste Manuscripts' which Oldsey has described as a 'hundred-page stripped-down novel functioning as an adaptation script for a movie'.[45] The subject was spies in Trieste at the end of the Second World War but the authors were pipped at the post by the release of such films as *Diplomatic Courier* and *Night Train to Trieste*. The very idea of scripting a spoof spy movie identifies a common thread of comedy which runs throughout Heller's work for the cinema and television. After the publication of *Catch-22* more offers were made. Columbia bought the movie rights and hired Heller to write the screenplay. Then in 1962 he was invited to write a pilot script 'PT73 Where Are You?' to help launch the television series *McHale's Navy*. When the producers put an additional writer on the script and revised it without Heller's consent a legal wrangle began which dragged on as late as 1969. In the mid-1960s Heller went to Hollywood to work with David R. Schwartz on the script of *Sex and the Single Girl* (1964), a comedy starring Natalie Wood and Tony Curtis about a battle between an author and the publisher of a scandal magazine. One peculiarity of this film was its use of stars in minor roles and it was subsequently repudiated by Henry Fonda and Lauren Bacall. One scene revolving around a beauty contest in a New York restaurant was cut from the script for reasons of economy but director Richard Quine later bought back the scene from Heller, even giving him the onerous task of selecting the beauty candidates himself.[46] Although Heller enjoyed the extraordinarily high wages he was receiving he apparently took a very quick dislike to the movie colony because, as he explained: 'The last thing they need in Hollywood is a writer. Movies are pictures; for the most part, they want nothing to do with words'.[47]

This was not yet the end of Heller's involvement with the cinema, however, since Charles K. Feldman asked him to work on the James Bond spoof *Casino Royale* (1967). After rewriting a number of scenes Heller discovered that Feldman had approached several other writers and that Woody Allen had actually been working on the same scenes as himself! The result was that Heller created a comic fiction out of his own experience publishing it as a mini-novel under the title 'How I found James Bond, lost my self-respect and almost made $150,000 in my spare time' in 1967. Heller casts himself as a gullible fall-guy, victim to Feldman's large promises of wealth. Feldman is quickly identified by the following exchange as a paranoid obsessive straight out of *Catch-22*:

> [Heller is speaking] 'Let me read the script and I'll see what ideas I can come up with.'
> 'You can't read the script', Feldman said.
> I was startled. 'Why not?'
> 'Because I won't let you', he replied. 'Everybody's stealing my ideas and putting them into their own spy pictures. I don't want anybody to know what's in the script'.
> 'Not even me?'
> 'Especially you!' he shot back. 'I don't even know who you are!'[48]

Contradiction is used here, as in the novel, to protect the subject (here Feldman) from imagined betrayal. Heller plays off his fictional voice against Feldman's throughout the narrative as a contrast between calm and frenzy, restraint and mania. When Feldman is telling Heller of his associates' diametrically opposed opinions of the original script Heller relates this impasse to a 15th century anticipation of catch-22 called Morton's Fork. This was a stratagem devised by Henry VII's chancellor to impose a war levy on the gentry in 1491. Francis Bacon summarises it as follows:

> There is a tradition of a *dilemma*, that bishop Morton the Chancellor used, to raise up the benevolence to higher rates; and some called it his fork, and some his crutch. For he had couched an

article in the instructions to the commissioners who were to levy the benevolence; 'That if they met with any that were sparing, they should tell them, that they must needs have, because they laid up; and if they were spenders, they must needs have, because it was seen in their port and manner of living'. So neither kind came amiss.[49]

However the gentry entertained the inspectors their behaviour could be interpreted to mean they were capable of contributing. Similarly, however Heller objects to Feldman's script his opinion can be countered.

The identical double bind raises the question whether there are broader similarities between this piece and the novel. If Feldman replaces the military hierarchy, then his promise of a huge fee is the equivalent to the promise of being sent home after completing the bombing missions; and equivalent to Cathcart's raising of the missions is Feldman's changing his mind about the nature of the film. Hence speed becomes ironic in this work just as in *Catch-22*. The more frenziedly Heller works the more the film shifts and recedes. Partly this is expressed spatially. Feldman leaves for California but sends telegrams from England. Rapid movement gives a farcical tempo to the narrative because in each meeting between Heller and Feldman the groundrules have changed. There is even a self-reflexive dimension to this comedy because, instead of sailing through an easy fortnight's work scripting a spy film, Heller finds himself caught up in a ridiculous melodrama of secrecy where he is shadowed by Feldman and his Bulgarian bodyguards, and where he reads the script for *Casino Royale* behind drawn blinds. Heller has quite clearly structured this narrative like a miniature novel in spite of its brevity, dividing it into 16 chapters and an Epilogue. The chapters usually end on either a note of expectancy or on an ironic twist both of which help to create a rhythm of alternating forwards and backwards movements. Each step towards revising the script is reversed by Feldman's unpredictable changes in attitude, and both characters are to an extent engaged in a game of mutual self-deception. Heller's doubts are smothered by his desire for the goal. When he reads the script he notices that 'the style of writing changed almost from page to page, as though a number of talents had already been involved'. 'As though' is a pointedly ironic phrase because it turns out to be true — the climactic scene is Feldman's admission that 12 writers are involved — and because

Heller never pursues his suspicions. On the contrary, in spite of the script being 'the most confusing thing I had ever read', he tells Feldman that it is 'great'.[50] Similarly Feldman anticipates Ralph in *Good as Gold* by telling Heller that *his* script is 'great' also. The ironies pile up when it becomes obvious first that Feldman doesn't like the script and second that it isn't even *Heller's* script that he has been reading. 'How I found James Bond' is a narrative of self-deception which draws clearly on Heller's first novel for its ironies and tempo. It ingeniously salvages comedy from his financial disappointment.

Apart from being invited to participate in the making of *Doctor Strangelove*, Heller did two other pieces of writing for the cinema in the 1960s. He worked on a screen adaptation of his friend George Mandel's novel *The Breakwater* (Mandel had also helped him with the writing for *Casino Royale*). And he collaborated with Tom and Frank Waldman on the script for *Dirty Dingus Magee* (1970), a spoof Western starring Frank Sinatra. Heller has frankly admitted that he only worked on these scripts for the money and has even expressed very strong reservations about the cinema as an art-form: 'Movies aren't really serious things anyway and movie writing isn't an art', he declared in 1967.[51] And in a later interview he put forward a different reason for disliking them: 'Movies I distrust very much because there's a kind of pandering that goes on to public taste...'[52].

Given these doubts we might wonder how he reacted to the filming of *Catch-22*. Heller was so little interested in writing the script that he waived his contractual right. He was shown a copy of the script which Mike Nichols and Buck Henry had produced and had an opportunity to discuss it with them. Among other things Heller pointed out that it was three times the length of an average script and also that there was too much incidental comedy in the opening scenes. Heller stayed well away from the actual filming and reports differ about his general opinion of the film when it was released. He has expressed reservations variously about the changed characterisation of Milo, the use of gratuitous comic effects, the absence of interrogation scenes, and cinematic references like the use of music from *2001*. Because of the cinema being a visual medium Heller admitted that the whole notion of 'Snowden's secret' was lost in the film; on the other hand he admitted: 'I think the film does work out the very slow death and the discovery of death in a most effective and dramatic way'.[53] Negative and positive comments almost balance each other. He has several times singled out the scene of the old woman in the brothel as making a particularly powerful comment on the whole situation of the novel: 'There's such a philosophical weariness in what she's saying – that everything's been smashed and there's no way to stop it'.[54]

Just as Heller created comic capital out of his work for *Casino Royale* so he wove a fiction out of the financial dealings over the movie rights for *Catch-22*. In 1963 he published a sketch of the agent Irving Lazar which begins with a stylistic flourish of symmetrical contrasts: 'Hollywood's biggest agent is also its smallest. What he lacks in stature he makes up for in vagueness. What he lacks in nobility he makes up for in disinterest. What he lacks in sincerity he makes up for in lethargy'.[55] Heller uses the literary form of the portrait to avoid clear portraiture. The epigrammatic appearance of these opening lines is entirely misleading because their witty bravura actually conceals oblique criticisms (is *vagueness* a positive quality?). In fact the whole essay skirts nimbly round overt criticism, hinting at paradoxes, even suggesting that Lazar is working on a level where normal values simply do not operate. Once again there is a debt to *Catch-22*, perhaps to Milo Minderbinder, in this portraiture. Lazar is just as all-engrossing, a ubiquitous presence in the movie business (hence Heller's title 'Irving is Everywhere'), and a character who speaks intermittently only to deflect criticism. He will answer the charge that he only works hard for the already successful ('That statement is a lie!') and then relocates the emphasis in his rejoinder to transform it into a virtual acknowledgement: 'I will work hard for *anybody's* most successful authors'.[56] Lazar emerges as a comically determined and obsessive manoeuvrer whose reactions are as Pavlovian as Milo's. Where the former identifies commodities, Lazar immediately associates any name he hears with deals. Heller even (again compare Milo) links Lazar's name with the US Government as if the two were of equal scale and power. His very energy leads to an indifference towards his clients' immediate wishes which in turn creates a ludicrously topsy-turvy form of communicating. Heller comments: 'My way of getting in touch with Irving is to fire him. In fact, now I fire him *only* to get in touch with him'.[57] It would be wrong to try to find a satirical dimension to this essay because Heller's comic method actually pays a round-about compliment to Lazar's industry and success. On the other hand his portrait draws directly on the methods of *Catch-22* and his skill at manipulating the news media looks forward to characters in Heller's later novel *Good as Gold*.

4

Something Happened

BUSINESS AND FAMILY STRUCTURES

Only a year after the publication of *Catch-22* Heller had his idea for a second novel and he had soon planned out the whole book.[1] In the event *Something Happened* was not published until 1974, being delayed by Heller's script-writing, political activities and above all the production of *We Bombed in New Haven* which caused a two-year interruption to his writing. Although he had written some 172 pages of the new novel after *We Bombed* had been produced he went back and rewrote the whole work afresh.[2] On the face of it nothing could be further from *Catch-22* in method and subject than this extended monologue by a bored middle-aged business executive but Heller gives Bob Slocum (the protagonist/narrator) a background of wartime experience in the US air force which originally was much closer to Yossarian's than appears from the final novel. A preliminary version of the opening chapter published in 1966 identifies Slocum as a former bombardier flying missions over Italy and France. Heller subsequently erased these references and attenuated Slocum's experiences in Italy down to a time of lost sexual prowess and a symbolic time of freedom. 'I was outside my family,' he reflects, 'had no wife, job, parent, children, met no-one I cared for. I had no ties'.[3] By contrast Slocum's present situation is *all* ties in his business and in his family life.

Slocum's memories of the war are tenuous but they do offer a point of comparison with one of the most famous postwar American novels to deal with a similar subject, Sloan Wilson's *The Man in the Grey Flannel Suit* (1955). Thomas Rath is, like Slocum, a successful business executive who is dissatisfied with his lot. He is married to a wife who criticises his lack of satisfaction ('we shouldn't be so *discontented* all the time'), living in a house which he hates (again like Slocum), but without ever being able to articulate the roots of his dissatisfaction. Wilson expresses this disparity between material wealth and unhappiness in terms of a fracturing of Rath's life into four distinct areas:

There were really four completely unrelated worlds in which he lived ... There was the crazy, ghost-ridden world of his grand-mother and his dead parents. There was the isolated, best-not-remembered world in which he had been a paratrooper. There was the matter-of-fact, opaque-glass-brick-partitioned world of places like the United Broadcasting Corporation and the Schanenhauser Foundation. And there was the entirely separate world populated by Betsy and Janey and Barbara and Pete [Rath's wife and children], the only one of the four worlds worth a damn.[4]

His conclusion is premature because his experiences as a para-trooper – the excitement of combat and a love-affair in Rome (Slocum remembers Bologna with a similar nostalgia) – exert a strong emotional pull, particularly as his restlessness with the present mounts. The process of changing his job heightens his self-examination; indeed it even demands it since Rath has to write a short essay beginning 'the most significant fact about me'. His difficulties in deciding how to answer this stem from the separa-tions in his experience and the novel poses the question: how, if at all, will Rath bring his four worlds into harmony? The final out-come is disappointingly convenient. He defeats a rival claim on his grandmother's house, organises payments for a child he had by his Italian lover (who remains safely distant), and stays in his new job, but not as a personal assistant to the president of the company. The pat resolution does not adequately resolve Rath's feelings of dissatisfaction over his work. He is afraid of becoming another anonymous man in a grey flannel suit ('the uniform of the day') and is so weary of writing and rewriting a speech (again cf. Slocum) for his new president (which comes to seem a 'penance from which he could never escape') that he takes a risk in criticising the speech. Luckily the risk pays off.

In many important ways Wilson's novel helps to locate the socioeconomic situation which underpins *Something Happened*. Rath is both tempted into a new corporation and uneasy about his position in it. According to William H. Whyte, whose classic study *The Organization Man* (1956) used *The Man in the Grey Flannel Suit* for its accurate description of a business executive, this unease is created by a conflict between the traditional ethic of individual self-advancement and the new facts of business life where 'the way to success in an organization life depends upon being aware that most of the decisions that affect one's destiny are made by others. . .'.[5] Wilson sentimentalises this issue by packing it into one point of decision where by criticising the speech Rath simultaneously salvages his self-respect, satisfies his wife and confirms a secure job for himself. Heller faces this conflict more honestly when Slocum comments of Andy Kagle, the man whose job he has been offered, 'he is a self-made man and unable to hide it'. The latter's personal obsolescence in the company reflects a change in business ethics. It is significant that Kagle is rather a nonconformist but also fatal in a context where the individual is subsumed into the corporate structure. Where Rath can at least find some solace in his family life, perhaps because it is so separate from his work, Slocum experiences the same separation but is alienated from both worlds.

When we move from Wilson's novel to Heller's a change in emphasis becomes immediately apparent. Where Rath was working on a speech it has become Slocum's local ambition to deliver a speech at his company's annual convention, but its content is never specified. We know approximately the subject of Rath's activities but we never know what Slocum's company sells. When questioned by his son about his job Slocum simply replies that he 'sells selling'. Near the beginning of the novel he ironically outlines the company pyramid as a hierarchy of fear but then declares: 'the company is benevolent. The people, for the most part, are nice, and the atmosphere, for the most part, is convivial. The decor of the offices, particularly in the reception rooms and anterooms, is bright and colorful' (18). In a way he is right that the company is benevolent but it is also very rigidly regulated, being run by a system of rules which resemble those of a miniature society, hence the close connection between the decor of the offices and the decorum of those in the offices. There are clear conventions as to when to use first names, which and how to talk about sex and also what clothes to wear. Instead of recoiling from uniformity like Thomas Rath, Slocum actually lectures Kagle on what sort of clothes he should be wearing. When Kagle asks what difference his sports jacket makes Slocum answers: 'more than your good sales record'. His days are numbered because 'he has no tone' and because 'his manners are not good'. More than that he is inept at business politics for the whole emphasis on appearance and style is nothing more than a façade of 'niceguymanship'. Where Kagle is the failure in this system Slocum's immediate superior Jack Green forcibly expresses the principle of subordination which should be at work: 'God dammit, I want the people working for me to be worse off than I am, not better. . . . I don't trust deference, respect, and cooperation. I trust fear' (414). Heller had originally planned to have Slocum take over Green's job but his retention was crucial because Green voices the masked absolutism of the company's practices. A faux pas will lead *inevitably* to demotion, extended leave and so on. In contrast with his family life Slocum positively enjoys the certainty and predictability of the company's rules.

As part of a necessary preamble to Slocum's monologue he summarises typical years in the company's life and personnel, mimicking the language of statistical reports. Even his flirtation with a girl from the Art Department is the latest in a series which changes according to the fiscal period. Slocum is thus participating in a system which validates itself as it goes along. The personnel know that the company is prospering because the Annual Report says so. The company even functions on collective fictions, the most obvious case being the sales reports. The section head Arthur Baron wants these reports because he 'has no other way of keeping familiar with what the salesmen are up to (or say they are) and a no more reliable source of knowledge on which to base his decisions and reports, even though he is certainly aware that most of the knowledge on which he bases his decisions and prepares his own reports is composed of lies' (51–2). Of a passage such as this Elizabeth Long has commented: 'the work process has evolved towards such abstraction that only its bureaucratic aspects have reality . . . and the void is filled by an overwhelming paranoia'.[6] Heller shows this abstraction by systematically excluding any reference to product so that the company has only a generic or bureaucratic identity.

Soon after the novel was published Heller was reported as stating that Time Inc. was the model for Slocum's company but specifics are irrelevant to such a generalised and anonymous institution.[7] Subsequently Heller corrected the impression that this admission caused: 'I wanted to use a company that was not harsh, but beneficent. I took Time for the book because of the six or seven companies that I worked for, Time was the most generous with vacations and pay and nobody was ever fired. I did not want to write a book about economic exploitation. I wanted a neutral corporation'.[8] Even this correction should be modified in the light of what Heller has said in interviews about his business experience. While working for *McCall's* and *Time* as a presentation writer Heller would mount slide and film shows to demonstrate promotional techniques and gave one such demonstration at the 1961 sales convention in Nassau.[9] And while working at Remington Rand his duties consisted 'of writing and supervising the production of advertising and sales promotion material'.[10] This is exactly the sort of activity which Slocum wishes to do at *his* annual convention and in the first version of the novel's opening Heller retained Nassau as the location of the most recent convention (he subsequently altered it to Florida). In other words Heller seems to have drawn on his experiences in at least two different companies for his sketch of Slocum's company but then during composition (as he did with *Catch-22*) he revised names so that the autobiographical parallels would be reduced. Much more important, however, is Heller's careful evocation of an institution which is not hostile to Slocum. Unlike Yossarian Slocum is not defined *against* his context. Rather he looks to the company for reassuringly predictable roles to adopt. The fixed order in the company constantly contrasts with the shifting and uneasy structure of Slocum's family. In neither case does structure suggest community but rather it triggers off more and more anxieties about his self-image and status.[11]

Since no end-product is named in this company our attention is focused again and again on the company's internal procedures. Slocum's answer to his son is a metareferential one, substituting transaction for product (the selling of selling) and his desire to deliver a speech is a desire to perform a role whose significance is defined internally, within the politics of the company. Here is Elizabeth Long again: 'the picture is of work so routinized that process has completely eclipsed product, leaving only the struggle for money and position to motivate and satisfy.'[12]. While she is certainly right about the deadening effects of routine in this novel it is debatable whether money acts as an incentive to Slocum. A much stronger pull is exerted by status even though he simultaneously knows that promotion will only cause a minor ripple in the company hierarchy.

In *Catch-22* we have already encountered cases of self-enclosed systems – in the military bureaucracy and in Milo Minderbinder's M & M Enterprises. Slocum's company similarly seems to exist to perpetuate its own processes. It devotes a lot of energy to internal analysis, to the copying and distribution of these internal reports.

And it takes its external information from statistical organisations such as the US Census Bureau, that is, from larger but similar bodies to itself. External reality is either ignored or accepted fatalistically: 'People in the Market Research Department are never held to blame for conditions they discover outside the company that place us at a competitive disadvantage. What is, is − and they are not expected to change reality but merely to find it if they can and suggest ingenious ways of disguising it' (28–9). Now it very rapidly becomes clear that the subject of *Something Happened* is not this company but Slocum himself. The focus of attention is steadily directed inwards. Even here, however, the company provides a model since we hear of the *internal* results of their techniques of persuasion. Instead of encountering an effect on a notional public we see how crucial appearances within the company become. Those few naïve individuals who wholeheartedly believe their own propaganda actually become less efficient operatives because they fail to understand that the company does not deal in truths but in perceptions ('what mattered was what people *thought* was true'). This helps to explain why Slocum is so preoccupied with impressions, shadow-realities and half-truths. His narrative tactic of reversing perspective, so that we either receive the hypothetical views of the character under discussion or Slocum's own views from a different angle, is a consequence of the heightened, even hypertrophied awareness of personal style forced on its successful employees by the company. Since how they act becomes far more important than what they do Slocum sums up his ironic sense of behaviour patterns in the figure of a dance: 'We come to work, have lunch, and go home. We goose-step in and goose-step out, change our partners and wander all about, sashay around for a pat on the head, and promenade home till we all drop dead' (30). Originally Heller had used an analogy with 'varnished goose-stepping mechanical dolls' but the dance is a more effective comparison because it choreographs movement according to patterns which are an end in themselves.[13] They do not lead to goals.

In the initial description of Slocum's company the fools are those who believe in the truth of what they are doing. Heller firmly directs our attention away from effects, products, truth-value, etc. towards the internal structure of the organisation. In his 1963 novel *The Boss Is Crazy, Too* (1963) Mell Lazarus follows a slightly different tactic by presenting his protagonist Carson Hemple as quixotically honest within a publishing company which is riddled with dishonesty. Lazarus follows to its extreme conclusion the logic of his comic cynicism in having the boss wilfully destroy the company to keep safe other financial deals he has made. His chosen instrument in achieving bankruptcy is the hapless Hemple who has to go through a whole series of lessons on how to steal, fiddle and defraud. Lazarus in effect gives an inverted parodic version of commercial success. As Hemple learns his lessons he becomes more and more popular in his company and so prosperous that by the end of the novel he can set up in business in his own right. The key to his success is abandoning all moral scruples and participating in the general system of organised theft. The watch-words of commerce ('time is money', and so on) become ironic comments on Hemple's own individual progress towards prosperity through a series of comic episodes which are usually at his expense. Heller knew of this novel and endorsed (if ambiguously!) Lazarus on the novel's dustjacket as the 'second-funniest writer in America'. *The Boss Is Crazy, Too* perhaps stands behind some of the comic details of *Something Happened*, especially in its emphasis on business as theatre. In the former the presumption of honesty has to be knocked down; in the latter the presumption of meaning.

If Slocum was in his late teens just before America's entry into the Second World War this would give him approximately the same age as Heller himself and also would identify him as a child of the Depression when the pressure to find a job was unambiguous and when there were clear national idols. Contrasting his own childhood with his son's predicament Slocum reflects: 'At least I had people like Joe DiMaggio, Babe Ruth, Joe Louis, and Cordell Hull I could want to be when I grew up' (259), whereas now his goals have either disappeared or become confused. Ernest Becker comments on this problem of realising idealistic goals: 'If you can't be a hero within a communal ideology, then you must be a nagging, whining failure in your family'.[14] Slocum's ironic self-awareness makes him see through the nature of company success with the result that he takes out his disillusionment on the hapless members of his family. As Heller subsequently explained, 'Slocum has achieved what he has been taught ... would be success but without gaining the expected sense of satisfaction'.[15] Slocum feels disabled from advising his son what to do by his own uncertainty about his purposes. This is where we come back to his ironic use of statistics. Slocum sums up his family situation in the following way: 'We are a two-car family in a Class A suburb in

Connecticut. Advertising people of the US Census Bureau [which also supplies his company] prepare statistics that include us in the categories of human beings enjoying the richest life' (341). As in W. H. Auden's poem 'The Unknown Citizen' any mimicry of statistical information in this novel implies that something is left out, a qualitative seepage which has nothing to do with material satisfaction. Slocum does not even enjoy these satisfactions anyway, mocking the pseudo-rusticity of his suburb. Upward mobility is a process which he feels induced even trapped into accepting, all the more absurd because it has lost touch with needs. The size of the land he owns, for instance, becomes primarily an indicator of his salary and business status. If he mocks progress then he is also mocking goals and Slocum is left in the uncomfortable position of simultaneously desiring a symbolic achievement (making a speech at the annual convention) and recognising that it has no importance. When he finally does make the speech at the end of the novel not surprisingly the result is an anticlimax.

As he fails to identify his own individual purposes Slocum projects this absence of continuity on to the national scene. Every time that Slocum makes a generalised comment on the decline of American life his outburst is locally stimulated by his individual problems. Worry over his bad feet shades into worry over crime and city riots; nostalgia for the stability of childhood is triggered by his more or less constant family rows and rationalised, for instance, as an adulteration of wholesome food with additives; paranoia leads to reflections on FBI telephone tapping. In all these cases externalisation represents an attempt on Slocum's part to reassure himself that he is not enduring marginal problems but that – even in a negative sense – he is keeping in touch with main currents of contemporary experience. The most substantial passage on national decline (one which Heller published separately as a self-contained article) hypothesises an entropic process of decay ('the world is winding down') which is again demonstrated in food ('butter tastes like the printed paper it's wrapped in', and so on).[16] This choice of examples has more to do with Heller himself than Slocum to whom food is not particularly important. Heller on the other hand has for years been in an informal group of gourmands who meet regularly in New York to sample the delights of mainly Chinese cuisine (Mel Brooks, a close friend and member of this group, has recorded Heller's expert comments on egg creams).[17] Slocum then launches into a parody of Katherine Lee Bates' poem 'America the Beautiful' which begins:

> O beautiful for spacious skies,
> For amber waves of grain,
> For purple mountain majesties
> Above the fruited plain!
> America! America!
> God shed his grace on thee
> And crown thy good with brotherhood
> From sea to shining sea!

Slocum's 'revision' reads:

> From sea to shining sea the country is filling
> with slag, shale, and used-up automobile tyres.
> The fruited plain is coated with insecticide
> and chemical fertilizers. . . . Money talks. God
> listens. God is good, a real team player.
> 'America the Beautiful' isn't: it was all over
> the day the first white man set foot on the
> continent to live. . . Depreciating morals, junked
> automobiles, and quick-food joints grow like
> amber waves of grain. (483–4).

Bates' sublime expanses of open space are filled with junk, the detritus of modern civilisation; the animate is smothered by the inanimate; and a god who should be endorsing national destiny is reduced to a role of subservience to commerce. Instead of a crowning apotheosis Slocum can only imagine anticlimactic endings which he articulates by systematically blocking every positive image in the patriotic poem. The problem with this passage is that it raises more issues than the novel can deal with. For a more substantial treatment of the European settlers as spoilers of the landscape and of the symbolic role of junk we would have to turn to the fiction of Thomas Pynchon, which Heller knows and admires. Heller's satirical landscape should rather be seen as an extension of Slocum's business activities and an expression of his disillusionment. Just as in *Catch-22* the administration was so counter-productive that it produced an entropic drift towards disorder, so Slocum's company weaves more and more interpretative variations on statistical data; and so Slocum weaves more and more variations on his own memories and fantasies. James Mellard rightly cautions us against reading the text as a diagnosis of American society: 'The "reality" of the world Slocum projects is inconsequential to any analysis of *Something Happened*. . . for readers are forced to regard all his utterances as symptoms of his ailment.'[18] The contrast in the description quoted above between extremes of romantic plenitude and industrial waste gives us the hint that it fits appropriately into the opposing extremes of his monologue. Just as Slocum parodically defaces an earlier rhapsodic text so he articulates his progressive disillusionment from earlier hopes. The polluted and junk-ridden landscape becomes a collective metaphor of his current state of mind.

If dissatisfaction is one feature of Slocum's present predicament boredom is the other. Boredom is both the consequence of achieving goals which he no longer values and also the premise of his narrative. Like Yossarian at the beginning of *Catch-22* he tries to vary his office routine with games which are also fanciful exercises of power. Slocum composes a utopia from names of personnel which are occupations or designs 'happiness charts' maliciously based on the animosities between the members of staff involved, thereby compensating in his imagination for the absence of initiative open to him in his actual job. Ironically the very free time which might be the goal of Slocum's labours turns out to be the worst problem. Although he is a member of a comparatively leisured class he reflects that 'spare time is ruinous'. Heller has taken a tremendous risk in writing such a long novel about monotony where Slocum's sheer verbosity could be taken as an attempt to fill the time.[19] He even tries to extract self-mocking humour out of this state: 'Apathy, boredom, restlessness, free-floating, amorphous frustration, leisure, discontent at home or at my job — these are my aphrodisiacs now' (p. 385). His disillusionment with either of his contexts (home and office) results in an unlocalised narrative situation. Unlike *Lolita* or *Portnoy's Complaint* where the narrative voices emerge from a fictitious trial or a session of psychoanalysis, Slocum's voice issues from a void. In his interview for the *Paris Review* given during the week when *Something Happened* was published Heller explained that Slocum was 'utterly unset, undefined, ambivalent'.[20] Accordingly 'there is almost no action in the whole book except introspection and recollection'.[21] The time span of the novel's present covers a brief period between Slocum's being offered Kagle's job and his acceptance of it, but this sequence could

hardly be called a plot. Rather it is used as an anchor for Slocum's
free-flowing thoughts and memories.

His narrative consists of a rambling and segmented monologue
which Patricia Merivale has located within a confessional genre,
finding a common pattern in *Something Happened* and the fiction of
William Golding, Camus, and others.[22] One work which clearly
stands behind it is Dostoievsky's *Notes from Underground* (Heller
used a passage from Dostoievsky as an epigraph to the first
published excerpt from the novel). Dostoievsky's narrator, like
Slocum, is constantly arguing with himself, overturning earlier
statements and using asides, digressions and parentheses to anticipate the reader's responses. Again like Slocum he finds a refuge in
reverie and dream to compensate for the dissatisfaction of his daily
life and he too attacks a statistical account of life as grossly
inadequate. Paradoxically he constantly addresses an audience of
'gentlemen' and claims that he is writing only for himself. One
difference from Slocum lies in the fact that he has arrived at a more
formulated general notion of human nature as characterised by
perversity and striving rather than attainment and the enjoyment
of happiness. The shorthand term for this wilfully perverse, almost
masochistic substitute for happiness is 'underground', a state
rather than a location which he explains in a key passage:

> But it is just in that cold, abominable half despair, half belief, in
> that conscious burying oneself alive for grief in the underworld
> for forty years, in that acutely recognized and yet partly doubtful
> hopelessness of one's position, in that hell of unsatisfied desires
> turned inward, in that fever of oscillations, of resolutions deter-
> mined for ever and repented of again a minute later − that the
> savour of that strange enjoyment of which I have spoken lies.[23]

Where Dostoievsky's narrator waxes sarcastic about the enlightenment which knowledge brings, Slocum constantly mocks the platitudes that age brings wisdom (partly by posing as a small child)
and that material prosperity brings happiness. Both narratives
have satirical margins where unthinking conformity is ridiculed,
but Slocum is debarred from the other narrator's ironic crispness
because he continues to perform the very roles he criticises. He
both attacks the company's stereotypes and participates in the
processes which will convert himself into just such a stereotype.
As such he is an excellent personification of the waverings and
oscillations diagnosed by Dostoievsky's narrator. Richard Hauer

Costa has produced an excellent account of the similarities between '*Notes from Underground*' and *Something Happened*, finding
a common tone of voice, a common attitude to external life as a lie,
and even a parallel between Slocum's parentheses and the antici-
pated refutations of Dostoievsky's narrator.[24] Just as 'underground' suggests covert resistance to all social conformity Slocum
has made a private mental withdrawal from the values he continues to practice. His is a narrative of personal dislocation where
his external actions have lost any correlation to the feelings he
admits within the privacy of his monologue.

Slocum's own narration is obsessed with time. He is haunted by
transience and by the lost opportunities of his youth. As memory
shades over into sexual reverie it seems that retrospective reflection offers a means of reliving the lost excitements of his youth. It is
appropriate then for Slocum to survey a number of possible
psychological beginnings in the short preliminary chapter of the
novel. These beginnings are primal scenes of sexual revelations (of
his brother, sister and parents). The doors which open on to these
scenes blur together into a composite psychological image charged
with sexual significance. The darkness of the coalshed where he
stumbles over his brother having sex is repeated and intensified in
the basement storeroom of his first job where another office boy
(Tommy) enjoys regular sex with one of the secretaries. An early
significance to doors very quickly emerges given this heavily
emphasised sexual context. If we take up Freud's explanation
('doors and gates ... are symbols of the genital orifice') then
Slocum's handing over of the key to the storeroom door to Tommy
becomes a sexual mime, a relinquishing of sexual initiative which
Slocum does not acknowledge so early in his narrative.[25] His
memories return again and again to a beautiful girl named (almost
allegorically) Virginia sitting directly under a clock. She is thus
juxtaposed against the broad perspective of time, an association
strengthened by the fact that she used to ration their contact to a
few hasty moments. The recurrence of Virginia's image confirms
her subjection to transience ('It would have passed, sooner or
later', Slocum reflects, 'just as she has passed already, just as I am
passing now': 88). Slocum gradually admits more and more details
about her which question her innocence (her willing participation
in a gang rape, for instance) and slowly empty her of sexual allure:
'I try to think of pink and fecund Virginia and can't: she is all silk
and exotic fragrance when we begin, but my imagination lets me

down and she withers rapidly in my mind into what she would be today. . .' (267). It is significant that a conscious effort at recall fails and the passage of time accelerates so as to exaggerate Virginia's ageing. The exercise of memory then does not revitalise through repetition, enabling Slocum to live through moments of the past, but performs a kind of erasure whereby figures from his past are recalled only to be obliterated. They are 'filed away' in his mental equivalent of a dead records store. Sooner or later these memory sequences come to bear on death, the ultimate eraser. One reason why Slocum feels comparatively free to toy with memories of Virginia is that he knows she is dead and so can never fulfil his sexual yearning which is anyway shown to be very ambiguous. His first reaction on hearing of her death is relief. Similarly his flirtation with Jane in the Art Department is also largely a matter of verbal innuendo, and consciously pursued as a reversed form of his relationship with Virginia (this time he is older and he is in charge).

The gaps between Slocum's blocks of narrative correspond to the blanks between his periods of memory which he reifies as enclosed spaces and then as the physical fragments of an identity so that discontinuity becomes tantamount to dismemberment:

> There are long gaps in my past that remain obscure and give no clue. There are cryptic rumblings inside them but no flashes of recall. They are pitch black and remain that way, and all the things I was and all the changes and things that happened to me then will be lost to me forever unless I find them. No-one else will. Where are they? Where are those scattered, ripped pieces of that fragmented little boy and bewildered young man who turned out to be me? (134)

Slocum tries constantly to assemble continuous sequences because only in this way can he find his identity. His narrative should thus be seen as a series of attempts to construct a continuous sequence, to bridge over the gaps referred to in the passage above. As he fails to find authenticity even in remembered sequences they recede into a 'children's story' about someone else. Slocum's most terrifying single thought is of the period of deep unconsciousness induced by an anaesthetic for an operation. This appalling rift in mental experience haunts him as a temporary lapse from reality itself, all the more terrifying because he does not share William James's confidence in the ability of consciousness to bridge over such gaps. As his monologue progresses Slocum's problems with memory increase. He imagines isolated frames of arrested motion as if a film had slowed down to a stop. The strangest example of these static images is Slocum's dream of a frozen Christmas dinner tableau where all the members of his family are gathered round the table. Before this can be registered as an image of longed-for family unity the other figures present shade into 'sceptical shadows' and even 'sit like ruins in a coffin in their high-backed chairs' (402). Although Slocum insists to himself that he is in control of the scene he is simultaneously helpless to act, frozen into a posture of immobility over the turkey he is carving. The anxiety deeply embedded in the image gradually emerges through the juxtaposition of opposites: life and death, control and immobility, vitality and decay.

In the course of assembling his contracts between then and now Slocum repeatedly notes absences. His imagination is packed with thoughts of death (compare the Christmas dinner), the ultimate irreversible loss. Examples accumulate rapidly from the suicides of Virginia's father and herself, through the inexplicable murders reported in the newspapers to deaths actually witnessed by Slocum. A man collapses from a heart attack before his eyes; another is caught in the doors of a subway train and dragged to his death. And throughout the novel Slocum, like Stephen Dedalus, is haunted by guilt feelings over his mother's death, of which more in a moment. Deaths are the most dramatic examples of a whole series of disappearances which are constantly taking place in Slocum's experience. Unable to locate a firm continuity between say the boy who discovered his brother in the coalshed and himself now, Slocum visualises these early episodes as the experiences of quite separate selves who have somehow vanished. One meaning to the novel's title is expressed as a question: What happened? What caused these earlier selves to disappear? It is a question which echoes throughout Slocum's monologue, but one which appears to carry a misleading implication. Walker Percy answers it in the following way: 'What happened? We are not sure, but whatever it was, it was not a single event in the usual sense of events in traditional novels... It is more like some aboriginal disaster, the original sin of the twentieth century'.[26] By implying a singular cause Slocum almost composes a personal mythology where he falls from happiness through some primal wrongdoing, but in fact the more he reflects on his past experiences the more we see unmistakable signs of the ambivalence which determines his character in the present.

Here we need to note that Slocum's monologue is not a direct confession but more an enquiry into the origins of his dissatisfactions. For all its rambling digressions it takes the direction of introspective self-analysis. Questions arise again and again because Slocum encounters apparently inexplicable surges of emotion or patterns of behaviour. If *Something Happened* is in part a fictional exercise in diagnosis a brief comparison with one of the most notorious contemporary confessional novels — *Portnoy's Complaint* (1969) — should be helpful. Alex Portnoy presents himself as a psychic cripple, obsessive and guilt-ridden thanks to the constant self-sacrifice of his parents. But voice is crucial here. Portnoy renders his parents and his own 'sufferings' absurd by inflating them into comic fictions through a characteristic tone of voice which brilliantly sustains shocked incredulity. Complaining ('kvetching') involves composing momentary self-images and situations which build up to local climaxes and which Portnoy makes explicit when he pleads 'spring me from this role I play of the smothered son in the Jewish joke!'.[27] It is a broad ethnic irony in the novel that the comedy of misfortune should be directed against Jews as the creators of suffering not the victims, because of dietary restrictions, a cloying family consciousness and an ingrained habit of sacrifice. Obviously this marks an important difference from Heller's protagonist who is a carefully composed everyman without any defining ethnic or religious characteristics.

Heller has explained that he wanted Slocum to be undefined because 'he was a typical human being in a typical situation, leading a typical, uneventful life in which things are going his way'.[28] This difference being admitted, there are aspects of Slocum's monologue which resemble Portnoy's. He shows the same self-dramatising intelligence, casting himself in exaggerated roles (leering sex maniac, lost child, etc.) which internalise the theatricality — the mask of friendly manners — he practises at the office, his improvised composition of anecdotes, his shaping of situations and even his occasional evocation of personal exposure through facetious newspaper headlines all resemble Portnoy's recitation, though in a lower key. Where Portnoy articulates himself as being trapped inside a joke which he must repeat endlessly Slocum interjects humorous asides with the consciousness that his joking is forced and repetitive. The 'ha, ha' which concludes many of these asides is a signal to the reader that Slocum has gone through the form of a joke but without actually believing in its comedy (in spite of the fact that some of these jokes were taken from Heller's friend Mel Brooks).[29] It becomes partly a defence mechanism (convert the unattractive into comedy before you can be condemned) partly a stylistic procedure to go through when his true feelings are elsewhere. In his review of *Something Happened* Kurt Vonnegut noted that 'Slocum is invariably sober and deliberate during his monologue, [and] does not seem to give a damn who hears what he says'.[30] Thomas LeClair has made a similar point in declaring that: 'Slocum appeals to his reader's curiosity and gains his confidence by revealing a privacy rarely breached. While the anxieties, desires and ambivalences Slocum admits may be common, the attention he gives to the minutiae of his life ... exceeds the requirements of verisimilitude, defamiliarizes his ordinariness, and achieves a "reliability" that far outweighs the distance such revelations may create'.[31] What is at issue here is the extent of Slocum's self-revelation and its consequences for the reader's reactions. Heller has admitted that when he started the novel he intended Slocum 'to be a fairly loathsome person' but was surprised how his and the reader's sympathy grew for him.[32] Neither Vonnegut nor LeClair adequately recognise the extent to which Slocum hesitates in his revelations – now disclosing, now concealing – and all the time exploiting the gap between action and feeling to admit his faults notionally while persisting in the behaviour which exemplifies them. Slocum, like Portnoy, demonstrates a well-developed sense of audience in anticipating criticisms of himself. In both novels the implied reader shades into a part of the self which functions as censor and critic. For Portnoy this is an internalised form of his mother's voice which becomes the voice of conscience and which plays dialectically against the voice of desire. Philip Roth subsequently explained that Portnoy uses obscene vocabulary 'because he wants to be saved'.[33] If his mother articulates restriction and taboo he uses obscenity to try to break through that restriction and liberate himself. A similar process takes place within Slocum. As his monologue progresses he gradually admits thoughts into his consciousness which had previously been suppressed. The signs are not directly verbal as in Portnoy's case but a series of changing figures which express disturbing and unattractive impulses. When he feels a desire to kick Andy Kagle in his deformed leg he attributes this impulse to 'something cankered and terrifying inside me' and the course of the novel expands this 'something' into a 'crawling animal', and

'elusive imp', and a shadowy male figure — the father conspicuously absent from his family memories: 'This one watches everything shrewdly, even me, from some secure hideout in my mind in
which he remains invisible, and anonymous, and makes stern,
censorious judgements, about everything, even me' (135). The
presence of this censor figure explains Slocum's speed to criticise
his own account and his reluctance to state certain things to others.
His monologue offers an opportunity of thinking the unthinkable,
of articulating hidden hatreds through a kind of silent speech. The
situation is further complicated and further differentiated from
Portnoy's by the fact that Slocum is both a son and a father. In the
latter role he feels obliged to act as censor on his son, to teach him
moral behaviour even though the justification can be entirely
circular: 'We actually put him on notice that, not to punish him,
but only to teach him a lesson, we were going to punish him, but
only to teach him a lesson' (282). Tautology and contradiction in
these scenes reflect Slocum's scepticism towards a role which
biological circumstances have forced on him.

At one point when Slocum is reflecting on his hidden impulses
he demonstrates a familiarity with the terms of psychoanalysis:
'My id, suppurates into my ego and makes me aggressive and
disagreeable' (395). Elsewhere he throws out confident allusions to
the Rorschach ink-blot test and the Oedipus complex, thereby
complicating a psychological reading of his monologue. Portnoy
too incorporates Freud into his narrative — literally so since he
reads his works while masturbating! Portnoy takes Freud (and
specifically his essay 'The Most Prevalent Form of Degradation in
Erotic Life') as a normative voice related to his mother's and
therefore to be argued against. Freud's authority is undermined by
the ludicrous context of the quotations from his essay and from the
equally ludicrous use of a fictitious psychoanalyst ('doc') as the
addressee of Portnoy's monologue. Slocum also incorporates a
brief session with an analyst who does little more than sigh 'ah' to
Slocum's admissions. At the time when he was writing this particular section of the novel Heller was reading *The Ambassadors* and
by his own account borrowed the analyst's verbal mannerism from
James's characters.[34]

These details raise a broad issue about how to read *Something
Happened*. It cannot be approached in a simple psychoanalytic spirit
because Slocum has woven into his narrative an awareness of the
procedures of analysis and even converted them into comedy. This

does not mean that psychoanalysis becomes redundant but acts as a warning to keep the reader on his guard against reading a scene in too categorical a way. Take the example of the image of the door. In Slocum's preamble he develops the implicit sexual importance of openings. Later this significance is incorporated into behavioural tactics. Slocum uses open and closed doors as signals in his office or at home. The Freudian symbolism of the door gives way to its metonymic associations with privacy and concealment. His children shut themselves in their rooms which Slocum both regrets (because it implies independence and the end of their childhood) and welcomes (because more and more he does not want to know what is going on inside). The door is thus an object with open signification and also an indicator of Slocum's ambivalence: does he fear closed doors or open ones? Among other things the door can connote a protective barrier to the self as in Slocum's recurring nightmare when away from home that 'a strange man is entering illegally through the door, which I have locked, and drawing near, a burglar, rapist, kidnapper, or assassin' (169). A particularly helpful gloss on this dream has been offered by Joan DelFattore who sees it as expressing Slocum's dread of marital infidelity and an incestuous urge to seduce and dominate his daughter. She argues that Slocum's dreams are vital for revealing a set of psychic associations to the reader which revolve around fears. She continues: 'The dream figure of the dark stranger unites them all [the fears] and connects them with hidden aspects of his own personality associated with his need to dominate by means of sex and speech'.[35] We shall see that invasion and penetration are two such fears which grow stronger during the novel.

The main psychological development which takes place in Slocum's monologue is a progressive loss of identity. Heller has described him as a 'walking, throbbing nerve' and stated that 'his spirit is disintegrating'.[36] In his analysis of contemporary social figures Christopher Lasch, who takes *Something Happened* as a key text in his discussion, identifies a narcissistic personality as one who 'depends on others to validate his self-esteem' (Slocum describes himself as 'anaclitic' which amounts to much the same thing) and continues that 'his apparent freedom from family ties and institutional constraints does not free him to stand alone or to glory in his individuality'.[37] Slocum tries to show an independence of family ties by going with prostitutes but the attempted therapy always fails because their routines remind him of earlier promises and are never realised. Early in the novel he admits a mimicry reflex, an unconscious borrowing of the mannerisms of others and wonders whether he possesses any characteristics of his own. This develops into a positive fear of fragmentation and Slocum repeatedly depicts his mental activities as involving different personifications, a subject and watcher. He creates a whole inner landscape whose drama contrasts forcibly with the monotony of his external life, figuring the former variously as story, film, soap opera or melodrama. The climactic passage describes a private hell:

> Vile these evil, sordid, miniature human beings who populate my brain, like living fingers with faces and souls. Some wear hats. People suffer. I suffer. Children wander. Women weep. Mothers lie on deathbeds. I am afraid – I have been afraid – a screaming, wailing, or sobbing might start at any instant inside my ears, be taken up by other tortured voices from within, and never stop. I would not know if I was imagining it. Minikins move, and I can feel them, and dirty, cynical old men with sharp crutches and pointy beards pass with insinuating glints in their cruel, unscrupulous eyes. They hurt. Ugolino eats a head: mine (that son of a bitch) (536).

The reference here is to Count Ugolino de Gherardeschi whom Dante sees in the lowest circle of Hell gnawing at the body of a former ally who had betrayed him.[38] This allusion makes explicit the many images of torment (by streams of lice, ghouls and phantoms) which recur in Slocum's monologue and suggests that the passage quoted functions like an internalised and abbreviated version of Yossarian's night-time walk through Rome. Where he witnesses the signs of an institutional collapse into brutality Slocum's inner eye traverses a dungeon containing graves, a labyrinth of stone passages and an urbane miniature alter ego ('a worldly relaxed fellow with black silk socks and a grey pin stripe suit') who urges him on to sadistic acts. The landscape combines traditional Gothic elements (darkness, underground) with images introjected from daily life ('grimy, unshaven men expose themselves to me and to children of both sexes and go unpunished').

This collapse into mental anarchy blends in with Slocum's other symptoms of decline. His fears of fragmentation become a terror over loss. He has more and more dreams of helplessness, in one of which the family maid calls again and again for Slocum to come to the aid of his son, but without actually using his name. Slocum has castration fantasies and recoils from sexual contact. He begins to confuse inner and outer, starts talking in his sleep and repeatedly makes verbal jokes about the difficulties of locating his identity. About his son he reflects: 'At last he knows now that I am me, although neither one of us is all that positive who that me we know I am is' (p. 293). There is a poise to this expression of uncertainty which disappears in the last sections of the novel. As Heller explains: 'Whereas in the earlier portions he was punctilious about grammar and sentence structure, in those last sections he does have run-on sentences, the use of parentheses, he loses his logic, and he even begins having what amount to auditory halluci- nations. . . He's out of emotional control'.[39] Apart from the stylistic signs of breakdown (described below) Slocum makes a series of telephone calls to the company where he worked before the war. These games with the past (Slocum is enquiring after Virginia knowing full well that she is dead) involve trying on different identities and the game goes well until he asks for himself and is suddenly appalled by his own absence. The fluidity which has characterised Slocum's narrative so far, his ability to jump easily from subject to subject or to shift perspective, now turns into a liability and he figures himself as algae drifting helplessly. The detachment he could earlier manage from his own narrative now turns into an alienation so severe that he watches his own be- haviour as if it were that of another man.

If Slocum is experiencing breakdown can his family offer him any support? The simple answer is no, not because he 'reifies his children and wife' (as Frederick Karl argues), but because he engrosses them into himself.[40] They become alternative possible versions of Slocum. Heller stated that he 'tends to consider people in terms of one dimension; his tendency is to think of people . . . as having a single aspect, a single use'.[41] Slocum thus 'flattens out' the members of his family into simple roles and for this reason they are never named. To name them would be to individualise them. His daughter becomes the voice of conscience, seeing through all of Slocum's little self-protective fictions; his wife expresses his own yearning for a family harmony he constantly destroys; his son represents a best image of the young Slocum. The second section of *Something Happened* outlines Slocum's situation in his company, setting out the clear guidelines which ensure a kind of security. Although he later tries to apply the same formulaic kind of description to his family the attempt fails. Slocum never quite knows where he is with his wife and children and his family surely figures so prominently in his narrative because they cannot be easily brought under control. The most obstreperous member of the group is his teenage daughter. The following excerpt from one of their many arguments is typical:

> [Slocum advises her to conceal her actions from him so that he will not have to punish her and make himself unhappy]
> 'Why will it make *you* unhappy?' she wants to know.
> 'Because you're my daughter. And I really don't enjoy seeing you unhappy.'
> 'Really?'
> 'Yes.'
> 'Ha.'
> 'And because I don't like to waste so much time fighting with you and yelling at you when I have other things I'd rather be doing.'
> 'Like what?'
> 'Anything.'
> 'What?'
> 'Working. Reading a magazine.'
> 'Why must you say that? Why must you be this way?'
> (I don't know) 'What way?'
> 'You know.'
> 'I don't.' (I do.)
> 'Why can't you ever pay me a compliment without taking it back?' (145)

With such exchanges in mind Christopher Lasch comments that Slocum 'believes, with good reason, that his rebellious adolescent daughter wants him to punish her; and like so many American parents, he refuses to give her this satisfaction or even to recognize its legitimacy. Refusing to be manoeuvred into administering punishment, he wins psychological victories over his daughter'.[42] This is true as far as it goes but does not really explain the difference between this dialogue and the conversations Slocum has at work. The latter are not necessarily calmer or more comfortable (Slocum describes Green's style, for instance, as 'ego-baiting') but they operate within consistently maintained conventions which vary according to the status of the participants in the company hierarchy. Here it is typical that Slocum's daughter cuts through the verbal guessing games which he tries to practice with insistently sceptical questions which puncture his pose as long-suffering parent. Her aggressive intelligence identifies Slocum's tactics and prevents them from operating under the ostensible level of meaning. By making these tactics explicit his daughter manoeuvres Slocum into a lie (denying that he used them) and prevents them from succeeding. The fact that towards the end of the passage Slocum gives a voiced denial and a silent admission confirms that the daughter's voice actually shades into a part of himself which attacks his own posturing and egotism. Like Slocum she demonstrates an urge to attack which she does not seem to understand; and again like Slocum she breaks down into a stammer when she is out-manoeuvred. Speech becomes an exercise of power in *Something Happened* and its loss the worst sign of helplessness.

If Slocum's exchanges with his daughter are combative, his conversations with his son follow a completely different pattern. His daughter is almost an equal antagonist but his son constantly requires reassurance, hence the large proportion of repetition in their dialogue ('you promise?' for instance). Or alternatively his anxiety necessitates a coaxing out of words, a gradual bringing to utterance during which process (much to his delight) Slocum adopts the role of a Socratic tutor. Where the daughter uses speech to divide, the son uses jokes as a means of bringing the family together and partly for this reason has been happily described by one critic as the 'unacknowledged hero' of the novel and more fulsomely by another as a 'living metaphor for the idea that artless virtue is doomed in a hostile, antagonistic world'.[43] Slocum identifies so closely with his small son's anxieties that he takes them over into his own field of experience. *He* suffers (again and again) the trauma of his son's tonsillectomy and in a way regains contact with his own lost youth by sympathetically re-enacting his problems. One extended section devoted to the son's difficulties with sport at school turns out to bear directly on Slocum's own predicament. The son has no sense of tactics in sport which worries Slocum because competitiveness in sport is promoted as a model for progress in life. The son's generosity and exuberant sense of enjoyment prevent him from responding to the Darwinianism of his teacher which so enrages Slocum that he addresses the reader directly ('how would *you* like to be a tame, somewhat shy and

unaggressive little boy of nine. . .?'). The teacher acts like one of
Moses Herzog's 'reality instructors' but while Slocum is attacking
this ethic of competitive individualism (treated in similar terms in
Heller's next novel *Good as Gold*) he also remembers with nostalgia
that he had clearly identified sportsman heroes like Joe DiMaggio
to emulate (Alex Portnoy draws on the same model when he
yearns 'Oh, to be a center fielder'). His special solicitude towards
his son during this difficult period is explained by his dissatisfaction with the kind of success he has achieved and an angry
realisation that the role models have been superseded by current
business practice where conformity to the requirements of large
organisations is of paramount importance.

The other member of Slocum's family so far not mentioned is his
brain-damaged son Derek, the only one to be named. Derek is an
important suppressed presence throughout the novel. Heller has
stated that 'the damaged child is a reflection of himself [Slocum],
symbolically',[44] and Slocum virtually confirms this correspondence
when he admits that Derek has 'an incriminating resemblance to a
secret me' (391). Derek is frozen in the mentality of a five-year-old
suggesting that he is outside time itself, exempt from the transience that bedevils all other areas of Slocum's experience. If that
makes him the embodiment of an attractive possibility, he is also
the Benjy Compson of the family (Slocum's own comparison),
possibly the sign even of a curse put on the Slocums.[45] When
Slocum tries to imagine Derek's future he sees him as a grotesque
form of himself, an image which he consciously composes ('I color
his sweaters and jackets dark and his face pale'). But if Derek
represents a part of Slocum it is a part associated with guilt, an
internalised version of the guilt surrounding the issue of whether
to get rid of him or not. Slocum used to joke that they could kill
him but no longer does so when the folie appmanthos conscious
dunites.

If we thus visualise Slocum as positioned between two contrast
ing sons who embody opposite aspects of himself, we should now
consider the full significance of the novel's title and the fate of the
unnamed son. Obviously the title makes an ironic comment on the
uneventful nature of Slocum's life but the novel also plays on at
least four different shades of meaning in the verb 'happen': to
occur in the neutral sense; to occur *by chance*; to befall; and to become of someone. The permutations of the title (what happened?
what would happen? etc.) recur again and again through the novel

raising issues of causality and usually rationalising Slocum's passivity towards experience. He casts himself again and again in the role of voyeur (he prefers hearing Virginia's stories of her sexual experiences to actually having sex with her) and spectator. The following conjugation of an experience in his childhood is typical: 'I touched her gingerly. I molested a child. I was molested as a child. Everyone is molested' (339). Here he shifts his specific experience to the generic, the active to the passive, the passive to the universal, so that his responsibility for the original experience (comically slight anyway) is effaced by generalisation. Taking up such explanatory tactics Susan Klemtner has argued that Heller constantly undermines Slocum's fatalistic or deterministic accounts of his actions as evasive.[46] She rightly takes his generalising about entropy as a psychological convenience but decides rather hastily that Slocum's justifications for his actions waver between determinism and an admission of free will. For instance Slocum recognises that he took a decision to keep his disabled mother in a home but denies that he has a choice over accepting Kagle's job. As usual he wavers between opposing possibilities: responsibility saddles him with oppressive guilt; the imagery of drift and dreams of helplessness fill him with despair.

How does this dilemma bear on the death of his son? Klemtner makes out a cogent case that accepting Kagle's job is tantamount to accepting or confirming Slocum's 'bad self' as embodied in Derek, and to killing off the 'good self' embodied in his other son. When Slocum sees his elder son horribly injured in a traffic accident, clutches the child in his arms and by so doing smothers him to death, Klemtner interprets this action plausibly as the climax in a psychodrama. There is abundant evidence to support this version of the narrative. Firstly Derek is analogically linked to Kagle by the fact that both are cripples. Secondly the accident to Slocum's son marks the climax to a whole series of allusions to such accidents which punctuate Slocum's monologue (accidents to the son, the daughter, and other characters). These foreshadowings of disaster are realised in the penultimate section of the novel. And finally take the following mental sequence which takes place during one of the son's crises of anxiety while on holiday: 'I wanted to kill him ... then I wanted to clasp him to me lovingly and protectively ...' (336). During the son's accident the two desires find simultaneous expression in one ambiguous and fatal action. Like the governess at the end of *The Turn of the Screw* Slocum turns a gesture of protection into a fatal act. The death of the son takes place within a local context packed with references to disaster and suicide and also immediately after Slocum realises that he is beginning to pass out of childhood into adolescence (symbolised by him closing the door of his room on Slocum). Read against the many references to time in the novel Slocum's embrace could be taken also as an attempt to cling on to the child he loves, to prevent him from growing into independence. Heller received a letter from Bruno Bettelheim praising this episode for the psychological plausibility of Slocum's attempts to retain a love relationship.[47] It is already too late for his daughter. When he tries to embrace her she slips out of his grasp leaving his arms clutching at empty air. Ultimately Slocum tries to wrench his son out of time which of course he does – by killing him.

SLOCUM'S UNRESOLVED STYLE

The verbal correlative to Slocum's monotonous life is a simple present tense chosen by Heller to give immediacy, which also generalises a state rather than expressing transience.[48] A characteristic syntactical form in this novel is the simple declaratory sentence which describes (we are told of his son 'he is a gifted, hard-working student; he is inhibited; he is a quick, intuitive learner': 218) or which recounts typical actions ('I do such things to them ... even when I don't intend to'), emphasising a universal present of narration. Slocum is well aware of this when he explicitly collapses past and future together ('I am what I have been. I incorporate already what I am going to become': 402). If transience is excluded the narrative becomes descriptive and expository, and Heller runs the risk of mimicking rather than evoking monotony by using such a repetitive sentence pattern. In fact he creates progression in a number of different ways and varies the sentence pattern through oxymoron and parenthesis.

Oxymoron is primarily the rhetorical figure which articulates Slocum's endless ambivalences towards the various problems that beset his sex life (does he really want to make love to Virginia or not?) or his domestic experiences. In an earlier home he is puzzled by mice: 'I was afraid I would catch the mice...' and then in the next sentence 'I was afraid that I wouldn't catch the mice...' (9). Symmetrically paired possibilities cancel each other out because

Slocum did not know what to do about the mice. A typical sequence in Slocum's narration then is for a positive statement to be followed by its negative, not just in contradiction but as if he has momentarily switched round the perspective, as if he has declared 'on the one hand ... on the other'. The oxymorons in Slocum's style correspond to the contradictions in his behaviour. He simultaneously wants to succeed in his company and mocks that success. In that respect Slocum perfectly embodies an ambivalence which in 1968 Stephen A. Shapiro found to be typical of postwar American fiction: 'Oscillating between alienation and opportunism, between rejection and acceptance of self and society, between impulse and inhibition; tempted by simplicity and haunted by complexity, contemporary man has the choice of becoming a connoisseur of ambiguity or becoming paralysed.' While ambivalence, or at least the contradiction beween body and spirit, are nothing new Shapiro declares that the tone of contemporary fiction is significantly different because 'never before have we been so sophisticatedly aware of and tolerantly ironic toward the bewildering complications of our emotional, moral, and political lives'.[49] Drawing on Barth, Roth, Pynchon and Heller (although he has clear difficulties in reading *Catch-22* as a series of psychological portraits), Shapiro sketches out an anticipatory context for *Something Happened* and only one year before Heller's novel was published there appeared a book which Heller read and which sheds yet more light on ambivalence in the novel. Ernest Becker's *The Denial of Death* (1973) is a study of the contradictions at the heart of human life.[50] Man, he argues, is haunted by the thought that he will die and driven by the futile desire to escape from his own animality. Since this is impossible he spends his life oscillating between the opposing roles of mind and body. Becker supplies the ultimate pathological background to Slocum's hesitations; Shapiro puts his emphasis more on social values. Both accounts suggest that Slocum's predicament is not just a personal one, but rather typical of an era, and even of humanity in general. It is the style of his ambivalence which needs careful examination here.

When as a child he literally stumbles over his brother having sex in a coalshed he does not know whether to run away or not and so hesitates uncertainly until his brother comes out. This physical immobility anticipates what we might call a stylistic immobility where propositions are constantly neutralised in a way which contrasts ironically with Slocum's social and financial progress. At one point in the novel he begins a sentence 'I wish' and leaves it unfinished, thereby summing up a predicament which besets him throughout the novel, a state of unfocused yearning for unimaginable goals. He is on much safer ground when complaining about present ills than thinking of future pleasures and indeed his entire monologue could be read as a complaint against boredom, lost opportunities and lost purposes. The following passage, arranged so as to highlight its parallelism, is typical:

> I get the willies often in my spare time;
> I don't normally sleep well (although my wife tells me I do);
> I get the blues I can't lose; *they* decide when to leave
> (I either talk to myself or believe I might);
> I get depressed and don't know why;
> I mourn for something and don't know what; (506)

In spite of the insistence on the self Slocum's list, a sort of stock-taking of ailments, demonstrates a vulnerability to moods which are either personified as external forces (the blues) or whose reasons are hidden. The repetition of the verb 'get' glances back to the novel's title and suggests that pure chance is operating. Apart from its stylistic typicality the passage is also characteristic in presenting the currents of the self as mystifying processes.

Apart from Slocum's tendency to juxtapose contrary assertions and leave them unresolved he also expresses ambivalence through parentheses. The only critic to discuss this feature of his style, Lindsay Tucker has argued that, whereas parentheses contain nonessential information, Slocum's interjections are often as important as the statements outside brackets and therefore the informational level of the parentheses is reduced. The hierarchy between sentence parts is undermined and the declions collapse into nondifferentiation.[51] This is an argument which possibly takes its lead from the Fowlers who define the use of parenthesis as 'to insert, without damage to the root of the sentence, something that is of theoretically minor importance'.[52] The lesser/greater importance actually offers an inadequate means of approaching Slocum's parentheses even though the early version of Chapter 1 of the novel which was published in *Esquire* in 1966 does suggest that the parentheses were inserted into the text at a later stage of composition. The *Esquire* version contains virtually none and reads comparatively more fluently. It thus presents a Slocum who seems much more definite and — it should be said — much less interesting than in the novel. Slocum liberally peppers his monologue, for instance, with wisecracking asides which attempt to divert potentially solemn subjects (funerals, family divisions, etc.) into comedy. These particular parentheses are usually signalled as self-consciously forced jokes as if the jokes were part of a routine for staving off the emotional impact of disturbing thoughts. So we encounter near-contradiction — 'I really like and admire Green in many respects (even though I also hate and resent him in many others)' (31) because Slocum has suddenly reversed perspectives. Here we encounter the main purpose of these parentheses. Far from being minor insertions in the text, they supply Slocum with a means of attacking his own text, so that he can set up a proposition and then demolish it with a comment in brackets. The parentheses almost add up to a second narrative voice, mocking and questioning the assertions of the first.

One of the premises of the novel is that Slocum 'is able to see himself in a way that can only breed a great deal of self-contempt. . . He renders himself naked to his own eyes and that makes it very hard for him'.[53] Here we can locate the main difference from Heller's first novel. Where *Catch-22* attacks the corporate deceptions of a large bureaucracy from the outside, *Something Happened* sets up positive assertions by Slocum as targets for his parenthetical voice. Hardly has a flattering thought taken shape before it is contradicted by an abrasive counter-proposition. The parentheses expose the unreliability or ambiguity of impressions (by adding a comment such as 'or think I do'); or they admit thoughts that Slocum does not want to place in his more explicit text such as his desire to be rid of his brain-damaged son. The following passage takes up the praise of visitors for Slocum's healthy son. Note how the parentheses positively attack parental pride and then methodical parental guidance:

> We think so too (we are somewhat vain and braggarty about those precious intuitions and idiosyncrasies of his in which we can take proprietary delight) and (like rigid, high-powered machines not really in charge of ourselves) operate automatically to change him . . . (261)

What Slocum will half-admit in the main sentence the parentheses make explicit. *Something Happened* shows the dialogue of Slocum's mind with itself and in the above erosion of domestic pieties the effect is rather as if an argument over patriotism had taken place within Yossarian's mind.

All the way through the novel Slocum is finessing about what can be stated and what cannot, employing an elaborate mechanism of self-censorship. If one progression in his monologue is the relaxation of that censorship then we are now in a position to see why, as Lindsey Tucker rightly notes, the parentheses become longer and longer. Since they almost invariably contain fantasies, memories or secret admissions, their amplification reflects Slocum's tendency to take over the subject of his own narrative. Whatever local topic may be under discussion the focus easily switches round to Slocum himself. His son's difficulties at play group trigger off a digression on the size of breasts; the former's anxieties at school occasion a long memory-passage on Slocum's nightmares of immobility. Tucker tries to maintain a distinction between 'actual incidents' and Slocum's obsessions which is doomed to failure because first-person narratives, especially mono-logues, are inevitably and notoriously subjective. As Heller himself explains, 'Bob transcribes his own auditory hallucinations, so that parts of the dialogue are in fact imagined conversations'.[54] Slocum does not usually indicate the distinction and later in the novel seems to lose hold temporarily of the real. In informational terms Slocum's obsessions take over from other narrative subjects and his extended digressions become charged with psychological meaning. His reveries, memories, and such like reflect priorities. His digression on breasts joins a whole series of other references and images which suggest a nostalgia for a cherished object of childhood. Inevitably these parentheses retard the process of reading and complicate the structure of the syntax. One result of this is to set up a juxtaposition between material inside and material outside the parenthesis. Slocum places a digression on making love with his girlfriend Penny next to a passage on killing, on the wilful killing of small animals on country roads. The odd disparity between the two subjects is overcome by the recurrence of a key word, 'muff', in both passages, a recurrence which invites the reader to speculate on possible resemblances. Thus making love, which Slocum explicitly sees as an act of domination, becomes an act of hunting and murder. Slocum becomes a sexual predator, killing off his conquests.

In an interview given soon after the novel was published Heller

pointed out that his purpose had been to gear Slocum's prose style
to his mental state: 'At the beginning, the prose is very orderly,
very precise, very controlled. But as you move into the middle, as
Slocum becomes more emotional, the prose gets less orderly and
the sentences get longer'.[55] The following example from the section 'It is not true' is typical and occurs (again typically) within a
reverie about Virginia:

> I could have done it to her lying down and sitting up, frontwards
> or backwards, sideways frontwards and sideways backwards
> too, the way I'm able to do now with girls who are slim and agile
> and don't get cramps (if I don't put on more weight. And I hope I
> don't lose more hair, or I soon might not be able to do it any way
> with anyone but my wife. I used to be praised for my lush wavy
> hair. Now curls are the thing, and I don't have any), several
> times a day most days of the week – and had my sandwiches
> and *Mirror* on the desk top there too – with my leather shoes
> propped firmly against the *Personal Injury–1929* file cabinets for
> greater drive and mobility and my folded elbows cushioning our
> heads against a smash into *Property Damage–1930* (372–3).

The sentence begins with an exaggerated (and safe since it is an
impossible hypothesis) declaration of sexual prowess but as the
first mention of a physical ailment creeps in ('cramps') Slocum's
parenthetical voice takes over in a lengthy interruption which
drains the sentence of its confidence by undermining the syntactic
priority of the first clause. We have seen again and again how
obsessed Slocum is with time. Here the obsession surfaces in a
muffled anxiety about his declining physique where hair is temporarily identified with sexual potency. As he returns to the imagined
scene a second identification is hinted at between sexual activity
and the risk of personal injury. By the time we reach the end of this
sentence its true subject has been revealed as Slocum's anxiety
over his own physique and his substitution of hair for a more overt
recognition of sexual fear takes place in the silent drama of his
monologue. The main critical task in reading *Something Happened* is
to bring out the latent content in such passages, to examine the
implications of how Slocum expresses himself rather than take his
statements at face value.[56] Thus syntactic structure and style give
us reliable access to his real priorities. In the passage quoted above
Slocum is composing a static self-image rather than the description

of an activity with another person, where his imagined younger self is poised symbolically against reminders of the passage of time.

Once again we have come back to the central issue of control. Lindsey Tucker has performed a crucial task in pointing out how *verbal* an issue this is. We have already seen how dialogue can become a means of exercising power. As Tucker points out, an important area of fear for Slocum is literal speechlessness. He fears the inability to utter which blocks Derek's attempts to communicate and which descends on his mother after her stroke. Silence is so horrific it becomes associated with death, hence the underplayed irony of the title to the section where his son is killed − 'My little boy has stopped talking to me'. Slocum's finicky corrections to his own monologue and his criticism of others' bad grammar are reflections of his anxiety to preserve verbal fluency and superiority. His nervous jokes about echolalia try to convert verbal redundancy into humour, but silence not redundancy is the ultimate terror. Mimicry is raised as an issue during one of Slocum's exchanges with Green, where Green points out that even banal enquiries mark a latent content ('You know I wasn't asking you what was wrong before when I asked you what was wrong': 412). If we bear in mind the constant disparity between manifest and latent meanings in the dialogue of *Something Happened* an apparently trivial utterance can represent an exercise of tactics (playing for time, performing an expected role, etc.) and therefore becomes meaningful. It is this distinction between levels of significance which enables Heller to avoid monotony in the novel.

We have already seen numerous examples of Slocum saying one thing in dialogue and admitting its opposite in the privacy of his monologue. It now remains to be considered how that private utterance itself starts to collapse towards silence. During the composition of *Something Happened* Heller read Beckett's Trilogy and has since declared that he found the novels (especially *The Unnameable*) similar in tone and mood to his own work.[57] Beckett constantly links physical debility to a weakening epistemological certainty. His narrators decline through weakness to total immobility just as their capacity to narrate deteriorates. Beckett is preoccupied with imminent endings reducing his narrators to positions of minimal certainty about their own experience and existence. Hence Malone starts composing stories but falls back on 'aporetics', expressions of uncertainty which pack *The Unnameable* to such an extent that virtually all utterances are negated as soon as they are made. Where Slocum's contradictions express ambivalence, in the trilogy they articulate the loss of a Cartesian faith that intelligible reality depends on a single perceiving consciousness (hence throw-away jokes like 'what about trying to cogitate?'). Heller's novel lacks the philosophical density of Beckett's Trilogy, which, for instance, stresses that language precedes any individual consciousness. Hence it becomes 'their' language and fair game for the narrator's corrosive logic games. Monotony in Heller is caused by the circumstances of his narrator; monotony in Beckett is the general reaction to the disappearance of meaning. In both cases narratives are undertaken to pass the time. Where Beckett presents a dwindling self whose physical exhaustion corresponds to the futility of narrating ('if only this voice could stop. . .') Heller shows how Slocum's gradual admission of illicit thoughts increases his ambivalence to crisis point so that he begins to break down physically (headache, hallucinations, nightmares) and syntactically (ambiguous pronouns, shifting parentheses, inordinate digressions).

Surveying contemporary first-person narratives Richard Pearce has argued that the previously clear distinction between narrator and frame breaks down: 'The narrative voice loses its independent and dominant status. And what the reader sees is no longer a clear picture contained within the narrator's purview, but an erratic image where the narrator, the subject, and the medium are brought into the same imaginative field of interaction, an image that is shattered, confused, self-contradictory but with an independent and individual life of its own'.[58] Pearce takes the Trilogy as one of his prime examples of this process which is useful because it enables us to distinguish between the formal collapse which takes place in Beckett and two ways in which Heller modifies the consequences of Slocum's decline. He divides Slocum's monologue into nine sections which set out an orderly sequence, starting with a psychological preamble (with a glance at origins) and running through a section on his company and then a section related to each member of the family. There next follow two short sections containing his acceptance of Kagle's job and the death of his son, and a final epilogue. This structure ingeniously combines a survey of Slocum's situation with an attenuated plot where narrative hints are fulfilled in the climax of the son's death. Heller takes Slocum towards collapse but brings him back out of it. Appropriately enough he has explained the ending in terms of control: 'That last section was deliberately terse and controlled to show he's back in authority, not so much in the company, but trying very hard to control himself'.[54] Ironically the sign of control is not simply more systematic sentences but an act of concealment in hiding the facts of his son's death (the section is entitled 'Nobody knows what I've done'). Slocum's monologue has gone into reverse. Instead of harmonising inner and outer, a fresh surge of guilt has been suppressed by a sudden acceleration in business and domestic success. Again ironically this success has been triggered by the death of the member of his family whom Slocum loves the most — his son. That event both liberates him and prevents his monologue from reaching a resolving conclusion. Slocum's return to stylistic orderliness is actually a return to concealment, to the divorce between action and feeling.

5

Good as Gold

Heller's next novel combines elements from both *Catch-22* and *Something Happened* in a bitter indictment of political ambition. It presents an ironic and bleakly futile version of a success story pursued by its Jewish protagonist Bruce Gold in his efforts to penetrate the world of Washington politics. Washington represents an updated variation on the bureaucracy of Heller's first novel and displays just as many idiocies. What complicates *Good as Gold* (1979) is that the protagonist increasingly displays Slocum's ambivalence about achieving his original goals. Whereas Yossarian personified an ideally simple point of view, Bruce Gold demonstrates a dissociation of his ambitions from his critical intelligence and is consequently an unreliable commentator on his own experiences. A second complicating factor is the plot of the novel. Reflecting on the success of *Catch-22*, Heller has admitted that if he were to rewrite it he would 'try to make the early chapters a little more coherent' so as to avoid the reader's initial difficulties with the text.[1] Accordingly *Good as Gold* reads like a far more linear and orderly narrative than either of his preceding novels, partly because Heller could assume that the potential trajectory of his protagonist's success would be relatively clear in the reader's mind. This method risks making the novel seem simpler than it is just as the style at times appears deceptively realistic, but realism in *Good as Gold* regularly functions as a prelude to exaggeration and caricature. In that sense the novel exemplifies a quality located by Malcolm Bradbury as being characteristic of 1960s American fiction which 'becomes fantastic through its assault on the historical and the real'.[2]

Good as Gold is the first of Heller's works to engage with Jewish characters and, perhaps reflecting some diffidence on Heller's part about venturing into a territory prominently occupied by Saul Bellow and Bernard Malamud (the latter is quoted in one of the novel's epigraphs), Heller avoids realistic portraiture of Gold's family and instead pushes the most prominent memoirs towards grotesque caricatures. This tactic brought down the wrath of critics

like Pearl K. Bell who lambasted Heller for his ignorance of the
Jewish tradition and for wielding his 'free-floating cynicism like a
machete'.[3] Gold is an unfixed character and like Bob Slocum
wavers between two contexts. All the way through the book he
oscillates between Washington (a place full of future possibilities)
and New York in scenes with his family which relate primarily to
the past since Gold has lost meaningful contact with them. In an
interview of 1980 Heller summarised Gold's situation as follows: 'It
was a novel which would almost contrast the two worlds, the
intimate world of a large almost suffocating immigrant family
whose successive members have experienced different stages of
American life and assimilation, and contrasting that with the very
garish political public life of the celebrities in Washington
politics...'[4] In this description 'intimate' is a grimly ironic term
because physical proximity within the Gold family guarantees
nothing but friction and antagonism. This is revealed through a
series of meals which should enact togetherness but which actually
supply the occasions for this antagonism. Heller throws out in-
numerable ironies against assimilation here. Joannie, the one
member of the family who has rebelled against paternal authority
to the extent of going to Hollywood in pursuit of a film career, tells
Gold over lunch that she belongs to California temples for civic
reasons ('we make it a point never to pray').[5] There is no need for
Heller to underline the ironies in such statements because they
carry their own in-built pathos. The urge to blend effortlessly into
the mainstream of American society involves the fragmentation of
the Gold family so that paradoxically conformity leads to the isolation of its individual members, and none less than Gold himself.
He responds to the same fears which beset his relatives of drifting
into utter loneliness. The ritual of eating which should be a shared
experience and which should counter this drift only gives the
merest glimpses of the family feelings which are usually referred to
as absences.

In general the Gold family is defined by its inconsistencies. They
pride themselves on Jewish cookery but eat pork at a Chinese
restaurant; they admire Bruce for being an academic success but
treat him as the child of the family; the father scrupulously
observes Jewish holidays so that he can stay with his children
although he is an atheist — a 'Jewish atheist', he proudly boasts.
These inconsistencies, with their attendant mockery of the Jewish
immigrants' faith in education, amply justify J. W. Aldridge's claim

that the members of the family 'have long been displaced from the realities that formed them and gave them some sense of common purpose, and now they have become abstracted into caricatures of hostility and self-interest.'[6] Heller reveals this process by stylising their speech as in the following sequence where Belle (Gold's wife) tries to divert Gold from his daughter's tactlessness:

> 'Nobody's eating Esther's noodle pudding', said Belle, in a diversionary alarm.
> Like earth-moving equipment, arms reached forth over the table simultaneously for helpings of Esther's noodle pudding.
> 'Nobody's settled my hash,' said Muriel.
> 'And I brought nothing,' lamented Rose.
> 'Harriet takes the cake,' said Belle.
> 'And Belle chimes in,' Ida said.
> And now Dina [Gold's daughter] fled. (102)

Every detail sharpens the roles played out by the different members: Belle is the diplomat, Esther the one everyone feels sorry for. By converting references to food into colloquialisms Heller dramatises the tug of character against character. The characters are anyway kept flat, Muriel identified by her corned-beef hash and Rose (the subject of the party) through her monotonous refrain of regret.

Although Heller has stated that he wanted to convey incongruities in these meal scenes the examples he gives are quite consistent with realism, whereas in fact most of the scenes are comically heightened towards caricature.[7] Two of the most striking members of the family, the father and stepmother, turn out to be the least realistic but most powerful figures. The father dresses like a business magnate, grotesquely at odds with his past history as a failed tailor. He too is defined through Dickensian mannerisms: an obsessive hatred of cracked china which leads to a disaster in a Chinese restaurant, a stabbing forefinger and the repetition of *fartig* (that is, 'period') to strengthen his dogmatic style of laying down the law. It is crucial to realise that the father is both a tyrant and a truth-teller. At every meeting with Gold he engages in a tactic of contradiction which is aimed at belittling his younger son or simply humiliating the whole family. The following exchange is unique in making the verbal strategy involved so explicit. Gold suggests going to eat at a local fish restaurant:

'Let's go to Lundy's,' he suggested, 'It's right here. We'll have a good piece of fish'.
'What's so good about it?' said his father.
'So' — Gold declined to argue — 'it won't be so good.'
'Why you getting me fish that's no good?'
'Black,' said Gold.
'White,' said his father.
'White,' said Gold.
'Black,' said his father.
'Cold.'
'Warm.'
'Tall.'
'Short.'
'Short.'
'Tall.'
'I'm glad,' said Gold, 'you remember your game.'
'Who says it's a game?' (94)

Although Heller took care not to repeat the comic methods of *Catch-22* this exchange would stand comparison with some of the dialogues in the earlier novel and with the verbal sparring in *Something Happened*. It is absolutely typical in forcing Gold on to the defensive; even his decision not to argue backfires on him. Following out his simple rule of contradiction his father outmanoeuvres Gold whether the latter uses the same verbal counters or not. And he even refuses the apparently innocuous proposition that the exchange is a game. To do so would be agreeing a common level of seriousness, a complicity (to play together), and would also be stopping the game. By not agreeing on the rules Gold's father keeps his son at a permanent disadvantage since it is impossible to break out of the circle of contradictions. The exchange can never end; it will simply go on and on for ever with only temporary intervals.

Many of the conversations between Julius Gold and his children revolve around their efforts to get him to move to Florida, not for altruistic reasons. In other words it is a struggle for authority between the father and his children who want to determine their own lives. The father's fraudulent validation of his own status by laying claim to business successes he never had and to being a caring parent does not wipe out the cynical truths he keeps thrusting on Gold: that money is the source of power, that a Jew will not have any success in Washington, etc. The 'mad tailor of Coney Island' (Gold's phrase) demonstrates anger not insanity, rousing fury in Gold because his truths are so unwelcome. The peak of the latter's anger is a fantasy of torture: 'He should be locked up! In a prison, not a hospital! In handcuffs! To the walls of a dungeon he should be chained, that crazy fuck of a bastard, fifteen feet off the ground!' (181). One narrative theme in the novel is the father's stubborn refusal to be disposed of, his refusal to stop expressing the very doubts which Gold is trying to smother about his own fate. Although Heller decided to change his emphasis in the characterisation of the father away from that of a simple tyrant, Julius Gold is never just a caricature but is given the least attractive articulation imaginable of points of view endorsed by the novel as a whole.[8]

Gold's stepmother Gussie, who neatly avoids one comic stereotype firmly caricatured in Philip Roth's Sophie Portnoy, is similarly a truth-teller and a gratuitously cruel character. The most dominant members of Gold's family possess a common desire to embarrass and humiliate him. Gussie expresses the unmentionable, reminding the father of the nearness of death and even suggesting to Gold the possibility that he is a foundling, unrelated to the family which has been tormenting him for years. Presiding over the family gatherings as a grim and imperturbable presence, Gussie functions as a latter-day Clotho knitting the fate of Gold. Meetings between the two usually trigger off disquieting reflections on destiny and Gold's inability to break free from her power is acted out in gesture when she persuades him to hold her wool. Like Julius and Sid (Gold's older brother) Gussie is a joker at Gold's expense, denying a maternal relation.

Paradoxically Gold only possesses a family in name. His mother is dead, his mother-in-law rejects him, and his father displays him to his friends as an example of failure. Because Gold does not act consistently on his desire to escape from the family their gatherings demonstrate a disparity between his feelings and actions, and reduces his role to that of a frustrated observer. He is the point-of-view character in all family scenes but only passes silent comment, partly out of self-defence since every time he speaks he renders himself vulnerable to mockery by his father, mother-in-law or brother Sid. In the latter case a respectful and affectionate manner goes hand in hand with a constant desire to trap Gold in verbal games which he constantly loses. Thus when Sid misquotes from Pope, Gold's immediate reaction is to identify a tactic which he cannot resist:

> Gold saw in a flash that he was totally ruined. It was check, mate, match, and defeat from the opening move. He was caught, whether he took the bait or declined, and he could only marvel in dejection as the rest of the stratagem unfolded around him as symmetrically and harmoniously as ripples in water. (36)

Yossarian had exactly the same reaction when the principle of catch-22 was explained to him. Gold's plight is worse because the specific subjects of Sid's word games are so unpredictable. The game references in the quotation make it clear that the subject is irrelevant since Sid's tactic remains the same, inducing a bewildered paralysis in Gold which is the verbal dimension to his unchanging family situation. For this reason it has been described statically here. There is no real progression from scene to scene; rather a gradual unfolding of the basic situation and a repetition of the same conversational strategies which drive Gold to desperation.

If the members of Gold's family personify different social possibilities Gold's two main friends from college days, Lieberman and Pomoroy, represent alternative versions of himself. On the one hand Lieberman demonstrates Gold's ambition as a grossly physical gluttony and his self-regard in starting a series of autobiographies. Where Lieberman functions as a rival writer whom Gold can put down and thereby bolster his own confidence, Pomoroy acts as his intellectual conscience by directing short incisive questions at Gold. The difference in role between Lieberman and Pomoroy emerges in their physical appearance. Lieberman is a 'hulking' compulsive eater who gradually covers himself with gravy stains and sprays his listeners with half-chewed peanuts when he speaks. His messy appearance bespeaks a personal incompetence which contrasts with Pomoroy's leanness (an 'upright cadaver') which suggests a probity he demonstrates when he cuts through Gold's evasions and half-truths. All three characters are would-be intellectuals — Lieberman the editor of a little magazine, Pomoroy a publisher, and Gold a disillusioned academic. Section III of the novel gives a resumé of their 'success' stories and the stories of others to underline common predicament. Like Bob Slocum 'all had gotten what they wanted, and felt dissatisfied . . .

All were successful, and felt like failures' (65–6). All three register a common feeling of having missed out, of having lost opportunities, but it is only Gold who tries to put this into words by undertaking a book about the Jewish experience in America.

Since ethnicity is an explicit matter of dispute throughout the book it is predictable that one critic, Wayne C. Miller, has found a moral value in the family. He sees ethnicity as an 'alternative to the value of the corporate order of the modern nation-state' as represented in the Washington scenes and argues that Gold ultimately finds salvation in the family after the death of Sid.[9] There are many problems with this interpretation, not least with the fact that the Golds, as we have seen, are scarcely held together as a unit (ironically their main common bond is a problem – what to do with the father), have lost touch with their religion, and are riven by petty jealousies. Since every issue in the novel comes to bear ultimately on Gold it is consistent that he should register how problematic his family relations are in two main ways. The key to succeeding in the logic games with his father constantly eludes him and, secondly, the more he tries to find out about his own past the more difficult it proves to locate memories. The members of his family either cannot remember or say 'it didn't happen that way'. Even his own individual memories of the past turn out to be mistaken and Gold has to endure a series of bitter revelations towards the end of the novel, demonstrations of how unpopular he was as a child. Since the question of ethnicity relates primarily to the past it becomes impossible to argue plausibly that Gold regains contact with his roots since he cannot even come to terms with his individual past.

Gold is terrified by the thought that his brother Sid might die leaving him to manage the family and when this fear is realised, just when Gold is on the verge of meeting the President, it is still impossible to read this shift in responsibility in positive terms. Rather it is an ironic twist of events at Gold's expense which throws him back on the family without altering the dissatisfaction which is the premise of his characterisation. There follows a period of casting off projects (the book on Kissinger, etc.) and a visit to his mother's grave but here again Heller is careful to deny that Gold learns nothing. The headstone is in Hebrew; 'the earth had no message for him' (446). The last image of the novel is of *yeshiva* students playing softball, that is, an image combining traditional Jewish and American elements. There is no suggestion that these are harmonised or even typical of the American Jewish experience. To the very end of the novel ethnicity remains problematic, elusive, and controversial. In his review of the novel Leonard Michaels has commented rightly that Gold even embodies this ambivalence in possessing a Gaelic forename and Jewish family name. In contrast the Protestant characters are 'essentially unproblematic and mechanical'.[10] The most obvious and broadest irony in the novel is that Gold's anxious pursuit of the Jewish experience in America may *be* that experience. The searching, the arguing, and the uncertainty of allegiances may be the only defining characteristics which the Jewish characters have in common.

Nothing demonstrates Gold's incapacity to find his bearings among his family or friends so much as Heller's complication or inversion of predictable roles. Again and again Gold silently reflects that characters are insane, a reflex which says more about his own incredulity and helplessness. His father clearly demonstrates an inverted family pride in his younger son; his daughter Dina shows a precocious awareness of Gold's sexual activities (revealed in a comic play of her tough and profane verbal register against Gold's futile efforts to maintain his own verbal dignity); and his friend Dr Mursh Weinrock traps him into acting out the (absurd?) role of adulterer by inverting the results of his medical tests. The strangest Jewish character in the novel is undoubtedly Greenspan, the FBI agent who dogs Gold's steps once he seems within reach of high office. Introduced in Section VII, Greenspan functions, as Stephen Potts points out, as an 'Orthodox Jewish conscience', grotesquely overturning Gold's expectations of meeting a minor functionary.[11] Where Gold expects a member of the Washington establishment Greenspan actually tries to send him back to his other context in his family sometimes by acting out a comically melodramatic role:

> '. . . I remember my own dear departed father'. The memory detonated in Greenspan a final shot at bathos, and he came blubbering back toward Gold with a face drenched in revolting piety and goodwill. 'If you won't do it for me, at least do it for your sweet old father. Give up sex', he entreated with outstretched, shaking arms, 'and go back to your wife. Adultery might be all right for *them*, but not for us.' (269)

Where too many things are at stake for Gold to take this appeal as comic the reader is given the detachment necessary to identify the ironies in Greenspan's quasi-paternal role. Apart from absurdly misdescribing Julius Gold, he is unaware that Bruce Gold is trying to escape from his father, to move forward not back; and of course he is reminding Gold of the very ethnic distinctions which he is trying to overcome (or evade). Greenspan's repeated phrase is an accusatory one ('You're a *shonda* [that is, disgrace] to your race'). The first time Gold hears this it comes, needless to say, as a shock. Perhaps one significance of Heller making Gold an academic is to set up in him expectations of consistency, rationality, and predictability which, as we shall see more and more, the novel undermines through a series of comic shocks. For all his claimed knowledge Bruce Gold is surprisingly ignorant of contemporary sexual mores and political corruption.

In short Gold is a study in self-deception. He has marched on demonstrations against segregation but worries about blacks moving into prestigious residential areas. He mocks Lieberman for wangling a visit to the White House but does exactly the same himself. Heller leaves the reader in no doubt from the very beginning of the novel about Gold's capacity to turn with any wind: 'Gold was flexible and unopinionated now and able – with just a few minor adjustments in emphasis – to deliver essentially the same speech to an elderly reactionary religious group that he had given the day before with equal success to a congress of teen-aged Maoists' (46). Here and elsewhere in the novel the narrative voice nudges the reader towards spelling out the very contradictions and ironies which Gold's vanity induces him to conceal. Having stated this facility, a capacity to conceal his drift towards the political right with euphemistic phrases, Heller then allows narrative events to confirm Gold's hypocrisy again and again. The motive behind his self-deception and his desire to penetrate Washington politics is to escape from his fears of marginality in his family, in his own city, and even in his childhood. Gold is a figure caught between two worlds – three if we include that of his university. Melvin J. Friedman has summed this up with excellent concision: 'Gold negotiates three geographies: the university, the family, political Washington, D.C. They are all verbal constructs, with their own special grammars'.[12] Certainly each area of his experience has its characteristic syntax. At moments of pressure with his family Gold has recourse to Yiddish inversions and vocabulary ('In my mouth to ashes the food is turning!': 33). In the world of Washington, Gold starts using by contrast much less exclamatory sentences which gesture towards possibilities but which take on the contradictions associated with the place (of which more later): 'I'm going to work for the government, you see. It's absolutely definite now, although I can't be sure.' (213). Like Herzog Gold is intellectually self-involved but unlike Bellow's character he possesses a layered vocabulary which repeatedly reverts to profanity. Reflecting the irrelevance of his education this intellectual patina is so thin that it can be comically pierced at any time and Gold is repeatedly mocked for the disparity between his status and vocabulary. Heller even creates two voices within Gold to express his conflicting impulses once his political hopes are raised. Significantly the warning voice is Yiddish: 'A voice inside cautioned, *Zei nisht naarish* [don't be stupid]. Where does someone like you come off being Secretary of State? What's so crazy? he answered it brashly. It's happened to bigger *schmucks* than me' (124).

The discontinuity between Gold's different verbal registers is part of a much bigger discontinuity between the different areas he inhabits. Heller creates short episodic units which pay comparatively little attention to transitions from one scene to the next so that even the gaps in the novel's text signal a characteristic of its protagonist's experience. While Friedman was right to stress the importance of language we should also recognise that Heller uses setting in the second half of the novel to contrast the worlds of the American Jew and of the WASP. The main opposition is that between Coney Island and the Virginia estate of Gold's lover in Washington, Andrea Conover. The latter is an updated plantation presided over by Andrea's father as a feudal lord. The enormous spaces of the house and grounds are only populated by his negro retainers and the gargantuan buffet where Gold has breakfast is set for 500 although he is the only one to eat. In his description of the food Heller stresses the containing vessels (creamers, gallipots, kegs, bins, basins, and so on) as if the main importance of the food was sheer quantity. It also represents a throwback (indicated by archaic terms and such dishes as a pig's head on a platter) to an earlier manorial epoch. The contrast with the dishes prepared by Gold's sisters involves much more than differences of cuisine. In the Conover house food seems to have lost touch with its consumption. The WASP characters in *Good as Gold* show no interest in food as if they are cut off from some crucial dimensions to experience. The Conover mansion sums this up in its silence; everything is smothered and thereby life-denying. To the Golds as a representative Jewish group the preparation, presentation, and above all consumption of different dishes is a dramatic and engrossing process. The contrasting sets of cultural rules which determine the working of both worlds are reflected in Heller's attention to space. The Golds, like Heller himself, are from Coney Island and the last part of Section VII is devoted to a discussion of the deterioration in the area over the past 40 years by Gold and some childhood friends. Racially embattled, they squeeze into a small Italian bar and agree on the borough's decline, which is confirmed when Gold drives round the area contrasting it with how it used to be. Partly he registers disgust at decay, partly he senses dispossession from his own past as buildings have been razed and new ethnic groups have moved into the area. In Section VII Gold generalises these reflections into a gloomy vision of entropic decline where the area has become filled with rubbish and where new institutions take on a diseased life of their own: 'Office buildings rose as spectacles where there was no lack of office space, and organizations with Brobdingnagian names were sprouting like unmanageable vines and spreading like mold with sinecures and conferments for people of limited mentality and unconvincing motive'. (325) Here, as in *Something Happened*, landscape evokes cultural disease but now the image suggests a social vision rather than a psychological state. Ironically a vision of urban blight triggers a vision of a flourishing bureaucracy, a kind of parasite life. Again as in Heller's preceding novel, however, this vision must be set in an ironic dramatic context. In spite of Gold's professed dismay he still pursues the chimera of an appointment within this corruption. Heller's topographical contrasts suggest that to a certain extent this is a pursuit of personal space, a point which will recur when Gold's reactions to Washington are considered.

Although Gold knows notionally that success depends on luck he persists in believing that he is fitted to high office. Heller's new version of *Great Expectations* follows a similar narrative arc to Dickens' novel in tracing out the rise of the protagonist's hopes and their abrupt deflation in his physical collapse. Again like Dickens' novel Heller positions a series of characters who explicitly warn Gold not to build up his hopes. Their warnings and exposure of his evasions form the internal correlative to the broad ironies of the novel's plot. Gold simply will not act on his bitter recognition that success has nothing to do with intellectual ability. *Good as*

Gold, for all its comedy, is Heller's bleakest novel to date because it dramatises Heller's stated view that in America there is 'no relation between those who have authority and the exercise of it'.[13] In an article published the same year as *Good as Gold* Heller also asserted that 'those qualities which are important in achieving public power have little to do with creative intelligence or integrity of purpose'.[14] He thus locates two disparities: between the retention and the exercise of power; and between intelligence and power. A vision of America emerges as a country where political power is retained by an ethnic elite, one of the most exclusive aristocracies in the world.

Given this bleak vision the failure of Gold's expectations is implied from the very start and Heller uses three main devices to reveal this futility: the use of running as a metaphor of social striving, the confusion of direction and size, and the references to names. Gold (again like Heller in the late 1970s) goes jogging at his local YMCA and, while running, implicitly relates his actions to social purposes: 'Goals, he muttered as he pounded along steadily on the short oval course while the pain departed from his chest and settled and throbbed in his dangling kidneys, we ain't got any real ones' (64–5). Gold's absence of purpose is enacted in his circular laps around the track but once the tempo of his life quickens the running metaphor accelerates into a sprint. His physical collapse takes place later in the novel on this very track where his attempts to juggle different strands of his experience wear him down. It may well be that Heller is alluding obliquely here to Bud Schulberg's 1941 novel *What Makes Sammy Run?*, a narrative of financial success where the protagonist Sammy Glick sets his sights firmly on Hollywood. In a novel where social purposes have become ambivalent it is appropriate that Gold's direction should be circular, that his progress should be correspondingly ambiguous. We have already seen athletics being used in *Something Happened* as a training for engagement with social competition. Bob Slocum's son cannot excel at games at his school because he has no idea what career he wants to follow in life. *Good as Gold* begins with a protagonist who has lost his sense of personal purpose, introduces a goal, and simultaneously questions that goal. In the scene in the YMCA track Gold is tricked by his childhood friend Spotty Weinrock into running himself into the ground. Weinrock hides in the corners of the room and then sprints past Gold as if he is constantly lapping him until Gold collapses. Even at his point of collapse he dramatises his failure in pseudo-heroic terms: 'The ground rose to meet him with sways and undulations as he felt his legs wobble and give way, and, like a wounded warrior plucky to the last, he ran almost fifteen more yards on his knees before toppling to the track and lying still as a stone with his eyes staring, as though he had been brought to his doom by a mortal fright' (412). The analogies are pointedly ironic because Weinrock has simply outsmarted Gold and thereby demonstrated Gold's social naïveté. The dogged way in which he plods round the track reflects an absurdly inappropriate faith in winning under his own efforts whereas Weinrock's stratagem is much more consistent with the society of the novel.

The second ironic technique Heller uses is an extension of routine metaphors in the language whereby rising connotes an increase in hopes and falling their diminution. Judith Ruderman has usefully pointed out this theme noting that Gold is confused about up and down because the world itself has been stood on its head: 'Going to Washington will be a step up for Gold in status and prestige, but this elevation of politics and denigration of family are subversive of both politics and family in ways that Gold refuses to see'.[15] An argument with his family (which characteristically confuses representation with reality, humour with seriousness) and a conversation with Ralph Newsome, Gold's college friend and means of entry into Washington politics, make the confusion between up and down explicit, and any number of narrative details fill out this ironic theme. Gold's spirits sink when he goes to family dinners, his hopes literally descend with him in the elevator from Ralph's office, and, as we have just seen, his loss of hopes is expressed through physical falling. Rising and falling carry strong connotations of quality and social mobility in this intensely status-conscious novel. Gold's father is constantly asking him who is better than him, sadistically forcing his son to place himself on a vertical social scale. But Gold is partly aware of the confusion of values which is expressed by Heller in directional terms and after a visit to Andrea Conover's father wonders: 'How much lower would he crawl to rise to the top?' (378).

A surreal variation on this theme revolves around size and comes to the fore when Gold (described by Heller as a 'small Jewish guy' partly modelled on his friend Mel Brooks) takes Andrea to an expensive restaurant, sees the prices, and immediately feels small.[16] By contrast one of his college friends Harris Rosenblatt joins them. Although he is Jewish, Rosenblatt has somehow metamorphosed into a WASP. To Gold's astonishment he had 'grown lean with rectitude and tall and ramrod-straight with probity and . . . manifest puritanical social self-righteousness' (250). This change has been self-induced and is the physical expression of a cultural, even racial, transformation whereby Rosenblatt forgets his Yiddish and becomes associated with Nordic or Germanic Protestantism. Where he becomes taller, Andrea has become shorter — because of her contacts with Gold. Size here to a certain extent suggests self-esteem and of course status.

Heller also underlines his racial themes by drawing attention to names. Gold's sister Joannie has adopted an assimilationist alias in the name Toni but Gold might go a considerable step further if he joins the Washington administration since he will become 'unnamed'. The anonymity forced on him would deny his family, even his own individuality, since Heller is careful to stress the physical uniformity of Washington officials. The strangest episode which revolves around names, however, takes place during Gold's meeting with Andrea's father in Section VI. Masking his anti-Semitism with a polite façade, he mocks Gold's attempts to escape from his ethnic identity by calling him different Jewish names which are initially permutations of his own (Goldberg, Goldfarb) and which become more and more abusive, culminating in 'Ikey-kikey'. This exchange where Conover simultaneously acts out the roles of host and Jew-baiter has more than a personal reference, since Gold and Conover start bandying lists of names in an attempt to identify the number of Jews who have penetrated the Washington establishment. A crisis of identity in modern fiction is regularly signalled by the distortion, diminution or total loss of name, but it is one of the many ironies of *Good as Gold* that its protagonist should *pursue* anonymity and ethnic name-calling so whole-heartedly.

What are the determinants of Washington and what is it about this world which attracts Gold so strongly? Initially it is a question of verbal promises held out by Ralph Newsome but his words have a habit of slipping through Gold's grasp. After they have met several times Gold tries — unsuccessfully — to pin Ralph down to specifics:

> 'Ralph,' said Gold, with skepticism predominating again over a multitude of other concerns, 'do you ever really see the President?'
> 'Oh yes, Bruce,' Ralph answered. 'Everybody sees the President'.

'I mean personally. Does he see you?'
'The President sees a great deal, Bruce.'
'Do you ever see him to talk to him?'
'About what?' asked Ralph.
'About anything.'
'Oh, Bruce, you can't just talk to the President about anything,'
Ralph chided. 'The President is often very busy. He may be
writing another book.'
Gold persisted rationally in the face of a gathering fog of futility.
'Well, Ralph, if you did have something of importance to discuss
with the President, could you get in to talk to him?
'About what?' Ralph asked again.
'About whatever you had that was important – no, don't stop
me – like war, for example.'
'That's not my department,' Ralph said. 'That's out of my area.'
'What is your area?'
'Just about everything I cover, Bruce.'
'What do you cover?'
'Everything in my area, Bruce. That's my job.' (209-10)

Unlike the exchanges within Gold's family where the guiding
principle seems to be antagonism, Heller now sets up an opposition between rational enquiry and the voice of political experience.
The more Gold tries to specify his questions, the more easily Ralph
slides from meaning to meaning with the constant implication that
Gold's questions are naïve. Not only does he assume a knowledge
of the political establishment on Gold's part (implying an insider/
outsider distinction which whets Gold's ambition) but he avoids
direct answers by semantic shifts so that the verb 'see', for instance, is used in three quite distinct senses here. He manoeuvres
from 'anything' which is a lexical invitation for him to give an
example to the denotation of something of no importance. The
answers are always askew of the questions and when Gold finally
does suggest an example this leads the dialogue into complete
circularity. Ironically eager to communicate, Ralph's replies – repeating a rhetorical pattern set in *Catch-22* – actually block off
progression and deny access to information.
    Ralph's speech repeatedly uses three rhetorical figures: circular
or symmetrical propositions such as the lines which close the
passage above; comparatives whose reference is elided; and
oxymorons. He will constantly seem to refer to Gold's Jewishness

but deflect the innuendo, or will 'promote' Gold even though no previous appointment has been specified. Or again he will make an offer to Gold which is immediately qualified or contradicted ('You can have your choice of anything that's open that we're willing to let you have. At the moment, there's nothing': 117). Walter Nash has explained Ralph's peculiar verbal facility as follows: 'Ralph's character is nothing that can effectively be described *by* words. It resides *in* words; his soul is a self-adjusting verbal frame-work which is never allowed to pull out of balance...'[17] Ralph's rhetoric constantly tends to close off external reference and to become a self-contained system. Nash usefully points out that this system maintains its own equilibrium, which has the political consequence of maintaining the status quo. In effect Ralph divorces political processes from the rational procedures of the language itself and thereby articulates a discontinuity which Heller evidently finds in American politics. In 1975 he gave an interview to *Playboy* magazine where he spoke at length about his disgust with politicians but respect for political reporters who are the only group to emerge with credit from *Good as Gold*. Heller's most scathing sarcasm is reserved for the ambitious, again entirely consistent with the general ironies of the novel, and he generalises his disenchantment in a statement about the lack of communication in government: '... now there's too much distance between the citizen-voter and his elected representative... the Presidency has become a kind of public-relations enterprise for the party in power'.[18]

In *Good as Gold* the President's role is veiled, muffled and reduced. Ralph Newsome is the front man of government, a press officer who parries Gold's questions as if with an intention to give out as little information as possible. The fact that Heller published a news briefing as a preliminary section of the novel in 1976 suggests that Ralph is based on a specific figure, on Nixon's press officer Ron Ziegler.[19] A former tour guide in Disneyland, even Ziegler's appearance is repeated in Ralph but political commentators have put him on record primarily for his verbal agility. Joseph C. Spear has argued that Presidents in the 1970s have carefully controlled and manipulated sessions with the press in a growing preoccupation with secrecy. He locates the beginning of this tendency in the Nixon (i.e. Ziegler) years. For Helen Thomas, a leading political commentator, the beginning of this secretiveness lay in the presidency of L. B. Johnson and was caused specifically by the Vietnam War.[20] Once again this position harmonises closely with Heller's comments on the political events of this period. In his preface to the dramatisation of *Catch-22* he identifies a tension between political reporting (disclosure) and government, as exemplified in the revelation that Johnson had 'cruelly and systematically lied to the press' over Vietnam.[21] The case of Richard Helms, the former director of the CIA who lied under oath, thus assumes a symbolic importance in the novel as a public example of governmental dishonesty. Ziegler used different tactics in responding to questions so as to avoid overt lying. Joseph Spear has explained his style as follows:

> He was a master of Madison Avenue prattle, speaking an impenetrable language peculiar to the advertising trade. He leaned on such terms as *time, frame, input,* and *program.* Many questions met with such responses as, 'I am completed on what I had to say,' or, 'This is getting to a point which I am not going to discuss beyond what I have said'. He once accused a reporter of 'trying to complexify the situation' and firmly disallowed one query with, 'I won't be responsive to your follow-up question on the original question to which I told you I wouldn't be responsive'.[22]

In recognition of Ziegler's extraordinary verbal performances the press corps coined terms for his rhetorical strategy − a noun ('zieglerism') and a verb ('to ziegle').

Heller pays no attention to Ziegler's jargon, concentrating rather on his tactics which he parodies in the press briefing in Section VI. The *Wall Street Journal* for December 29, 1969 carried a detailed report on Ziegler's press conferences quoting his words verbatim to demonstrate his elaborate reluctance to admit facts, even such uncontroversial issues as whether the president showed anger in private.[23] Ziegler's avoidance of specifics and his mannerism of making negative statements rather than affirmations ('This ... is getting to a point which I am not going to discuss beyond what I have said') are picked up by Heller. Ralph begins his briefing with an oxymoron ('I have to announce that I have no announcement to make') and then makes two negative statements ('there is no news today' and 'I don't know'). Heller satirises the press officer's evasiveness but also the press corps's willingness to be fobbed off with his answers (Ralph is even thanked for his frankness!). The session breaks down into verbal farce:

[Journalist] 'Well, is there anyone in the Administration who does know?'
[Ralph] 'What?'
'Anything.'
'Would you repeat that question?'
'Anything.'
'Is that a question?'
'Is that an answer?'
'I don't know.'
'I forgot my question.'
'I'll withdraw my answer.' (203–4)

Stalling gives way to discussion of style not content which predict-ably confuses the questioner (but not Ralph). By emptying the exchange of content Heller foregrounds the verbal tactics of the briefing which become so introverted that they are a dialogue about dialogue, each speaker arguing about the nature of his own speech-acts. Heller includes sideswipes at administrative ignor-ance, the press media machine, and the general collusion over playing the game; but his main emphasis, as in the dialogues between Gold and Ralph, is on rhetoric entrapment.

Where the satire of the news briefing is entirely verbal Heller's parody of the Presidential Commission on which Gold sits follows different procedures. First he mocks the diversity of the personnel who are all token figures (deposed judge, athlete, etc.) apparently chosen without any conceivable reference to ability; the implication being (although it is one which Gold pointedly does *not* draw) that Gold is there as the token Jew. Next Heller satirises the inefficiency and expense of the procedure (they conclude without any discussion and are allowed up to $1000 a day in expenses). As the members of the Commission leave the their allows their parodic roles to emerge in one of the novel's numberless divergences from realism:

'Will I see you at cocktails, Mr Special Prosecutor?'
'No, Governor. We're going straight to the banquet with the Comptroller and the Queer. Will you be at the ball?'
'The Mrs and I will be detained at the orgy. But perhaps at the supper.'
'If I'm able to get there. I'll be shooting the shit with the Adjutant and the Bailiff. Let's say hello to the Crook and goodbye to the Champ.' (198–9)

A disparity emerges immediately between the tone of polite social pleasantries and a noun like 'orgy'. By capitalising all titles Heller slyly equates political appointments with grotesque type-roles.

In Gold's liaison with Andrea Conover Heller explores the sexual side of power. Power as possession is introduced by an epigraph from L. B. Johnson ('I've got his pecker in his pocket') and repeated by the stony-eyed governor on the commission who takes control of Gold by putting his hand on his shoulder. Andrea repeats this action in her sexual grip even though Gold does not realise it. For him Andrea is the fulfillment of a fantasy image, a blond WASP princess ('a floating seraph of ageless and ethereal beauty') who he sees as ministering to his sexual needs. These increase as the novel proceeds, demonstrating the aphrodisiac effects of power which the novel builds up to a farcical crisis of sexual competence. Andrea voices the gender imbalance in American power structure by identifying the penis with 'action'. She is preoccupied above all with technique, intending originally to become a model in pornographic films. So fellatio for her (and perhaps for Linda Book, a teacher who functions as a duplication of Andrea) becomes a means of tapping into power and consuming it. Andrea and Linda grade Gold's sexual performance while his uncomplaining wife Belle docilely accepts the diminution of their sex life without a murmur. Andrea and Linda, however, do not represent unambiguously positive sexual possibilities for Gold. Their availability identifies them with a generation from which he feels excluded where sexual activity has become a matter of routine and casual conversation. As the generation gap grows more and more marked between Gold and Andrea he throws himself back on the role of a romantically old-fashioned, middle-aged man. Like Yossarian he is constantly falling in love.

The other main character to be related to the world of Washington is Henry Kissinger. Originally Heller planned to introduce him as a 'minor figure of no importance'.[24] In the event Kissinger grew into a major figure, partly perhaps under the impetus of Heller's distaste for the man (in 1984 he declared: 'I would think the antipathy I had towards him, and a great deal of contempt, was shared by every man of conscience and intelligence'.)[25] Kissinger becomes the focus for Gold's ambivalent feelings about achieving power. He is simultaneously hated and envied, the embodiment of cynicism and ethnic betrayal, and at the same time a personification of a political possibility. As Heller has explained: 'Kissinger was not simply a target of Gold's envy; he was a model for what could be achieved'.[26] Bearing in mind that Gold is an academic, nominally at least, and therefore a member of a quite distinct sector of American professional life, it is important to recognise that the vista of orderly desks and impeccable staff which he gets from Ralph's office both literally and metaphorically opens up new possibilities. A year after the novel was published Heller explained that 'the highest point to which a college or university professor can climb today in America is to be a member of the President's cabinet or a national security adviser. So we've had Kissinger from Harvard and now we have Brzesinski and Brzesinski is now the swinging celebrity of the Carter administration'.[27]

Every detail of Gold's feelings for Kissinger is ambiguous. He collects a dossier of cuttings (as a critic or as a fan?) just as he collects other clippings from newspapers as a sign of American social change; the cuttings quoted at the end of Section IV, for instance, exemplify inverted values which the novel exploits. Heller's use of quotations in the novel's text from newspapers becomes complex. On the one hand they give glimpses of Kissinger's overweening pride; on the other they raise questions about his identity. The one image which is repeatedly referred to is of Kissinger kneeling to pray with Nixon in the oval office. Within the novel's context of gestures of abasement this image encapsulates Kissinger's denial of his race (by not observing the conventions of prayer) and individual abasement to the WASP establishment. As usual in *Good as Gold* details bear directly on the protagonist without Gold admitting that relevance. In speculating about Kissinger's Jewish identity Gold in effect speculates about his own. For Gold's father the issue is clear. Kissinger compares himself to a cowboy; no Jew was ever a cowboy; therefore he is not Jewish. For Bruce Gold, however, the application of national myth to his own experience has a strong attraction. The cowboy is essentially an individualistic mythical image and quite appropriate to Kissinger's arrogance in taking decisions single-handedly, bypassing Congress in matters of national importance. Gold's own attempted version of the log cabin to White House myth (at one point he even imagines his inauguration) contradicts a truth which he has grasped theoretically. Myth implies pattern whereas Gold denies pattern and sequential causality, finding pure luck as a basis of success. Apart from his political and ethnic significance Kissinger, like David Eisenhower, Gerald Ford and others, is a rival author for

Gold. When he learns that Kissinger is writing his memoirs he privately claims credit for this work as if he were Kissinger's ghost-writer, or even as if he had taken Kissinger's identity on himself. In fact one of the many ironies of the novel is that potentially Bruce Gold's experiences are repeating those of Kissinger. Nixon invited the latter to take office after being impressed by his book *The Necessity for Choice*; in 1974 Kissinger married Nancy Maginnes, the tall blond daughter of a New York lawyer. Like Andrea she was a former student of Kissinger's at Harvard, and again like the novel the newly-weds spent their honeymoon in Acapulco. Such parallels create an ironic gap between Gold's actions and his stated sentiments, the one contradicting the other.

In theory at least Gold tries to empty Kissinger of value, hence the title — *The Little Prussian* — for his Kissinger book reflecting his subject's reduced stature and crypto-fascism. But as usual this text remains a hypothetical one, only in Gold's imagination a rival to, say, Marvin and Bernard Kalb's biography of Kissinger which is quoted at one point and which Heller used for many of his details.[28] The main part of the novel where this takes place is in Section VIII where quotations alternate with sarcastic glosses:

KISSINGER CHARGES UNTRUE, HANOI AIDE IN PARIS SAYS

Hanoi was correct and Kissinger was not.
Q. What concessions did the United States make to get this agreement?
A. What concessions did the United States make? The United States made the concessions that are described in the agreement. There are no secret side agreements of any kind.

There *were* secret side agreements. (Jews, by reputation, made much better bargains.) The lonesome cowboy was *ba-kokt* again, and it was his allies in South Vietnam who would not accept the *tsedreydt mishmosh* of a truce he had *ungerpotchket*. So, *Moisheh Kapoyer*, the North was bombed to placate the South and salve the hurt feelings of the *mieskeit* and his *umgliks*, and not, as Kissinger falsely indicated, to force new concessions. (353)

Judith Ruderman has given an indispensable explanation of Heller's Yiddish allusion here to a cartoon character from the *Jewish Daily Forward* who made 'upside-down' comments. Since Gold is working with secondary information (the Kissinger biography, articles by various writers, etc.) he cannot adopt the role of an investigative journalist. Instead he casts himself as a second Moishe Kapoyer (literally 'Moses backwards') to extrapolate the evidence of lying and inversion. Verbally this consists of playing off a Yiddish voice against the figure of Kissinger. Ruderman has pointed out that Yiddish is one of the European languages most removed from power so that Heller's wordplay has a pointed political irony.[29] Also in a phrase like 'the lonesome cowboy was *ba-kokt* again' Heller forces Kissinger back towards the ethnic vocabulary he is trying to avoid. Sarcastic terms like *gonif* or *shlemiel* are not simply abusive but relocate Kissinger in a context of sordid trickery. The Yiddish vocabulary counters media images of him as a sex symbol or TV star and scale him down through a particularly skilful expression of indignation.

Kissinger then ambiguously embodies an ultimate stature for Gold (when the latter went to Columbia University he was first impressed by its *status*) and simultaneously the possibility of great wealth. In 1980 Heller commented that money and fame went hand in hand in a shift in postwar values: 'The system of public social values in the States have changed very radically between let's say 1950 and today. The apotheosis of money has been extraordinary, money and fame in America, and money is one of the surest ways to fame, and these are the primary indications of success.'[30] In a novel with the title *Good as Gold* it is not surprising that Heller should make extensive references to money and wealth. Broadly speaking he draws a contrast between two periods – the Depression and the present. In the Depression payment for goods or services had to be immediate because no-one's credit was good. So Julius Gold, the voice of those years, insists on the literal and immediate value of money. When Gold and one of his sisters think of their parents emigrating to America they can scarcely conceive of the journey without credit cards, and here we come to the dominant financial characteristic of the present for Heller. America is now an economy and a society run on credit. Heller draws an analogy between currency and words so effortlessly that the two components of the analogy come together in Gold's efforts to sell his own writings. Since his cynicism about their value has reduced them to mere commodities to sell, his haggling with Lieberman and Pomoroy in Section I represents the first sign of a financial ambition which Gold is ironically eager to criticise – in others. For him the cry of the Coney Island traders ('If you've got money, come out and buy, / Got no money, stay home and cry') sums up the callousness of American society by drawing a sharp distinction between the 'haves' and 'have-nots', but in fact such a distinction cannot be maintained by Gold whose financial dealings revolve around debts or promises. Past and future payment smothers any clear sense of a financial return for goods, hence the irony in Gold declaring to Lieberman: 'And I want the three hundred that's still coming to me for "Nothing"' (13). Gold's relations with his family and the other Jewish characters are regularly complicated by questions of debt − he still owes his family for financing his university studies. As usual in this novel the issue is made bizarrely explicit in Gold's attempts to recover a loan from Spotty Weinrock who offers to repay him handsomely, but in a promissory note for the benefit of the Inland Revenue since he is going bankrupt. In the meantime *he* asks *Gold* for more money to tide him over, explaining, in words worthy of Milo Minderbinder, that 'it's one of the ways I maintain my good credit in the industry. By going bankrupt regularly' (310).

When Gold enters the world of Washington it is as if he is entering a new system of commerce. A newspaper item describing Kissinger's sponsorship of minting a series of medallions usefully hints to the reader the possibility of a new kind of coinage. Gold's asset, his one and only asset here, is a gift for phrases. Words are the currency of Washington since the business of government is shown to be the promotion of empty official statements (one of Heller's reasons for despising Kissinger, was because 'he does not know the meaning of the words').[31] As soon as Gold uses a phase which catches the eye of the establishment it becomes a commodity to acquire and use and use again. No other novel of Heller's before *God Knows* is so full of threadbare epigrams and proverbs (quoted in rhymed couplets by Andrea Conover's father) as *Good as Gold*. Inevitably puns on different notions of value abound. A new 'Gold standard' is set in Washington by Bruce Gold's coinage of catchy phrases although the verbiage associated with the establishment is repetitive and inflationary. Ralph's circular explanations and ambiguous promises of promotion lead Gold to assume he has reached a new echelon of the wealthy and of course the play on inflation and deflation offers one more variation of Heller's references to rising and falling, but with a new dimension added. If verbal meaning is roughly correlated to monetary value then

Gold's grandiose claims of sexual prowess and political progress represent a devaluation of his own verbal currency. For this reason Conover mocks him by reducing his name to a base metal, calling him first 'Silver' and then 'Brass'. Heller's repetition of the novel's title phrase resembles this inflationary process but in fact adds to the novel's meaning by strengthening the puns on the protagonist's name and reminding the reader of the question of value. The phrase suggests substitution and also of course favourable comparison. It is used to suggest Andrea's sexiness but ironically her father reverses the connotations by inviting Gold to *geld* some of his horses. Heller's choice of a name for his protagonist is pointed because it makes it impossible for the reader to ignore the financial dimensions to his ambition. The latter reaches its culmination in fantasy at the end of Section VI where Gold imagines himself transformed into a jewelry store through a dream of redemption:

> The land would rejoice. A child had been found. He might even be a prince. The people who attended him with such devotion and bliss were all multi-millionaires.
> 'You are not Bruce Gold,' they assured him soothingly. 'These people are not your people and these relatives and friends are not your true relatives and friends. You are Van Cleef and Arpels,' they said. 'You are a stunning, sparkling jewelry store on Fifth Avenue, and it's all yours. The wealthiest people come from everywhere to shop in you'. (256)

Gold erases his own identity and that of his associates to convert himself into an image of glittering financial and social centrality. This can only be achieved by a commodification of the self, in effect a denial of his own humanity which is the ultimate price he is prepared to pay.

Gold's dream is a modification of a literary stereotype drawn from Victorian fiction, the narrative of a foundling whose identity has been concealed until the end of the novel when he or she is restored to the rightful place in family and society. One possible model for Gold's imagining might be Esther in *Bleak House* which Heller read in 1974, that is, around the time he was beginning to work on his novel.[32] Such an analogy with Gold's destiny would be far too positive in tone for such a bleak novel. As Heller has explained: 'For *Good as Gold* I intentionally read English comic writers — Austen, Dickens, Wodehouse and Waugh. I was looking for certain kinds of "literary cliches" '.[33] Instead of using a redemptive ending Heller draws on another stock device of Dickens' fiction, the revelation of a hidden relation between characters. The allusions to Dickens and overt reference to him as a 'long-winded novelist . . . whose ponderous works were always too long and always flawed by a procession of eccentric, one-sided characters' (378) by no means confirm the implications of Heller's admission that he 'stole from Dickens with a great deal of confidence' in this novel.[34] Far from indicating a desire to imitate his works, these allusions give an important *lack* of authenticity to Heller's narrative. Because it reads in part like a pastiche of Victorian novels of social discovery and achievement the inauthenticity of the narrative suggests the hollowness of such goals. The ironies of *Good as Gold* then even erode its own narrative status as, for instance, with the discovery that Conover has been the former lover of Gold's stepmother Gussie. At the very point where the revelation is made Dickens is mentioned and, as if to make the artifice as conspicuous as possible, Heller even gives Gussie the name Goldsmith. Heller simultaneously reminds us that Gold is subject to the directions of the author and that he would be substituting one sadistic father for another in Conover.

Where the Dickensian interconnection between characters stands out pointedly for the reader (but not for Gold) because there is no context of similar revelations, Gold's request for Andrea's hand in marriage similarly resembles an earlier literary text, this time Evelyn Waugh's *Vile Bodies*. Adam Symes wants to marry Colonel Blount's daughter but, on arriving at the family hall, is mistaken for someone else. The oscillation between politeness and aggression is less startling than in Conover's case but Adam like Gold is subjected to a probing interrogation of his financial reasons for wanting to marry. On his second visit Adam fails to communicate with Colonel Blount because of the latter's obsession with film-making. In effect Adam fails to penetrate Blount's discourse so that he (Adam) is always referred to as a third person (an 'ass of a fellow'). Where Waugh exploits the comic cliché of an absentminded country gentleman, Heller increases the aggression in Gold's future father-in-law to such an extent that requesting his daughter involves him in the most abject humiliation.

These literary parallels proliferate. Gold finds his family so incredible that he starts 'reading' its members as if they are characters from famous novels. The temporary replacement of their names with fictional ones heightens their already exaggerated characteristics and joins other literary allusions in the novel to Pope, *Our Mutual Friend* (Ralph, like Eugene Wrayburn, taps his nose while speaking to Gold) and *A Tale of Two Cities* (Gussie is compared to Madame Defarge). The suggestion of fictions within fictions establishes a context for an interruption in the narrative which Heller makes in the middle of Section VII:

> I *was* putting him [Gold] into bed a lot with Andrea and keeping his wife and children conveniently in the background. For Acapulco, I contemplated fabricating a hectic mixup that would include a sensual Mexican television actress and a daring attempt to escape in the nude through a stuck second-story bedroom window... and I would shortly hold out to him the tantalizing promise of becoming the country's first Jewish Secretary of State, a promise I did not intend to keep. (308)

Heller has commented: 'From the start I planned injecting the first-person pronoun into the novel fairly regularly, and doing so in a way that would incline the reader to infer that the first-person voice belonged to me, Joseph Heller. I wanted very much to have some kind of sustained, perhaps disconcerting, reminder to the reader that this *is* only a story, that it shouldn't be taken too seriously'.[35] As he worked on the book he decided that the effect might become monotonous or too obvious and so reduced the 'intrusions' to one. Since Heller includes his own name at one point in the novel among a list of literary celebrities the temptation in the above quotation is not necessarily to identify the narrator with the author. The narrative voice throughout *Good as Gold* functions as an ironic commentator on the protagonist, unobtrusively indicating the evasions and inconsistencies which Gold is trying to hide. It is a narrative voice which constantly move at the expense of Gold and the narrator's explicit comments simply modify this role so that the narrator becomes the voice of Gold's ironic destiny. It is absolutely consistent with the general direction of the novel that he should fall victim to sexual farce and to narrative betrayal since Gold is the gull of his own ambitions.

The literary allusions and the narrative comment discussed above obviously foreground the fictiveness of the novel temporarily and by so doing harmonise with a general strategy which Heller follows throughout the novel, namely to introduce a title within the text which then becomes the title for the succeeding section. Heller has explained his plan as follows: 'I thought that one of the unifying structures for the novel would be to have – ideally – every section deal with something Gold was going to write or had written and use that as a title for that section or the following section.'[36] Thus Gold's title for an article, 'Every Change is for the worse' introduces a series of success stories. 'Nothing Succeeds as Planned' (again devised by Gold) sets up a more complex kind of referentiality in Section IV. One of the main episodes is a family meal where Gold's most admiring reader (Esther) thinks Gold's article is a story. 'Nothing Succeeds' thus becomes the subject of discussion even while it is demonstrating itself. Heller undermines Gold's capacity to reflect on patterns of causality from a point outside his own experience by converting his own titles into comic comments on his fate within the novel. The several references made to *Tristram Shandy* strengthen this particular irony since the protagonist cannot experience his life and write it at the same time. Bruce Gold is in a worse predicament since he cannot have the Jewish experience and even *begin* to write about it. Gold as author produces plagiarised or mangled texts, or plans potential ones. An article sent to the *New York Times Magazine* is changed, abbreviated, and retitled – but at least paid for twice after being boosted in the *Congressional Record*. More typically, as we have seen, Gold is skilled in devising phrases and titles. His writings are always referring to other texts and never completing themselves. As Heller points out, 'Gold uses clippings because he hates doing research.'[37] In that respect Gold's efficiency as an author contrasts most strikingly with that of Heller himself. The opening of the novel autobiographically invites such a comparison by narrating the actual origin of Heller's idea for the book – suggested to him after a reading in Wilmington, Delaware.[38]

Bruce Gold's ambitions attempt to reconcile two incompatible roles. On the one hand he tries to cast himself as a hero in the rags-to-riches myth even while he admits the inconvenient fact that his family was not poor. On the other he tries to function as a detached intellectual critic of his own culture. Sam B. Girgus has usefully outlined a pattern of engagement with America by Jewish writers. He argues that there has been a consistent felt need to explain America, or criticise it for failing to measure up to its own ideals. The tradition of the jeremiad, he continues, has been adopted by Jewish writers although in very different ways, and he

finds a new variation in Heller's novel: '*Good as Gold* itself constitutes an inward turn by being a jeremiad against a prospective new
Jeremiah'.[39] Instead of using an intellectual protagonist like Moses
Herzog to question contemporary assumptions in American culture Heller creates a phony intellectual in Bruce Gold who is the
object of relentless ironies rather than the source of critical challenge. Heller himself has stated his purposes quite clearly: 'What is
being ridiculed, deplored, by me if not by my characters, is a moral
corruption, a disavowal of responsibilities, a substitution of vanity,
folly where other people's lives are concerned.'[40] Heller's choice of
terms invites yet another Victorian comparison. Gold slightly
resembles Becky in *Vanity Fair* who pursues the ultimate point in
London society (presentation at court) while at the same time
seeing through that society's hypocrisy. In spite of her mistakes
Becky is a superb social tactician whereas Gold is shown to be inept
and disabled by his own ambivalence from the very start. The only
prosperous figures in the novel are the cynics but the desire for
that prosperity, however hollow it is shown to be, is common to
most characters. Gold is only a particular example of a general
impulse, hence Heller's repeated juxtaposition of him with alternative versions of himself. The techniques of the novel revolve
around discontinuities and disparities, whereas Gold's drive is to
connect with the central sources of power. The surreal episode
where he sprints against Spotty Weinrock and simultaneously tries
to juggle sexual liaisons in Acapulco induces a physical collapse
leading to 11 days in hospital. This period reveals the pathos in
Gold's ambitions and the depth of his failure to form any connections because all his family and friends take his absence for
granted.

The bitter comedy of *Good as Gold* is technically unified by
consistent verbal and thematic motifs and by a tendency within the
narrative to veer constantly towards caricature. Although Gold's
hopes collapse it would sentimentalise the novel to take his family
as a bedrock which he can return to for moral comfort. Ultimately
Gold is suspended in a void, incompletely related to any of the
contexts which might give him definition and in that respect is
related to the uncommitted ironies of the narrator. Peter Prescott
objected that in *Good as Gold* 'the tension between what should be
and what is has disappeared' but it is difficult to see how this can
turn into an adverse evaluation of the book.[41] For Heller to have
implied an absent norm would show his faith in at least a hypo-

thetical alternative possibility in American life, but the novel is in fact written from a pessimistic vision of an America gripped by social decay and economic stagnation. Its comedy overlays a profound gloom about the contemporary situation.

6

God Knows

When *God Knows* was published in 1984 it suffered the odd fate of promptly becoming a bestseller and of being greeted by largely hostile reviews. Almost to a man, reviewers compared the work with Mel Brooks' comic monologue 'The Two Thousand-Year-Old Man' but then divided over the novel's wisecracks and anachronisms. It was described as 'entertaining but centerless', as showing an 'elephantiasis of the whimsey', and as having too many one-liners.[1] The novel's frivolousness, complained Roger Kaplan in *Commentary*, stops the novel from 'grasping its own theme'; and in the *New Republic* Leon Wieseltier decided that Jewish-American humour had gone quite far enough and declared roundly: '*God Knows* is junk'.[2] Virtually the only reviewer who made any attempt to examine the novel on its own terms was Mordecai Richler and even he suspected that the anachronisms were overdone.[3] Such reservations and downright hostility were clearly not universal, for in 1986 the novel won the Medici Prize for the best piece of fiction by a non-French writer in that year.

God Knows marks a new departure in Heller's career since it consists of an extended monologue by the aged King David on the verge of death. The origins of this idea may lie back in Heller's childhood since his friend George Mandel has recounted how he would read the Bible and retell the stories to Heller, one of the latter's favourites being the narrative of David's flight from Saul.[4] The earliest sign of any attempt to convert a biblical story into fiction comes in 1974 shortly after the publication of *Something Happened*, when Heller was considering a novel beginning: 'The kid, they say, was born in a manger'. The notion of playing off an aggressively modern idiom against a familiar biblical narrative clearly looks forward to *God Knows*, but Heller abandoned the idea apparently when he remembered T. S. Eliot had already done something on these lines in 'The Journey of the Magi'.

In fact, although the Bible has replaced a contemporary subject in Heller's fourth novel, there is a very strong thematic link with his earlier works. We have seen how Heller returns again and again to related issues of authority and justice. Now he relates them to the archetypal father and embodiment of authority in Western culture – God. In Heller's novel David is preoccupied to the point of obsession with God's justice and with his own position in a series of disputes between fathers and sons. Fathers begin to figure conspicuously in *Catch-22* where Major Major is facetiously named by a parodic WASP father, a Calvinist who sees himself as the sole exception to predetermination and who actually plays God in a joke at his son's expense. This joke develops more and more absurd consequences through Major Major's subsequent life. In the section of *Catch-22* which Heller cut out of the draft and published as 'Love, Dad' he parodies the paternal advice offered through a series of ludicrous letters from Nately's father. This latter-day Polonius (who actually quotes *Hamlet*) voices platitudes of honour, patriotism and economic opportunism ('war . . . presents civilization with a great . . . challenge').[6] Heller juxtaposes the letters to Nately's actual experience and then cuts off the series abruptly with the official stamp 'killed in action'. In both these cases the fathers are so obsessed with their own purposes that they never really recognise their sons as human beings. By the time of Heller's play the issue of paternity had become charged with bitterness. *We Bombed* was written out of the conviction that the Selective Service Act was being aimed at the nation's sons but that the well-placed were pulling strings to have exceptions made.[7] This conviction directly influenced the generational character oppositions in the play.

Something Happened deals with this theme more obliquely. The original opening sentence of the novel read: 'I get the willies whenever I think about my father' but this was dropped on the advice of Heller's editor Bob Gottlieb who insisted that this was not the real subject of the novel.[8] If the revised opening sentence more accurately establishes the issues of closure and disclosure, one of the sights revealed by an opening door to the young Slocum is that of his father in bed with his mother. It is introduced as a possible primal scene which might have influenced Slocum's subsequent development. Fatherhood is a role which Slocum hesitates and agonises over, sometimes trying to avoid, sometimes speculating about the Oedipal desire of a father to kill his son. Slocum's ambivalence over the exercise of paternal authority is reversed in *Good as Gold* where the perspective is from the son to the father. Bruce Gold is victimised paradoxically by an inversion of the traditional Jewish respect for scholarship. His father's role is to argue aggressively against Gold's ambitions and hinder as far as possible Gold's search for a substitute WASP father. When he does find one Conover's anti-semitism and his obvious connection through a love-affair with Gold's stepmother throw Gold back into his family. The death of his elder brother leaves him with an abusive father and a mother who refuses to allow him to address her as such. In other words Gold becomes the head of a family which is constantly denying its own structure.

In the works preceding *God Knows* fathers take on more and more prominence as the embodiments of an authority — familial and even, in *Good as Gold*, religious — which is either abrogated or ambivalently maintained. Throughout Jewish-American fiction the father is the focus of the problematics of familial and spiritual obedience. At one extreme stands the domestic tyrant of Anzia Yezierska's *Bread Winners* who exploits his old-world status as religious head of the family to force his daughters into menial work to support him. At the other stands the case of Sholem Asch who introduces his collected stories with the following statement: 'The image of my father comes before my eyes every time I am in distress, in need of guidance. Any time I am in doubt, not knowing which is right or wrong, I need only call from the sea of my memories his lake-blue eyes.'[9] Asch's maintenance of religious belief is demonstrated by the lack of opposition between himself and his father. He internalises the latter into an idealised spiritual mentor modelled on 'Jacob of old'. A third quite different possibility is represented by Alex Portnoy's father. Philip Roth parodies his self-sacrifice on behalf of his son ('my liberation would be his') by reducing his suffering to the physical indignity of constant constipation.[10] Between the extremes of acceptance and rejection Herbert Gold's autobiographical novel *Fathers* (1967) steers a finely sophisticated middle course. Gold's father had already rebelled against his father in rejecting the past and starting over again. Gold's narrator reverses this gesture by attempting to reclaim his father's and his own past from oblivion. Paradoxically the very act of recording constitutes a break with his father's pattern and at the same time bears witness to the father's crucial participation in the boy's experience: 'Gradually my father's life echoes in mine; his shadow lies athwart mine'.[11] The most climactic moment in the novel comes when the boy, unable to bear the emotional pressure on him to help in the family grocery store, attacks his father. Gold brilliantly records this as an exercise of two simultaneous impulses — of love and of hate:

> I clung to his great neck to strangle it. His beard scratched my arms. He hugged my ribs, forcing them up — cracking! — pushing my hair out, lengthening my bones, driving my voice deep. Savagely he told me his life, wringing his childhood from me. I took this after his long day and had nothing to give in return but my unfleshed arms roped about his neck. We embraced like this.[12]

This engagement enacts the boy's rite of passage from childhood into maturity. The fight becomes an act of love, a tensed clasping before time forces the two apart for ever. Gold concludes later in the novel that all fathers struggle against death and participates himself in this struggle through his own narration.

In his review of *Fathers* and Chaim Potok's *The Chosen* Philip Toynbee relates such struggles to the issue of immigration: 'The tension springs from a typical hen-and-duckling relationship: fathers who have never been able to turn themselves into Americans are in loving but painful conflict with sons who are American by both birth and inclination'.[13] For Harold Fisch, however, the struggle has a much broader significance. It has to do firstly with the survival of religious faith: 'the Jew responding to the emancipatory trend of the time felt that he ... must reject his father and his father's God' and with this rejection 'the Jewish mother is gradually restored to the family to become the pivotal figure'.[14] Fisch cites *Portnoy's Complaint* as a text symptomatic of this shift and while his article sketches out a useful background to *God Knows* Heller's novel would not quite fit his paradigm. Fathers abandon sons instead of vice versa and mothers are scarcely mentioned. In fact fathers and religious faith figure as absences and Heller's plan seems to have been to investigate the state of loneliness which he describes as 'one of the great plagues of mankind'.[15]

Both Asch and Gold refer their experiences back to the biblical story of Jacob as archetypal father. Heller, however, chooses David for his subject because he had *three* fathers (Jesse, Saul and God) and lost them all. Like Slocum in *Something Happened* the narrating consciousness is fixed and makes a series of mental excursions into the past in an attempt to understand the present, to understand specifically how he lost Saul and God. The equivalent scene to

Herbert Gold's desperate struggle with his father occurs in Chapter
6 where David's music draws the king out of his catatonic melancholia. As Saul gradually comes alive David preens with satisfaction — but not for long: 'I felt redeemed — now he would be more
indebted to me than every before. I gazed at him in happiness. The
next thing I knew, the crazy son of a bitch was lunging to his feet
for his javelin and casting it at my head with all his might!'[16] The
sudden change from calm to murderous attack, from one verbal
register to another, is strongly reminiscent of *Catch-22*. David feels
himself 'enmeshed in absurdity' as he struggles to understand the
inverted logic of Saul's attacks. The solicitude of Jonathan and the
phlegmatic calmness of Abner (who plays Aarfy to David's Yossarian) only increase David's bewilderment and make it even more
difficult for him to find a causal principle in Saul's actions. This is
not a narrative of a son breaking away from the authority of a
father, but rather yearning for that father only to be rejected. David
generalises his own plight through mythical analogues (Saturn and
Chronus, etc.) but analogues carry no explanatory value in this
novel beyond suggesting a pattern. The absurdist vision of David
tonally resembles that of Yossarian in the sense that both characters voice incredulous shock at a pattern to events which they
perceive to be at odds with the expectations of commonsense logic.
David is drawn to Jonathan because he too is the victim of his
autocratic father, but at the same time as he recognises Saul's
mania David is drawn back to him irresistibly. In his review of *God
Knows* Mordecai Richler rightly commented that Heller 'doesn't so
much tell a story as peel it like an onion — returning to the same
event again and again ...'[17] The narrative equivalent of David's
physical return to Gibeah is his repeated examination of the figure
of Saul. The impulse is to gain bearings, to return from a mental
wilderness, even though David recognises: 'I was exiled forever
from the only nest in which I could ever dwell without feeling
myself estranged and adrift...,' (167). By trying to reclaim a lost
father figure David is also trying to cling on to a belief in rational
causality, but he fails. Saul remains to the very end a puzzlingly
manic figure triggering comically shrill expressions of incredulity
in David. The relation between the two figures is further complicated by Heller's presentation of Saul as a precursor of David, a
similar victim of an apparently unjust God. When the former
is punished for sacrificing without the presence of Samuel he
complains to David, asking some of the very questions ('Can

one reason with God?') that will apply to his subsequent predicament.

If God is the third father which David loses the reason is Bathsheba. The two main events in *God Knows* are God's withdrawal of favour from Saul and God's killing of the child Bathsheba bears from David. The biblical lexicographer William Smith has commented that 'the tragedy of David's life . . . grew in all its part out of polygamy, with its evil consequences, into which he had plunged on becoming king'[18] but Heller concentrates heavily on the specific story of Bathsheba. Nostalgically coloured by David's waning physique in old age, the image of her bathing naked on the rooftop recurs again and again throughout the novel to insist on the erotic necessity of David's actions. Bathsheba acts as a sexual tutor releasing him from inhibitions and opening up new verbal as well as physical areas of expression. It should be noted here that Heller was considering writing an erotic narrative on the lines of either *Portnoy's Complaint* or Updike's *Couples* but in the event simply wove an erotic dimension into *God Knows*.[19] David quotes liberally from the Song of Songs in a directly sexual context thereby resisting the traditional hermeneutic emphasis on the book as spiritual allegory.[20] Old age has made David very conscious indeed of his body, of its smells and impotence, and in recoil he turns to Abishag, the concubine/nurse sent to care for him. Abishag represents a youthful image of physical perfection which David celebrates through poetic comparisons (again on the model of the Song of Songs): 'Her face is as brown garnet, her hair like sable at midnight' (112); or through verbs of tracing, caressing and contemplating. Through the very act of description David takes erotic possession of her. Abishag represents the culmination of Bathsheba's initiation and brings about a late realisation in David that all his life he had wanted love. While Heller had admitted that 'the attitude in the Bible would be offensive to women', the attitude, that is, as exemplified in his biblical quotations, Bathsheba and David's other partners cease to exist purely as spectacle (as sexual images) once they start to speak.[21] His wife Michal becomes his enemy from their wedding day onwards. Heller develops the biblical hint of her contempt for David into a full-blown snobbish puritanism. Even Bathsheba has turned into a critical voice, constantly puncturing David's flattering images of himself and manoeuvring on behalf of her son Solomon.

Again and again in *God Knows* David casts himself in the role of victim, whether of Saul's perverse animosity or of other agents. The sequel to his love for Bathsheba is the contrived death of her husband Uriah but David blurs this possible source of guilt by suggesting that it was all Bathsheba's doing, that it was the 'work of the Devil', or that David was merely responding to the promptings of the voice of desire. The latter, dramatised through the brief introduction of Mephistopheles, conveniently externalises his impulse and so distances his own responsibility. Dialogue then performs an important function in questioning David's monologue. So when David claims 'I always was faithful to my wives and concubines' Bathsheba counters this assertion by retorting 'When you cheated with me?' (104) and then proceeds to list the legal prohibitions against adultery. David repeatedly projects himself as being at the mercy of scheming wives and sons, composing scenes which comically minimise his own awareness or responsibility. The question 'is it my fault?' echoes through his monologue, constantly trying to capitalise on the mitigating circumstances he puts forward and even the novel's title becomes a self-justifying exclamation. The implication of David's narrative tactics is that he is minimising his own responsibility so as to throw God's punishment of Bathsheba's child into maximum prominence as an unjust act. Even so it is only late in the novel that David can bring himself actually to call God a 'murderer'. It can then stand as a focus for David's indignation and a justification for his turning away from God. God has already withdrawn his favoured voice but from the death of the child onwards it becomes true, as Heller has stated, 'my David's at war with God'.[22] The vocabulary of moral remorse ('atone', 'repent', etc.) is only raised here and in connection with Saul to reflect David's confusion and bitterness. 'Repent for what?' he asks himself.

One central aspect of David's life which receives extended treatment by Heller is his dialogue with God. The very possibility of communicating with the deity exists within strictly stylised limits in the Old Testament. The following example is typical from 1 Samuel 23 (vs 2) where David is asking for military guidance: 'Therefore David enquired of the Lord, saying, Shall I go and smite these Philistines? And the Lord said unto David, Go, and smite the Philistines, and save Keilah'. The pattern is of an enquiry being followed by a predictive confirmation which repeats part of that enquiry word for word, and the pattern is so regular that Heller's David reflects, 'our talks went smoothly'. These so-called 'talks' enact the divine endorsement of David's royal destiny to establish the nation of Israel and a turning-point in his story is the symbolic transference of divine communication from Saul to David. The period between this change and Saul's death marks for Otto Rank (referred to by Heller in the novel) a time of conflict before the two roles of Messiah and divine king can be united in one person.[23] Saul recoils from God's silence by visiting the witch of Endor to communicate with the shade of Samuel who, like Nathan and Gad, has performed an intermediary role in dialogues with God, but Samuel's words only confirm the absence of God's favour and predict Saul's death. In any dialogue communication must necessarily move in two directions, to reveal man to God, or vice versa. The former is recognised by David in I Chronicles 17 where divine omniscience actually undermines the very need of utterance and results in the admission of speechlessness (vs. 18: 'what can David speak more to thee...?'). This admission goes hand in hand with a recognition of God's justness and perhaps for this reason the Chronicles narrative was rejected by Heller. His David dismisses it as a 'prissy white-wash' where he figures as a 'pious bore'. Heller's preference went to I and II Samuel and I Kings where David's faults are allowed to emerge and where there is more sign of David's restiveness against his divine calling. Accordingly his interests lie more with those figures who answer God back or even accuse God of injustice – Moses and Job – although in the event Heller makes surprisingly little use of the Job story.

In his old age Heller's David feels a need for an external voice to break the solipsistic spiral of his thoughts and the famous address from the burning bush is retold under the impetus of David's urgency to hear once again from the deity, but it is rendered comic by a stark contrast of roles between the hapless, stammering Moses and a God who sadistically delights in his own 'tyrannical prescriptions'. Complaint is followed by ironic question:

'It's a hard life You gave us'.
'Why should it be soft?' spake the Lord.
'And a very tough world'.
'Why should it be easy?' (22)

In place of an authoritative exposition of the future the notion of a guiding providence is replaced by a voice which challenges Moses' presumptions about God. Both voices co-exist on a common human level in a dialogue between spiritual confidence and scepticism. God's questioning of Moses repeats the same destructive interrogation of patriotism by Yossarian, the old man and others in *Catch-22*. Partly Heller's purpose is to reveal a 'concept of Jehovah ... [who] owes no explanation to man for any behaviour'.[24] He simply *is*; he exists without any need for justification. But at the same time that God's absolutism is revealed God's ludicrously colloquial speech register mocks not only Moses' expectations of rationality but also the very notion of religious belief: 'If you want to have sense, you can't have a religion' (24).

The narrative perspective which David establishes in these scenes questions the kind of authority which God expounds and works consistently against pious submission, endorsing Moses' own objections. The perspective also works against the sense of the book's title that God is the only repository of complete knowledge. David himself wants to know, wants to communicate with Moses and draw on his experience. A main crux for him in the biblical story is, as we have seen, Saul's visit to the witch of Endor and David decides to repeat this visit to summon up the shade of Moses. This wholly fictitious episode plays an important part in establishing a tension between desire and scepticism which the rest of the novel will develop. David's plan goes wrong and the shade of Samuel appears before him. There then follows a dialogue sequence where David alternates between wanting information and wilfully blocking his ears. Once again a source of expected spiritual enlightenment turns out to induce uncertainty ('There is no heaven. There is no hell... That's all in your mind': 55) and to attempt to induce a fatalistic belief in destiny. David reacts indignantly against both possibilities. Heller has stated: 'I do believe that there is something in us that wants a parental figure or God' and David certainly demonstrates this yearning.[25] He exemplifies William James's assertion that 'we want a truth' but the twists and turns which his exchange with Samuel takes multiply the questions he wants to ask by alternating enquiry with evasion, disclosure with concealment. Where the roles were more or less set between Moses and God now they shift from one speaker to the other. At one moment Samuel articulates scepticism, at another David.

Since the prophet Nathan plays such a prominent role in David's destiny it is not surprising that he too should be subject to irony and questioning. After extensively burlesquing his proverbial exchanges and prophetic style, Heller has David answer back when Nathan brings news of his impending punishment. In the biblical narrative (II Samuel 12) David admits his guilt after Nathan has authoritatively ('thus saith the Lord') delivered his message. Heller's David queries Nathan's credentials:

'In what language,' I asked, 'did God address you?' This was a trick question of my own.
'In Yiddish of course,' said Nathan. 'In what other language would a Jewish God speak?'
Had Nathan said Latin, I would have known he was fabricating. (288).

Once again authoritative dialogue, where the superior speaks to the accepting inferior, is replaced by an exchange between equals. David's questioning of Nathan enacts his refusal to receive him as God's chosen intermediary and reduces his message to a battle of wits, but not one that he necessarily wins as the throw-away irony suggests which concludes this quotation. A passing allusion to Gilbert and Sullivan immediately after this passage also draws our attention to verbal theatre. It is repeatedly implied in *God Knows* that Biblical characters are performers rehearsing their lines. In this way Heller draws attention to the familiarity of the narratives he is using, and here he specifically plays on different linguistic and verbal registers (that of the King James Bible, Oxford English, etc.).

In one of the very rare cases where Heller presents dialogue between David and God it is important to see in what ways the novel diverges from the biblical text. The following takes place during David's early campaigns to unify Israel, with direct quotations from the Bible being marked accordingly:

And I *inquired of the Lord, 'Shall I go up to the Philistines* just as I did the time before? *Wilt thou deliver them into my hand?'*
And the Lord said, 'No'.
For the moment I was shaken. 'No?'
'No.'
'What do You mean, no?' I was indignant. 'You won't deliver them into my hand?'
And the Lord said, 'Do not go up against the Philistines as thou did before.'

'What then?'
'But fetch a compass behind them, and come upon them over against the
mulberry trees.'
'A compass?'
'A compass.'
'What's a compass?'
'Encircle them. Ambush and aggravate them.'
'You're not going to believe this, O Lord,' I said, 'but I had that
same idea myself, of sneaking around them through the mulberry
trees on the sides of the plains and pouncing upon them from
there and aggravating them from the flanks.'
'Sure, sure you did.'
'What worries me, O Lord, is the noise we might make as we
move closer to them in the woods and prepare to charge. Is it
possible they won't hear us? Wilt Thou deliver them?'
'Didn't you already ask Me that?' (252) (II Samuel 5)

Two communications are conflated here to underline a divergence
from the expected pattern of query being followed by confirmatory
response. By having God answer in the negative Heller ironically
draws attention to the fact that this is the last time he will speak to
David. In the Bible the negative injunction is stylistically identical
to the laws ('Thou shalt not go up') and in the novel there is
repeated reference to this pattern. Again in the Bible David awaits
a signal from God (the emphasis being on power) whereas in the
novel God emerges as a military tactician. Also – even more
importantly – David recoils from acquiescence to his instructions.
He is indignant, curious and then tries to steal God's thunder by
claiming to have had the same idea. As frequently happens in the
novel the result is that the divine is diminished. The statements of
instruction are phrased either directly or indirectly in the language
of the King James Bible, whereas once David starts questioning
them God shifts into a modern register and the role of a sceptic
('Sure, sure you did'). David invites God to gloss his own instruc
tions but God only repeats them and from that point on David has
to struggle with silence. His dialogue with God shifts into the
conditional mode at the end of Chapter 10 as he imagines himself
playing a newly aggressive role. There he assembles quotations
from Job (38–41), rhetorical questioning of divine power which
David counters with 'what difference does that make?', but the
longed-for confrontation never comes. David's anger at God's

injustice (in killing Bathsheba's baby) cannot issue in speech and his inner feelings separate from his outwardly pious behaviour. His declarations of anger and indignation remain silent and silence itself is generalised into a metaphysical predicament: 'I could not make sense of the quiet in the universe' (287). The lack of response is even worse than a negative response. As Heller explained in an interview after completing the first draft of *God Knows*: 'Even though he's convinced God is dead and God doesn't exist, he still wants to be talking to Him again'.[26]

Saul's fate is of particular importance to David because it turns out to be predictive. Heller has noted a recurring pattern in the Old Testament narratives of a son being separated from his family and part of David's learning process involves noting parallels between himself and other biblical characters such as Abraham (though he is not so pious), Jacob (also the victim of rash sons), Moses and Saul. When Heller was interviewed in 1986 by Bob Azurdia he was asked whether David's dialogue with God was characteristically Jewish and whether it might stand comparison with Topol playing Tevye the milkman in *Fiddler on the Roof*. Heller did not answer directly but pointed out that 'even Moses did not get along with God too well and on at least two occasions he disagrees with God and succeeds in talking him out of destroying . . . people for very minor infractions'.[27] In other words Moses gets a response and it is this which David envies more and more. Ironically he unconsciously promotes the growth of his own spiritual doubts by suggesting to Saul that God is dead, i.e. voicing the very possibility that he cannot ultimately accept. At the peak of David's anger against God he is conscious that to rage aloud would be to imitate Saul. The conclusion to the novel demonstrates a complete repetition of Saul's predicament since he imagines his earlier self ('an eager, bright-eyed youth') come into his room to play on the lyre. If the youth is David then David the narrator has completely identified with Saul even to the point of searching for a javelin to hurl at the apparition.

This identification does not close off *God Knows* because Heller several times suggests the inconclusive nature of David's monologue, as in the following sequence which speculates on the value of his own meditations. It begins with a quotation from Jeremiah: '. . . the heart is deceitful in all things. Don't I know that from my bouts of self-examination? The unexamined life is not worth living, I know. The examined life is?' (174). The alternation between statement and question suggests a progression through a silent dialogue comparable to Bob Slocum's use of proposition and counter-proposition where, as soon as a proposition is formed, its rebuttal is considered. This alternation can only end with David's death but even as he feels his vital energies he denies a 'serene sense of natural completion' imagining himself rather pursued by invisible demons. Although David interprets Bathsheba's physical changes as an emblem of impermanence and although he repeatedly quotes from Ecclesiastes (as if he and not one of his sons were the author), he never demonstrates the latter's settled wisdom of old age, never in fact accepts the inevitability of impending death. Hence his consciousness of diminished power (residing only in the choice of a successor) and of helplessness. As Heller has stated, 'finally David is not a father figure, if anything he's a dependent child'.[28] The novel's epigraph from Ecclesiastes ('But how can one be warm alone?') is never answered. It rather establishes the state of utter loneliness that David is trying to escape in his old age.

So far I have been stressing the sombre themes of *God Knows* because the reviewers chose to comment on the superficially striking aspects of the novel's style – its anachronisms and its incidental jokes. The comedy of the novel overlies questions of the loss of faith, the search for a voice, impending death and the value of self-examination, none of which Heller ever mocks out of existence. He himself has explained that the anachronisms are 'a way of informing a reader of what the book is about and how to interpret it'.[29] Not all are comic. For instance the references to Freud, melancholia, inhibitions, etc. project a contemporary psychological awareness on to the narrative and form part of a general reminder that any reader of the King James Bible is going to experience a tension between 17th-century and late 20th-century idioms. Several passing comments and sequences of low comedy (such as the laboured joke that the user of '-eth' forms is lisping) draw facetious attention to exactly those aspects of the Bible which are obscure or anachronistic. For the same reason Nathan's cryptically proverbial style of utterance is burlesqued as is a formula phrase like 'and He spake'.

When Heller decided to use the Bible for his novel he must have been aware that he was taking on the most authoritative text in Western culture. The precedent of Sholem Asch's trilogy (*The Nazarene*, 1939; *The Apostle*, 1943; *Mary*, 1949) helps to explain by contrast what use Heller made of this prototext. For Asch retelling the story of Christ was an attempt to incorporate the beginnings of Christianity into the Jewish tradition. He combines realistic description with an exposition of Jewish duties. The following brief excerpt from the opening of *Mary* exemplifies a kind of lyricism: '. . . on the hills each leaf of grass could be distinguished as it trembled under the fresh dew, swaying in the breeze as in mute prayer, and irradiated by the selfsame glow with which it had been charged in the first hours of Genesis'.[30] Here there is no antagonism to Old Testament myths; on the contrary the celebratory link with Genesis suggests new beginnings, rhetorically indicating a kind of spiritual recurrence. It is absolutely symptomatic of Asch's devout piety that he should conclude *The Apostle* (about the life of Saul) with a prayer of thanks and dedication to God. In other words, Asch is working within a tradition and not against it. This is where the contrast with *God Knows* emerges.

Heller has demonstrated a constant awareness of the values embedded in the King James Bible and it is these values which his own narrative works against through burlesque, ribald mockery and anachronism. In an interview given in *Vogue* the year that the novel appeared Heller commented on one example of such values:

There are such musical, soothing phrases in the King James translation, being 'full of years and full of days'. I think implicit in that was a resignation that if one did live to the point where he was full of days, it was time to go. Jacob asked that his bones be carried back to Canaan to be buried by his ancestors. It's not what I would do on my deathbed.[31]

And it's not what David does in *God Knows*. The commission to Solomon in I Kings 2 to keep to the ways of the Lord delivered with exactly the implicit resignation spotted by Heller is replaced by querulous self-searching, yearning and a refusal to accept the fact of ageing. Instead of using the biblical story as an occasion for pious retelling as did Sholem Asch, Heller produces a running commentary on it where the recurring main event is a bizarre clash between two kinds of discourse — that of the Authorised Version, and a modern and irreverent speech idiom. The weakest parts of *God Knows* are those where Heller merely retells parts of David's life because this narrative can be taken for granted. It already exists in what Harold Bloom would call Heller's 'precursor text' (which is quoted constantly) and can be either left implicit or referred to obliquely through such phrases as 'back then' and through chapter endings which comment on the ironically unpredictable twist which was to be taken by subsequent events.

One way in which David resists the biblical text is again through an anachronism, by reference to the concept of Jewishness, although that only becomes relevant after the Babylonian captivity and by adopting — a second anachronism — a Yiddish voice. Heller has carefully placed Yiddish words and Yiddish mannerisms ('go figure him out', 'what then?', 'from your mouth to God's ears', and answering a question with a question) to undermine one of the central notions of the biblical story — that of covenant. When dramatic readings were given from this novel on BBC television's South Bank Show the actor-narrator (dressed appropriately) delivered his lines in a consistent style, whereas the Yiddish voice is only adopted temporarily by David and for quite specific purposes. Take the following lines:

Some Promised Land. The honey was there, but the milk we brought in with our goats. To people in California, God gives a magnificent coastline, a movie industry, and Beverly Hills. To us He gives sand. To Cannes He gives a plush film festival. We get the PLO. Our winters are rainy, our summers hot. To people who didn't know how to wind a wristwatch He gives underground oceans of oil. To us He gives hernia, piles and anti-Semitism. (40)

Through characteristically rehearsed antitheses — and we shall see shortly what a self-conscious stylist David is — covenantal promise is revised into a series of liabilities. Forward-looking hope is replaced by a wry retrospective voice whose Yiddish syntax, with the benefit of historical hindsight, implies the comedy of misfortune which grew out of the East European ghettoes. With a God like that who needs enemies? Where the notion of covenant implies a bond between God and his chosen few, this tone of voice recurs in places where God's purpose seems inscrutable, in other words to imply a gap between David and the deity. To return to an issue raised by one of Heller's interviewers near the opening of this chapter, such a voice seems to resemble at times that of Tevye the milkman whose story formed the basis of *Fiddler on the Roof*. In Sholem Aleichem's original narrative ('Tevye wins a fortune')

Tevye, like Heller's David, is constantly quoting the scriptures.[32] An ironic attitude to his own experience is offset by his references to proverbial wisdom which actually reinforce his solidarity with the folk. 'As the Bible says' shades easily into 'as we say', whereas David's quotations of proverbs are so obtrusive and frequent that they burlesque the stylistic appeals to a common wisdom, and hence this kind of folk narrative. For Heller to do otherwise might compromise the isolation of his protagonist.

The characteristic effect of Heller's comedy is diminution and reduction. Robert Alter has seen such reduction as a means of coping with adversity: 'Jewish humor typically drains the charge of cosmic significance from suffering by grounding it in a world of homey practical realities'.[33] Heller too denies cosmic significance to events but he also reduces the spiritual status of the main figures in the biblical story. Solomon, for instance, is inverted from the proverbial personification of wisdom into an obsequious moron who constantly tries to copy down David's words although he understands nothing. Samuel is dramatised as a bitterly cruel self-seeker indifferent to the fate of those around him. The plan to build a temple, of enormous symbolic importance to the covenant, is introduced as pure egotism on David's part and then mindless extravagance on Solomon's.[34] Above all the figure of David is scaled down. One reason why Heller was drawn to this biblical figure seems to have been a disparity. He has explained that 'the image that we have of David as the ideal ruler, a heroic ruler, is not justified by the story'.[35] In a panel discussion between Heller, Dwight Macdonald and others in the late 1960s the question of heroic qualities came up and the novelist Wallace Markfield declared: 'We are dealing in the modern novel with men to whom things happen, little men.... He is called in some parts the schnook, the schlemiel – again, the anti-hero'.[36] During the discussion which followed Heller questioned the assumption that the hero has a monopoly of integrity, courage and brains, implicitly attempting to transfer these qualities on to Markfield's anti-hero. The examples he gives are of Achilles' refusal to fight in the *Iliad* and Sampson (a 'chippy chaser').[37] This debate bears directly on David in *God Knows* who is revised into a modern man full of uncertainties and ambivalence about the meaning of his own experience. Robert Merrill draws a similar inference in seeing David as being basically a 'figure who wants to control his own destiny' but then concludes that 'the existence of God, Jewish or otherwise, is therefore peripheral to the meaning of *God Knows*'.[38] On the contrary the existence of God is an important focus for the authority that might validate David's experience which he at once hates and desires.

Heller is particularly concerned to reduce images of David, whether in Michelangelo's statue or in the Old Testament text, especially the image of him as a hero-king and his treatment of the encounter with Goliath is central to this process. First of all he subjects some of the biblical narrative to realistic scrutiny; why, for instance, would David need to pick up fresh stones if he was a regular user of a sling? Then he dramatises David's eagerness to fight him as an appetite for fame, a consciousness that all eyes were on him, after admitting ('the poor fucker was a goner') that if he did not kill him plenty of others would. The verbal confrontation is crucial to the biblical narrative, especially the following sections:

> And the Philistine said unto David, Am I a dog, that then comest
> to me with staves? And the Philistine cursed David by his gods.
> Then said David to the Philistine, Thou comest to me with a
> sword, and with a spear, and with a shield: but I come to thee in
> the name of the Lord of hosts, the God of the armies of Israel,
> whom thou hast defied. (I Samuel 17:43, 45)

The repetitive syntactic pattern of 'and . . . and' builds up a cumulative impression of inevitability in the narrative sequence as if a destiny is being worked out. Also the rhetorical dimension to this meeting is crucial. Goliath's haughty accusation is the verbal correlative of his physical stature, the articulation of his pride as a warrior. David's rejoinder must be equally stylised and equally poised because ultimately this is a confrontation between two notions of deity and an exemplum of God's guiding over Israel's destiny. Heller has already undermined this notion by compromising David's moral status and his position as chosen saviour. He further reduces the scene to comedy by making Goliath deaf so that questions have to be repeated, and reduces it yet again by having David comment on his own lines: 'My voice was filled with righteousness. Ask me to this day what I thought I was talking about when I said "Lord of hosts" and I still will be unable to tell you. I have many phrases whose meaning is likewise unintelligible to me, but rhetoric is rhetoric' (99–100). Since the spiritual meaning of David's act is embedded in its rhetorical expression, take away the rhetoric and the event itself collapses into farce. Instead of placing Goliath's defeat within the divinely guided history of the creation of Israel as a unified state, David only gives it a problematic personal significance as the starting point for Saul's inexplicable animosity against him.

Heller has paid the oblique tribute of all parodists to the stature of the text he has chosen to mock. The Authorised Version is the very model of sustained verbal decorum, so much so that when new translations of the Bible appeared the critic Ian Robinson railed angrily against them for collapsing into the colloquial and journalistic and losing the 'slow, measured rhythmic sentences' of the earlier text.[39] Heller deliberately sets up and exploits such cases of bathos as temporary transgressions of the King James version. As we have seen, part of his purpose is to revise David away from his general images and to present instead an existential narrative of his struggles to understand what is happening to him. By picking up brief enigmatic details from the biblical story (why, for instance, did Michal despise David?) Heller creates a kind of counter-narrative in a modern idiom where Bathsheba becomes a proto-WASP denying David self-fulfillment through sex. Another reason for Heller's approach must surely lie in the sportiveness of parody. As he himself admits: 'I suppose it's a blasphemous book to the extent that it has fun with the text'.[40] Accordingly Sarah, the wife of Abraham, acts as an important symbolic presence in the novel as the only biblical character to laugh in response to one of God's edicts.

Several reviewers of *God Knows* commented on the fact that David presents himself as an under-appreciated author. The opening chapter offers the reader a bill of fare ('I've got a love story...', etc.) which includes a whole range of narrative interest, but we have already seen that the novel itself does not work primarily through narrative. Accordingly David's promise of entertainment involves direction for the reader to check out the biblical stories. Instead of retelling them, the following passage gives us a typical example of what David *does* offer. The comments are occasioned by the praise lavished on David for being a better soldier than Saul (I Samuel 21.11: 'Saul hath slain his thousands, and David his ten thousands'):

Imagine how Saul took to that one. I didn't imagine, and the next thing I knew I was dodging javelins to save my ass and

running for my life. You think you've had problems with
in-laws? I had a father-in-law who wanted to kill me. Why? Only
because I was too good, that's why (6).

The first sentence addresses the reader directly, drawing him in to
a common understanding of David's situation which was not
available to him at that point, as the second sentence makes clear
with its play on 'imagine'. Then the passage alternates question
and statement as if a dialogue is taking place between the narrator
and the projected reader. This is the crucial point. Traditionally in
first-person narratives the 'I' as protagonist gradually converges on
the 'I' as narrator but here David maintains a constant distance
between his narrating and his earlier experiences – a distance
expressed as a difference between then and now, belief and scepticism, etc. – so that he and the implied reader can enjoy the latter
as spectacle. David can thus exclaim in mock disbelief at his earlier
gullibility and can anticipate conventional requests or expectations
from the reader, ingratiating himself with the promise of insider
revelation ('you want to hear the real story?') and constantly
conditioning his own expressions to give the impression of sincerity or spontaneity. It then follows that although David fears
loneliness and although he refers to his own narration in individual therapeutic terms (as being personally cathartic), the implied dialogue between himself and the reader prevents him from
ever reaching this state of utter isolation.

   David as author pays constant attention to verbal style, rhetoric,
literary analogues, and symbolism; David as monologuist presents
his narration as a verbal performance where the reader does not
only function as listener but also as audience. If David, as he
claims, has the best story in the Bible then the punch line to that
story is the conclusion that God's killing of Batholeba's child was
so unjust that it amounted to murder. Partly David's reluctance to
draw this conclusion defers it until Chapter 9; partly it is his desire
for maximum effect:

Yes, *murdered* is the word. When the good Lord made my baby
die in order to have me repent my sin, that was murder, wasn't
it? God is a murderer, imagine that. I told you I had the best
story in the Bible, didn't I? I have always known that He was.
Sooner or later He murders us all, doesn't He, and back we go to
the dust from which we came. (241)

Once again a dramatic narrating situation is briefly involved as if the reader has reacted with incredulity. David's insistence combines argument and also a sense of panache in delivering a conclusion that should match up to the promises he made at the beginning of his narration. His questions are now cues for the reader's implied agreement made all the more easy by David's generalisation of his individual suffering at the hands of God into the common fate of all humanity. In his 1974 *Paris Review* interview Heller declared that 'writing is performing for people' and we saw how Bob Slocum fractured his self into agent and observer so that he could assess his own experiences.[41] Now David is doing something similar but with a far sharper sense of performance and of the tactics of delivery so that he can pace and modify his own narration always with reference to this projected external audience. Inevitably a tension is set up between the comic histrionics of David's narration and his claim to the pathos and poignancy of his abandonment. The alternation between the two helps Heller's novel to delay monotony but the relation of the comedy to David's perceived betrayal remains problematic.

Since David's cherished role is that of victim he sees himself as an author cheated of his rights by the fact that he has no book named after him in the Bible. This sense of injustice becomes the comic occasion for self-aggrandising references outwards from his own story. Through quotation he gradually appropriates to himself the books of Ecclesiastes, Proverbs, and the Song of Songs. His diminution of Solomon to a passive copyist is thus an authorial tactic. David then quotes extensively from other works to extend the reference of his own narrative: from *King Lear* to extend the theme of ungrateful children; from *Doctor Faustus* to inflate his affair with Abigail; and from Shelley's 'Ozymandias' to comment ironically on Solomon's plan to erect buildings that would last for eternity. Quotation, however, implies no flattery at all. In spite of fairly neutral references to the *Iliad* David disposes of Homer as limited by the dictates of historical accuracy; Shelley's elegy on Keats is dismissed as 'revolting, sentimental *dreck*' (compared with David's own elegy on Saul, that is), and Milton's *Samson Agonistes* is attacked for giving the character an implausibly florid rhetoric. Browning's 'Saul' receives more detailed attention perhaps because it more closely resembles Heller's own narrative. This monologue by David narrates the latter's experiences in lifting Saul out of one of his states of melancholia through song. Browning images the latter in the attitude of crucifixion (which is attacked by Heller's David for being anachronistic) and leads David up to a moment of spiritual insight which explains this opening image. David has a vision of Christian love which suggests that the monologue is predictive, looking forward to the establishment of Christianity, whereas Heller's David claims the privilege of an eye-witness ('Why listen to him? I was there, Browning wasn't': 118) to relate the event to his own personal fortunes. David's longest outburst is against Shakespeare whom he reduces to a minor plagiarist and a *gonoph* (thief):

> A bard of Avon they called him yet. Some bard. *Him* I have to be measured against?. . . . O that mine adversary had written a book, instead of that mulligan stew of jumbled five-act plays with stupid plots cluttered with warm bodies and filled with sound and fury and signifying nothing. You watch. You watch. To him they'll give a Nobel prize for literature yet someday (146).

Adopting a stage-Yiddish voice David then uses a quotation from *Macbeth* to attack its author. Even in phrasing this attack his words are a patchwork of quotation ('sound and fury' of course has its own American context in Faulkner) from the book of Job and allusion perhaps to Gilbert Sorrentino's 1979 novel *Mulligan Stew* which assembles pastiches of a wide variety of writers and would thus be ironically relevant to the issue of originality.

Quotation then offers Heller's narrator a farcical means of re-dressing the low state of his own fortunes as a writer. He lifts passages from countless texts (Burke, Longfellow, Milton, 'The Star-Spangled Banner' and many others) without acknowledge-ment. Sometimes this novel gives the impression that Heller wrote it with a dictionary of quotations in one hand) and sometimes David gives a ludicrous impression that there is nothing he didn't write. He even theorises this practice ('there are only four basic plots in life anyway, and nine in literature': 129) and simultane-ously rationalises and exemplifies his position by quoting from Ecclesiastes 1: 'There is no new thing under the sun'. The very enterprise of taking up a biblical story implies a palimpsest and Heller's narrator delights in writing over (and against) the Autho-rised Version of his story. More opposition is involved in this than mere commentary. Mark Twain's narrator in *A Connecticut Yankee at King Arthur's Court* inscribes his story on an Arthurian manuscript and this textual erasure is the compositional equivalent of the parody, bathos and satire within Hank Morgan's story. The clear purpose is to mock Arthurian narratives out of existence. There is no evidence at all of Heller having a comparable animosity towards the King James Bible. Obviously his concern is much more light-hearted than Twain's but he too is setting up a narrative which comically flouts the authority and status of his own proto-text and of the leading works of European Literature. David casts himself as the archetypal protagonist and author.

One last aspect of David's narrative remains to be considered – his stance as a mock sage. Meredith G. Kline has explained that the wisdom books of the Old Testament present the thesis that 'wisdom begins with the fear of Yahweh, which is to say that the way of wisdom is the way of the covenant'. One way in which these books perform their explicatory function is 'by translating the covenant stipulations into maxims and instructions regulative of conduct in the different areas of life and under its varying conditions'. The central figure in these books is King Solomon who 'figures as royal patron of the wisdom enterprise in general'.[42] In *God Knows* David's presentation of Solomon (Shlomo) as a humourless simpleton symbolically undermines the whole wisdom enterprise and places David himself as a new personification of wisdom. The textual signs of this process taking place are David's obsessively frequent quotations of proverbs. His authorship of the psalms can be taken for granted so he turns instead to Proverbs and Ecclesiastes, but then gradually widens the scope of his 'borrowings' backwards and forwards to include Genesis, Job, Jeremiah and even the New Testament. His scope widens yet again to include more recent texts where passages have taken on a proverbial status to the point where David seems to be a latter-day Poor Richard, an aged sage who wants to pass on the benefits of his wisdom. The sheer range of his proverbs, however, militates absurdly against such a reading because they imply an unbelievably broad area of experience and awareness, one far too broad for an individual consciousness. Also Kline points out how important to the wisdom books is their 'common concern that their precepts be transmitted to successive generations through parental instruction of children', in other words through a generational continuity.[43] It is exactly this possibility which Heller burlesques and therefore questions in David's conversations with Solomon. Where the wisdom books imply communication between parents and children — Proverbs, for instance, consists of a series of exhortations from father to son — Heller repeatedly demonstrates *dis*continuity. Saul tries to kill David, God abandons him. Absalom rebels against him and Solomon and Adonijah jockey for his favours on his death bed. It thus seems to be the case that *God Knows* is a facetious piece of anti-wisdom literature. It renders absurd proverbial discourse and leaves ambiguous exactly how much wisdom David has gained. Although his narrative is absolutely packed with proverbs, a proverb implies transmission and application, but David literally has no-one left to address except the reader. His stance as sage is thus reduced to theatre, to part of his general verbal performance.

7
The Story of an Illness

On 12 December, 1981 Heller was returning to his New York apartment with his friend Speed Vogel when he experienced an inexplicable difficulty in opening the door and in pulling off his sweater. These were the first tell-tale signs of the onset of a serious disease of his nervous system, the Guillain–Barre Syndrome, which paralysed him completely within the next few days and which was to lay him low for months. The seizure interrupted Heller in the middle of writing *God Knows*, by coincidence the narrative of a 'character who is so weak he can't get out of bed'. Because it had all been planned out carefully beforehand, when Heller returned to the manuscript he began introducing a few new physical details about David's weakness, but otherwise the composition of the novel was comparatively unaffected.[1]

The account which Heller and Vogel subsequently wrote of this illness, *No Laughing Matter* (1986) is essentially a narrative of survival where the worst stage of the symptoms and the worst psychological period both occur within the first third of the book. More than most other illnesses this disease seized Heller suddenly, inexplicably, and developed silently within the heart of his organism following a sequence that seemed to have virtually no causal explanation. In his narrative Heller presents himself as ironically blessed with ignorance about exactly how serious his illness was or how long the period of convalescence would last. By opening the book with a letter from a fellow-sufferer Heller reveals this gap between the danger he was in and his awareness of it and initiates a whole series of startling revelations which took place during his paralysis and afterwards.

Metaphorically this illness is represented as a descent into a personal Hell followed by an ascent; Heller's transfer out of the Intensive Care Unit at Mount Sinai Hospital was 'like transferring from hades to paradise'.[2] And it is literally represented as a series of releases from the ICU to the normal hospital and beyond, which reflect Heller's regaining of greater and greater areas of mobility. Since he was so suddenly deprived of the physical actions which

181

most of us take for granted a large proportion of *No Laughing Matter* is devoted to Heller's laborious efforts to learn over again how to eat and how to walk. Getting up unaided becomes a major event. At about the point where Heller's symptoms stabilise he also experiences a crisis of fear which is one of the most moving points in the book:

> Between about four in the afternoon and ten at night, I thought I would die from the intensity alone of the fear I was suffering in secret as I struggled between a need for sleep so enormous it could no longer be staved off and a mortal dread of succumbing to it, the petrifying foreknowledge that if I drew that one more breath that would take me into dreamland, it was going to be my last (121).

Once again we encounter a double bind similar to those which recur throughout Heller's fiction except that this time it is the result of a felt separation between his mind and his body. His capacity to express contradictions lucidly ('what I longed for most in the world was sleep, and what I began to dread most was getting it') enacts the distance he has come from the original experience. Spelling out the contradiction has taken Heller a considerable way towards understanding his fears.

In a detailed review of *No Laughing Matter*, Dr Jay I. Meltzer concludes that Heller has been a totally passive patient during the onset of his illness, arguing that the lack of communication with his doctors actually increased his suffering to the point where he fell victim to an ICU syndrome: 'an altered mental state brought out by helplessness and withdrawal of the usual stimuli of life and its replacement by noise, constant activity, observation, and the feeling of being an object in an ambience of death'. He endorses Heller's friends' suspicion that he had temporarily lost his rationality in the ICU and sums up the cumulative effect of the book as presenting a 'picture of overwhelming denial — denial of death, denial of the most evident manifestations of his illness, paralysis and weakness, denial of fear'.[3] Dr Meltzer is, of course, giving a professionally expert opinion on Heller's account, examined from a medical point of view, and perhaps for this reason does not consider how far artifice may be playing a part in *No Laughing Matter*. The role of passive victim was no doubt attractive to Heller because it opens up all sorts of possibilities of self-mockery and irony in his account. Also it may well be the case that Heller was not actually in much danger of dying but, given his lack of direct communication with the doctors, he would not know that and would literally observe patients dying around him in the ICU. So even without recourse to, say, the theories of Ernest Becker who asserts that the denial of death is a universal human impulse (noted above in Chapter 4), it is not surprising at all that Heller would have experienced these surges of fear. Another problem for Heller in writing this book was the very fact that it was non-fiction. Again and again he has declared in interviews that he dislikes factual description and the few sketches he has produced (v. Chapter 3) have been light enough for his comic inventiveness to come into play. Heller subsequently admitted that he found *No Laughing Matter* 'much harder than fiction' because 'there's a precision needed when dealing with information'.[4] Apart from these factual restrictions Dr Meltzer seems to have been expecting a work like Norman Cousins' *Anatomy of an Illness* (1979), a book which was given to Heller while he was in hospital. Cousins suffered from a disease of the connective tissue which he combated in an almost ideal collaboration between himself and his doctor. The descriptions of his illness are given a didactic and analytical edge missing from *No Laughing Matter* as Cousins reflects on the nature of pain and placebos ('proof that there is no real separation between mind and body') to affirm the need to harness a patient's life-impulse in his or her treatment.[5] Heller and Vogel's account is more narrative and more heavily seasoned with comedy, bringing a comment from one reviewer that it was 'long on detail and short on insight'.[6] One interesting dimension, however, to *No Laughing Matter* lies in observing how Heller's comic vision persisted through his illness.

Here we need to consider the crucial symbolic importance of speech which almost certainly helped Heller to shake himself out of passive fear. As he acknowledges, his retention of the capacity to speak quite simply kept him sane and specifically helped him through this evening of crisis. Once he tells the night-nurse what he has been feeling the crisis begins to pass. Verbalisation becomes a way of controlling the impulses triggered off by the illness and the very act of narrating thus becomes both therapeutic and a means of retaining the immediacy of the experience. Heller's novelistic attention to setting and circumstances contrasts strongly with the terse abbreviations quoted from his medical record at this point. Indeed, one purpose of *No Laughing Matter* is to give an alternative record to the official one, to retain particularity and individuality which might be threatened as the authorities tend to turn Heller's case into just another medical statistic. His refusal to be bathed by strangers at one point is part of this general resistance to depersonalisation. Although *No Laughing Matter* is non-fiction it becomes obvious very quickly that Heller and his co-author Speed Vogel are using novelistic devices to compose a narrative where Heller is the leading character. The composition of scenes, the alternation between dialogue and reflective passages, and the use of chapter-endings to mark off phases or to glance forward to future events are all reminiscent of novels. Not that the intention is to aggrandise Heller. By these means he retains his individuality but also places himself in two contexts, within a circle of friends whose help was indispensable, and within a community of fellow GBS-sufferers whose existence he never suspected before his illness.

The device of alternating a chapter by Heller with one by Speed Vogel (the latter's were written first) at times sets up a kind of narrative dialogue where the one narrator is called on to confirm or deny the other's account. This can lead to good-humoured interruptions like a brief 'argument' about whether or not Heller tricked his friend into having to cook for an enormous dinner party; and it can present Vogel as a stooge for the comic parts of Heller's narrative. Most immediately it begins a running contrast between the two men so that, as he himself admits, Vogel becomes Heller's alter ego. He moves into Heller's New York apartment, dons his clothes, and even signs his cheques. He is the proficient cook; Heller is the gourmand. He is the housekeeper but 'Heller was like someone from another planet'. And as Heller falls ill Vogel's fortunes begin to prosper. Two plot lines diametrically opposed to each other reveal, for instance, Vogel going to the French Riviera to play the role of one then denied to Heller since he is only just beginning convalescence. In fact these contrasts are part of the book's situational ironies and allow Vogel to comically understate the great help he gave to his friend. Even more important, the alternation between narrators means that we keep moving backwards and forwards between internal and external perspectives. Vogel gives the most thorough descriptions of Heller as seen by his friends, admitting in retrospect how little he actually understood at the time ('I realize now that I was oblivious to most of Joe's awful experiences in ICU': 67). Many details in Vogel's chapters confirm this impression. When Heller left the ICU, for instance, the former comments: 'Joe was still behaving as though nothing much was wrong with him' (134). The key word here is 'behaving' since, as we shall see in a moment, Heller was putting up a front for his friends' benefit, and was also telling others (nurses, the hospital psychiatrist, etc.) the full truth about his crises. On the one hand Vogel and Heller's other close friends could only see what Heller allowed them to see; on the other, as Vogel humorously insists on pointing out, GBS was a turning point in Heller's character usher- ing in a new era of politeness compared with his previous abrasive manner.

The final role which Vogel adopts as the book progresses is that of writer. A preliminary article on Heller's illness in the *New York Times* in 1982 brings him temporary fame and also the idea of writing a series of connected sketches to be called *Poor Speed, His Friend Joe is Sick*.[7] When he asked Heller if he thought he was capable of this task Heller said no and then an editor at Bantam Books suggested the possibility of a collaboration. The main pur- pose in the book is obviously to set the record straight on the illness and on a number of other subjects like the Gourmet Club, the informal dining group including Mario Puzo and George Man- del which has been meeting regularly since the 1960s. By 1982 this had begun to receive attention by such journalists as Kenneth Tynan whom Vogel mildly takes to task. More important than this in- formation, however, is the way Vogel concludes his section of the book. The scene is outside Heller's home in East Hampton, Long Island. The two have just returned from the Caribbean and are shovelling the first snow of the winter. Vogel takes up the story:

> As I was momentarily at rest, my arms atop my shovel, I glanced in Joe's direction. He seemed to falter. Uttering a soft moan, he started to sink to the ground. I rushed to his side, catching him as he fell. His massive head rested upon my shoulder, his body was slack. With a peaceful smile, he turned his face toward mine and softly murmured, 'It's been such a wonderful year.' He looked up into my misty eyes and said, 'I'm going now. Thank you.' Slowly his eyes fell closed and he died in my arms. (333–4).

This brilliant pastiche of a sentimental ending shifts the style noticeably away from Vogel's usual direct vigour. The orchestration of the punctual peaceful demise and the tableau scene in the snow are of course pure fiction and neatly set up Heller's spirited rejoinder:

> I DID NO SUCH THING. What the hell's the matter with him? I have no recollection whatsoever of dying in his arms and I don't know why the damned fool keeps insisting that I did. What I did do that evening was enjoy a hearty dinner of the pot roast he cooked. . .

The serious point behind all this textual joking is that the possibility that Heller might die (in the background throughout the first part of the book) is now made explicit as comic fiction which simultaneously confronts the possibility and drains it of serious threat. Vogel grotesquely recasts Heller in the role of a passive sentimental hero which he in turn can shout down. There is then no need for him to sum up the state of his health after the profane energy of his denial.

How typical is this comic episode? The very title of *No Laughing Matter* (which Anthony Burgess rightly noted was a hackneyed one) raises, albeit negatively, the issue of comedy and it is useful to take bearings from *Catch-22*.[8] While illness has been an important theme throughout Heller's fiction, in his first novel it appears initially as comic theatre and farce. The most ludicrous and appalling casualty of the war is the soldier in white and it was with this 'character' that Heller's friends drew their comparisons on their hospital visits. The comparison stayed comic because Heller could talk, in other words because he was *not* like the soldier in white. As he puts it, 'I could hear, I could answer, I could joke' (8). The glide towards the horror of silence at the end of the first chapter is arrested by self-protective wisecracks and by a tactful portrayal of his friends as figures on the verge of caricature: the lugubrious Mario Puzo, the pedagogic Dustin Hoffman, and so on. The dialogues between Heller and Mel Brooks actually reverse the expected roles of patient and professional comedian so that Heller's attempted jokes about his friend's hypochondria fall flat before his solemnity. Brooks claims to be familiar with all the polyneuritises:

> 'How come?' I questioned him. 'I never even heard the word 'polyneuritis' before, and I've been a hypochondriac longer than you. I'm older.'

'How come?' He seemed surprised by my question. 'I've got my medical dictionaries, of course. Why are you looking at me like that? Lots of people have medical dictionaries.'

'But not everybody memorizes them,' I said as a joke. He took me seriously. 'I do. Was there any paresthesia anywhere before-hand? Did you have a respiratory infection of any kind? Any other viral infections? No bronchitis? No rabies shot? Get any other vaccinations? How about childhood viral diseases? Small-pox, measles, hepatitis —'

'Mel, Mel,' I broke in benevolently when it began to dawn upon me what lay most heavily on his mind. 'I know why you're here. I think I can give you what you've come for, the protection you want. I know how to immunize you.' I paused to clear my mouth with the suction tube. 'I'll have them shave my head and let you rub my baldy for good luck.'

The laugh he gave was perfunctory. 'It isn't funny, you know,' he admonished me somberly. 'Guillain–Barre is no joke.' (60–1)

Of course it isn't but the spectacle of Mel Brooks barking orders at the hospital staff is and likewise his stolid assumption that his knowledge and interests are the norm here. Heller's friends start calling him 'cripple' in recognition of his status as a black humorist and so he has to rise to this lead by actually entertaining his visitors. This gallows humour verbally fends off death which was constantly at Heller's elbow in the ICU, but it also traps him in a role with its own pressure and anxiety that his friends might no longer come to visit him. In the event this anxiety was completely groundless and *No Laughing Matter* bears impressive testimony to the loyalty and generosity of Heller's friends. During the same year in which the book was published he also declared that 'without that support system [of friends visiting regularly] I know I would have thought of suicide'.[9]

No narrative is complete without a love theme and a sub-plot and one of Heller's nurses provides the former. Valerie Humphries (as she then was) startled Heller by her conscientious care and by her formidable appetite for good food. Heller hints at the romance between them by noting in his narrative 'she remembers', impli-citly admitting that their relationship has continued beyond his convalescence. The progress of this romance is through a 'plot' hatched by Heller where he woos her verbally (like King David this is the only option open to him at the time and that is why he writes

'God Knows I talked plenty to Valerie. . .'), and vicariously through the ever-obliging Speed who escorted her to concerts and dinners. In a three-part article for *McCall's* Valerie Humphries added her voice to those of Heller and Vogel, putting on record her own sense of how important speech was: 'I knew right away that if I were to help him recover, I had to keep talking to him. . . . For anyone as vital as Joe, talking to a responsive, communicative person can be akin to therapy'.[10] Therapy gradually burgeoned into something far more lasting because Valerie accompanied Heller around the world on a tour to promote *God Knows* in 1985, and has since married him.

The sub-plot of *No Laughing Matter* concerns Heller's divorce trial which was interrupted by his illness. Heller has a consistently sharp eye for institutional absurdity, especially in the law, and as usual reveals that absurdity by playing off one verbal style against another. Here the main butt of his irony is his wife's lawyer who, in spite of being the author of *Uncoupling — A Guide to Sane Divorce*, accused Heller of 'raping' his Long Island home. Heller's method of portraying these hearings is to quote from the official transcript, commenting on the patent absurdities in a dead-pan voice. He suspends all wisecracks and even warns the reader 'now this is not a laughing matter' (265), but from at least Mark Twain onwards such warnings in American literature regularly act as a cue for more comedy. Here Heller's calculatedly calm tone functions as a foil to the mania of the opposing lawyers, one of whom tries to introduce *Good as Gold* into the trial as the 'Mein Kampf of matrimonial strife' when he is in fact quoting *Something Happened*! In these extracts it is particular individuals rather than a whole system which are revealed to be absurd and the irony ultimately rebounds on Heller when he receives his lawyer's bills. The enormous cost of litigation and the charge system of American medicine (which makes impairies of over $100 000 for GBS a 'bargain') are two more very good reasons why Heller had adopted a muted ironic style in this book.

No Laughing Matter is a far less adversarial work than Heller's previous fiction. It does not attack systems or projected public images; nevertheless the familiar self-mocking humour comes out when he is describing the progress of his illness. Because it carried no pain it was obviously difficult for Heller to think of himself as ill; but it was equally obvious that he was seriously incapacitated. *No Laughing Matter* makes repeated play of the disparity between perceptions of Heller's illness and the medical facts; and between such terms as 'paralysed' and the physical actuality. Paradoxically the illness resulted ultimately in Heller gaining an astonishing sense of well-being and happiness. Speed Vogel has testified to the great changes in his friend's character which took place during this traumatic period. It remains to be seen whether changes will also take place in the vision of Heller's fiction.

8

Picture This

Until his illness Heller's normal working rhythm had been to produce a novel every six to ten years. Now, however, everything changed. Within a comparatively short period he had completed both *God Knows* and his sections of *No Laughing Matter*, and had written an article on his illness for *McCalls* to introduce excerpts from the latter book.[1] He returned to the Gourmet Club and pursued his interest in food by contributing an article on the Theatercafeen, an Oslo restaurant, for the *New York Times* 'Sophisticated Traveller' series.[2] He was reported to be working on his new novel in November 1986 and apparently expecting to complete it the following February.[3] Considering how recently some of the source materials for this novel were published (a study of Dutch culture in 1987, for instance) Heller must have managed his research, drafting and revision in a remarkably short time. *Picture This* (1988) marks a second new departure in his career. *No Laughing Matter* was his first attempt at non-fiction; *Picture This* does not quite return to fiction, as we shall see, but it is clearly a very carefully researched work. The novel has a double subject — Rembrandt and Dutch culture in the seventeenth century; and the development of Athenian history from the Peloponnesian War to the death of Socrates — and every page bears witness to the meticulous care with which Heller has familiarized himself with the main historical accounts of both periods. Sections dealing with each period alternate, inviting the reader to make connections and highlighting the main themes. Two of these were identified by Heller during composition when he commented that the work was 'becoming a book about money and war'.[4]

Jacob Rosenberg opens his biography of Rembrandt with the statement that the painter's life, with its dramatic sequence of success and disaster, offers abundant material to the novelist', and we might expect Heller to have taken this hint to develop a novelistic portrait of the painter.[5] The fact, however, is that *Picture This* makes comparatively little attempt to create a realistic narrative of Rembrandt's life. There are very few scenes where

Rembrandt speaks and, although his biography does give Heller's book one source of continuity, the painter dies long before the novel closes, and Heller implies that the subsequent fortunes of his paintings – specifically of *Aristotle Contemplating a Bust of Homer* – are ultimately of greater significance. The evocation of Rembrandt's household in Chapter 13 where he jokes with his son Titus, talks to his patron Jan Six (then sitting for his portrait) while his lover Hendrickje Stoffels serves tea and biscuits, is a rare exception to this general rule that Rembrandt's life is described rather than recreated. Undoubtedly an important influence was exerted on Heller by two studies in particular. Gary Schwartz's biography of Rembrandt (1985) is the most systematic attempt to identify the milieu of the paintings and also the painter's sources of financial support. He declares that 'Rembrandt is an example of an artist who was marked by his associations with patrons – in this case, dissident Protestants', and he appears to have set a model for Heller in tracing out the tortuous connections between patrons, business interests, and the fluctuations in Rembrandt's commissions.[6] The second such influence was from Simon Schama's *The Embarrassment of Riches* (1987), a massive and scholarly study of seventeenth-century Dutch artefacts as historical phenomena. Thus the imagery of painting, for instance, is seen as a manifestation of the new republic's desire for self-legitimisation, and so he too stresses the all-important determining factor of the commercial and political milieu.

Heller follows approximately the same procedure right from the beginning of the novel where he relates Rembrandt to Amsterdam residential patterns, Dutch trade, and also war – the latter being one of the main motifs of the book. Chapter 6 ('The Invention of Money') develops the financial implications of Rembrandt's marriage and follows Schwartz in relating his prosperity to the rich businessman Hendrick van Uylenburgh; and Chapter 13 makes this method most obvious in its title 'Biography'. Here Heller adopts a simple technique of lateral linkage as can been seen in the following lines:

The Dutch East India Company was four years old when Rembrandt was born in Leiden in 1606 . . . Rembrandt graduated from Latin school two years before the resumption of the war with Spain . . . He did a silverpoint drawing of Saskia [his wife] . . . and when the island of Curacao was occupied in 1634, they married.[7]

In such examples Heller makes it impossible to read the facts of Rembrandt's life in isolation from contemporary developments in trade. Indeed the connection sometimes seems so close that Rembrandt's fortunes actually seem to parallel national commerce, an impression which is confirmed by the coincidence of a general recession and his own bankruptcy. The cumulative impact of this sort of rhetoric is that Rembrandt is constantly receding into his own cultural matrix and details which at first sight appear to fill out the local realism prove to have rich commercial connotations. To take one example from the household scene referred to in the preceding paragraph, the fact that Hendrickje is serving tea is an important hint of Rembrandt's extravagance since that commodity was so valuable that Amsterdam prostitutes preferred it to money. Secondly the biscuits she is serving are sticky with sugar, another key commodity in Dutch trade. Unfortunately its popularity led to a striking decline in the nation's health (Rembrandt, for instance, being described as a 'dental cripple') which Heller juxtaposes to Saskia's death.[8] The information necessary for all these connotations to be established is supplied within Heller's text with the result that it demands unusually close reading. It is characteristic of *Picture This* to follow what might be called an amplificatory rather than simple narrative method, whereby one section explains the details of another.

The dominant factor running through Rembrandt's life is money, according to Heller. Without ever quite discounting the former's love for Saskia, he presents their marriage as the prelude to a series of financial negotiations which reach their dismal conclusion in a section given the pointedly ironic title of 'Literary Remains'. This chapter (26) totally contradicts Rembrandt's words quoted as an epigraph to the novel ('An upright soul respects honor before wealth') since the only surviving documents in the painter's own hand are seven letters to Prince Frederick Henry's agent, Constantijn Huygens, concerning - what else but money? Here Heller adopts the stance of biographer (perhaps as a tribute to Schwartz's study from which the texts of the letters are quoted) asking what kind of inferences can be drawn from them.[9] And at the same time (as witness his facetious chapter title) he refers to them as an 'oeuvre' as if they represented a slim body of works handed down to posterity. What they actually demonstrate is a shameless pursuit of money through the most ingratiating and obsequious flattery, as in his third letter which begins: 'Because of the great zeal and devotion which I exercised in executing well the two pictures which His Highness commissioned me to make ... these same two pictures have now been finished through studious application ...'. Heller dryly introduces this letter as being written 'openly nine days after he bought the house, and after a silence of three years' (230). These details put Rembrandt's claim to 'zeal and devotion' into its proper perspective, that is, as a reaction to unusual expenses incurred by buying the new house. The remainder of this chapter, which concludes with Rembrandt's death in poverty and obscurity, finds only one saving grace in the man – his paintings. The other documentary records of Rembrandt in his last years are lawsuits once again revolving around money, but a bizarre disparity emerges between the serenity and brilliance of his paintings and the upheavals and constant financial manoeuvrings in Rembrandt's personal life. He completes, for instance, *Jacob Blessing the Sons of Joseph* (glossed by Heller as dealing with inheritance) the same year that he is declared a bankrupt.

If it is impossible in *Picture This* to consider Rembrandt apart from his historical context then we need to examine further how Heller evokes this setting. Four sections of the novel ('The Invention of Money', 'Rise of the Dutch Republic', 'The Herring in History' and 'Biography') give miniature sketches of the history of the Netherlands, concentrating on the period 1584–1652. Here as elsewhere Heller does not follow a simple chronological sequence. In the first of these sections he outlines the rapid changes that were taking place in Dutch society and the rise of a national banking system. One consequence for Rembrandt is a striking commodification of works of art, so that paintings become assimilated into a commercial system of credit as the signs of potential value. Hence it is not surprising that copies begin to generate their own prices although Heller jokes that this would be in counterfeit money. The boom period in Dutch trade (the first half of the 17th century) is synchronized with a corresponding rise in Rembrandt's fortunes, a period when he himself played the art market and speculated with disastrous results. The trade in artefacts could be compared with the tulip mania which swept the Netherlands (discussed elsewhere in *Picture This*) and which Simon Schama has explained as an example of speculation run riot.[10] The other chapters in this section discuss the 1652 blockade of the Dutch coast and the recession which followed; and add a short ironic coda on changing money values over the centuries.

The next three sections of *Picture This* return to this simple contrast between prosperity and depression, and flesh out the sequence starting with the achievement of Dutch independence out of a complex set of quite disparate factors. Chapter 11 is unusual in the book's Dutch sections since it uses direct quotations from a source text — Motley's *Rise of the Dutch Republic* — specifically to describe the pivotal event of William of Orange's assassination in 1584. Pursuing a consistent line of exposing contradictions and unexpected results in history, Heller highlights the irony that William was shot with a pistol paid for by himself, but that is a matter of detail. More interesting is his divergence from Motley's presentation of the House of Orange as a force working towards the causes of freedom and liberalism. 'So long as the Prince remained alive', he writes, 'he was the Father of the whole country.'[11] Possibly in mimicry of Motley's balanced prose style (on which he comments in this chapter), Heller presents the role of the princes rather differently: 'Each time there was peace, it was against the wishes of whoever was Prince of Orange' (97), and suggests that the princes were actually at odds with the new practices of the Dutch merchants.

Trade accordingly must be brought out in the following sections. Heller continues his role as chronicler to sketch out the astonishingly rapid development of the Dutch mercantile system and in the process establishes chains of connections which link all the diverse aspects of Dutch culture together and which bring them to bear repeatedly on money and warfare. One such chain would relate sea trade to discovery (the new telescope, vital for sailing) and even philosophy (Spinoza subsisted off his work as a lense-grinder). This procedure is reductive in the sense that Heller is questioning the naive idealization of this so-called 'golden' century of Dutch civilization. He achieves this effect through reminding the reader of the obverse to national prosperity ("Textile workers in Leiden dwelt in tiny huts with only a straw mat on a floor for furniture':113) and seizes on key details which, by implication, show the true purposes of trade. One such concerns Jan Pieterszoon Coen, a governor in the East India Company, who destroyed the town of Jakarta and who requested permission from the company to use all necessary force in subduing the Moluccas. Coen declared his principles in a letter: 'There is nothing in the world that gives one a better right, than power and force added to right' (111). Heller quotes this as a surprisingly blatant and cynical admission of brute force lying behind imperialistic aggression. His probable source for this material, C.R. Boxer, adds a rider to the effect that force was only agreed to in the Moluccas because the local rulers possessed no warships.[12] Evidently prudence was keeping a watchful eye on expansionism. The second symbolic event chosen by Heller for emphasis is Piet Hein's seizure of a Spanish treasure ship off Cuba in 1628, a masterpiece of opportunism which apparently did nothing to damage the trade between Spain and the Netherlands.

In all these cases Heller is locating disparities and double standards (the Dutch forbade domestic slavery but cheerfully shipped slaves to their Brazil plantations). Whether he is discussing Dutch trade or the Peloponnesian War Heller implicitly attacks such pieties of historical interpretation as providential guidance, or liberal progress and substitutes his own counter-statements. The following are typical examples:

> With the invention of money . . . people became free . . .
> to borrow at interest and go into debt. (52)
> One of the effects of capitalism is communism. (91)
> Nowhere in history is this assumption that human
> life has a value borne out by human events. (112)
> Democracy and free enterprise go hand in hand
> and are unfriendly to each other. (154)

Undoubtedly one reason why Heller singled out Socrates for prominence in this book was the precedent he supplied of an uncompromising sceptical intelligence and similarly he devotes considerable attention to Aristophanes as an irreverent literary commentator on his age. Some of the historical sections of *Picture This* resemble a Marxist analysis in that Heller so repeatedly reduces actions to self-interest. The statements like those quoted above which pepper the text rhetorically resemble the narrative generalizations in a Victorian novel as the points where specific examples converge on large truths. Most of Heller's epigrams are textually stressed by being given their own paragraphs and are both anti-humanistic and apparently non-logical. The oxymoron stands as a pattern behind these statements which often bizarrely unite opposites, and in that respect link *Picture This* to the verbal procedures of Heller's earlier fiction.

If the historical data about the Netherlands are brought to bear on Rembrandt the aesthetic issues focus on his central portrait of

Aristotle. Chapter 21 of *Picture This* becomes one of the most important in the book because it explores the nature of representation indicated by the novel's title. Here, in one of the few extended passages of dialogue involving Rembrandt, we return to the method of *Catch-22* where the voice of common sense confronts the voice of a counter-logic and collapses. Rembrandt's model finds a logical inconsistency in Rembrandt painting him but calling the portrait Aristotle. Rembrandt's answer is that the former's face seems 'more real'. He continues:

> 'I make changes in you. You smile more. I put red in your beard. Look at your clothes.'
> 'Were they his?'
> 'Are they yours?
> 'I don't complain of the clothes. I'm inquiring about this painting of me.'
> 'It's not of you. It's a painting of Aristotle' (182)

The absurdist techniques of answering question with question, or with rejoinders which undermine the other speaker's premises are marshalled here to complicate the reader's sense of reference. Pronouns and pronominal adjectives become hopelessly tangled in such exchanges and, since he wins the argument, Rembrandt's painterly autonomy is preserved intact.

However, more developments take place in this chapter than a simple destabilization of terms like 'real' and 'natural'. One area regularly exempt from irony in the book is Rembrandt's painterly skill, and by detailing how he mixed and applied his paints Heller pays tribute to the astonishing way in which representations take shape and depth on the canvas; so much so that a painted gold chain looks even more authentic than the model's. At this point a new complicating factor appears in the person of Govert Flinck, a former pupil of Rembrandt, whose paintings are now (that is, in 1653–4) selling better than his master's. It is at this point that Rembrandt shifts into the position of his model, shifts, that is, into bewilderment before an illogicality. If Flinck's paintings are imitations, the imitations are taking precedence over the genuine articles (Rembrandt's). Initially assuming that his status was secure, Rembrandt describes Flinck as his best pupil; checking the truth of the report with another sitter (Jan Six), Rembrandt reverses this estimate ('my most stupid pupil') and begins to suspect that he is losing his mind. Six then suggests that Rembrandt should take to painting like Flinck but does not want his own portrait altered; to which Rembrandt retorts, with an eye to the future: ' "No, let me make it appear like an imitation of what Flinck will do in imitation of me with the commissions he receives for portraits like yours in the style of the one I am doing of Jan Six after people see yours" ' (187). Understandably Six assumes that Rembrandt is joking!

In this episode Heller is playing jokes with the very concept of representation, as is confirmed when Aristotle's famous definition of tragedy is quoted as the imitation of an action. But there is an even closer connection between the *Poetics* and this scene. At another point Aristotle argues that 'as Tragedy is an imitation of personages better than the ordinary man, we in our way should follow the example of good portrait-painters, who reproduce the distinctive features of a man, and at the same time, without losing the likeness, make him handsomer than he is'.[13] Commentators on Aristotle have pointed out that there are downright inconsistencies in his use of the term 'mimesis' and Humphry House for one sees him as trying to straddle two positions: '(a) that characters should be "like" ourselves; (b) that the poet imitates men as they ought to be, not as they are'.[14] Heller has been familiar with the *Poetics* possibly since he took his degree at Columbia (where his studies included a course on classical influences on modern literature) and certainly since his spell in the Yale Drama School, where he gave classes on this text. In the scene under discussion he has Jan Six quote to Rembrandt exactly the above passage from Aristotle in order to validate the painter's claim of artistic licence; and of course the quotation also authorizes Heller's non-descriptive method in selectively heightening certain facets of Rembrandt's character. It is an important detail in this connection that the working title for Heller's novel was *Poetics*.

Since we shall see that Heller repeatedly pairs Aristotle and Plato in this work an alternative classical account of artistic representation is implied in this discussion, namely Plato's attack in Book Ten of *The Republic* on imitation. Here Socrates uses the example of the painter in an opposite way to Aristotle's, to argue that, for instance, the painter of a bed stands at three removes from reality since the painting 'imitates' a physical bed which in turn 'imitates' the one idea of a bed. Socrates' insistence on primal forms inevitably leads him to devalue objects of sense-perception and artistic representations but then the Platonic theory of forms was mocked early in the novel as an exercise in mystification. Chapter 5 of *Picture This* comments briefly on these issues and describes Aristotle (the Aristotle in the portrait, that is) experiencing a crucial realization that the portrait is a primary phenomenon: 'the painting of which he and Homer were part was much more than an imitation. It had a character uniquely its own, with no prior being, not even in Plato's realm of ideas' (p. 36). Heller substantiates this realization with his detailed accounts of how Rembrandt applied his paints to the canvas. In all cases the minute attention to brush-strokes, paint mixtures and so on convey a sense of a compositional process at work without reference to the sitter. Heller builds up an impression of Rembrandt's skill at creating shape and texture by ruling out any notion of copying.

It is probable that in *Picture This* Heller is also contradicting another attack made on the arts by Plato in *Phaedrus*, where Socrates declares that 'writing . . . has this strange quality about it, which makes it really like painting: the painter's products stand before us quite as though they were alive; but if you question them, they maintain a solemn silence'.[15] The fixity of script or painting for Socrates does not compare at all with the immediacy and versatility of the spoken voice. It is only through speech, he argues, that one can preserve his cherished dialectical method of debate. What he does not recognize is the dialectical relation betweeen artefacts, a relation which Heller is of course exploiting to the full in quoting and selecting from classical texts. By giving Rembrandt's painting of Aristotle a consciousness which can only be represented through the printed word he conflates exactly the two media which Socrates was criticizing and by having Rembrandt and others question the painting Heller is virtually burlesquing Socrates' statement. The so-called silence of the portrait emerges comically in Aristotle's speechless frustration when, for instance, he is not recognized, or, even less literally, when he is thought to have snorted with derision at the end of Section XV, 'The Last Laugh'. This anti-Platonic comedy ties in with the use of absurdist dialogue in Chapter 21 to question assumptions of a simple correspondence between originals and their artistic representations.

In Chapter 21 Heller is drawing attention to the procedures of his own book. Just as Rembrandt takes his sitter as a kind of base-figure which he can modify according to his own purposes, so Heller takes the same sitter and adds details such as a hoarse voice and a logical mind to transform the figure into a character. Where

he has a voice, the Aristotle in the painting is given a consciousness which further discourages the reader from seeing the
'character' as a copy. The sitter's preference for the bust of Aristotle
is neither logical nor realistic since this work would have been as
determined by the sculptor's purposes as Rembrandt's portrait
and, like the bust of Homer which Aristotle is contemplating, 'was
an authentic Hellenistic imitation of a Hellenic reproduction of a
statue for which there had never been an authentic original record'
(5). Indeed the latter portrait's prominence throughout the novel
acts as a reminder to the reader of the raw materials which Heller
has been using to make his own character of Rembrandt come
alive. In the case of his classical sources Heller repeatedly points
out disparities and divergences between accounts of Socrates' life,
for instance. The proliferation of texts in these sections develop the
implications of the chapter discussed above and remind us constantly of the unavailability of originals. Depiction thus spirals at
its most extreme into a *mise-en-abyme* of representations − hence
Rembrandt's ironic suggestion of making copies of copies.

Heller's apparently ludicrous dialogues over copying and originals where, for instance, Rembrandt shows anxiety over his own
signature, hark back momentarily to the chaplain's interrogation in
Catch-22, and elaborate on a historical complication in Rembrant's
life. Gary Schwartz has pointed out that there are in existence
paintings which seem to be the joint work of Rembrandt and
Govert Flinck, although in the former's style, as if the older painter
was helping his pupil's career. Evidently the lesson was learnt only
too well since 'starting in 1636 Flinck began encroaching on
Rembrandt's base of patronage until in the 1640s he conquered it
altogether'.[16] At the end of Chapter 13 Heller notes a striking
change in Rembrandt's style towards individualism which carries
an ominous indifference to his patron's opinions and, following his
principle of character-contrasts, he establishes Flinck as a foil to his
teacher. Where Rembrandt is pursuing a consistent interest in light
and shade, Flinck is a 'facile pragmatist' who 'changed styles with
the times' and accordingly rode out shifts in fashion with ever-
increasing prosperity.

The importance of the market-place in this discussion is signalled by the section being entitled 'Money Talks' and the fact that the
conversation is introduced by details of contemporary Dutch trade.
A commercial context for art is established here as elsewhere in
Picture This, partly to demonstrate how Rembrandt was enmeshed

In historical circumstances and partly to show specifically how he falls victim to arbitrary fluctuations in the market for portraits. The only possible reason why Flinck's paintings are 'better' is the tautology that they are 'more valuable', and assumption of logic in the transactions of trade collapses before an entirely mysterious commercial process. Here a distinction should be drawn between Heller's Rembrandt and the painter as described by the Marxist critic John Berger, for instance. Berger argues in *Ways of Seeing* that portrait-painting was inextricably tied to developing attitudes to property and indeed constituted a celebration of material prosperity, a position developed by Schwartz and followed by Heller. Against the limited role opened to them by their patrons, a few outstanding painters rebelled, went their own way, and suffered financial hardship as a consequence.[17] Heller by contrast presents Rembrandt not as an idealist but as a mercenary man preoccupied with the monetary value of his own works and possessions. That is why this particular scene opens with him trying to assess the value of his collection of busts. At the beginning of the chapter Rembrandt's model naively assumes a simple opposition between original and representation which is questioned by the painter. Later in the scene the roles reverse and this time it is Rembrandt who equally naively assumes he will maintain superiority over his pupil. But his arrogance blinds him to the market value of copies (it is perhaps significant that the term for painting a sitter's face was *conterfeiten*) and to the shifts in demand.

Before he had finished *Picture This* Heller was quoted as saying that his new novel lacked the pessimism of his earlier works, but this is a matter of tone and emphasis.[18] While it is true that the indignation with contemporary politics fuelling *Good as Gold* is absent and that the ironies of the new work are quieter, nevertheless *Picture This* directs its energies against idealized images of the ages of Pericles and Rembrandt. When discussing Dutch commerce Heller points out the existence of domestic poverty and the crude desire for imperial conquest. In the first block of chapters to deal with the Peloponnesian War a comparable progression is clear. Firstly Heller erodes Pericles' status as law-maker and patron of the arts, then he undermines his flattering titles ('the Olympian') with derogatory nick-names ('Onion-head'). Chapter 15 gives a brief summary of Pericles' era as one characterized by war. The next chapter then composes an ironic portrait of this ruler with a rhetorical method reflected in miniature by the following sentence:

'And then, in 433 B.C., Pericles, this leader of the democrats, builder of the Parthenon, sponsor of Aeschylus and Phidias, pupil of Zeno and Anaxagoras, and friend of Damon, in the belief that war with Sparta was probable, deliberately took steps to make it inevitable' (142). This sequence of titles collapses at the end of the sentence, implying a political wrong-headedness so extreme as to be criminal. In the next chapters Heller quotes and summarizes extensively from Thucydides and Plutarch (see table at end of chapter) selecting from the former so as to keep the struggle between Athens and Sparta constantly in the foreground. Heller follows Thucydides again in seeing the war as inevitable and caused by a desire for power but arranges the material in these chapters so as to build up to a climax.[19] After the 'portrait' of Pericles comes a description of the plague (Chapter 17), a natural disaster occasioning a breakdown in law and order. Then follow a series of conquests − of Mytilene (Chapter 18). The city of Plataea (Chapter 19) and Corcyra (Chapter 20).

During this sequence war has been established as a norm and a fitting culmination is reached in Chapter 20 with a depiction of the new war mentality. The crucial opposition here is between the demagogue Cleon and the satirical dramatist Aristophanes who stands behind Heller's own burlesque of the former's hawkish diatribes:

'Whose side are you on?' he snarled and growled, as he stamped about on the stage in the Assembly . . . 'What you have here', he bellowed from the podium, 'is a subversive influence allied with the Spartan government undertaking a very well organized effort to affect the vote in the Assembly.' (166–7)[20]

Heller captures the crude theatricality of this demagogue and renders him as a type-figure by introducing verbal details full of connotations from twentieth-century politics. His appeal to his audience's paranoia by suggesting an extensive and efficient network of undercover agents working against their own political system hinges on style entirely − on bombast, key words ('subversive') and an accusing question ('whose side are you on?') which actually reduces the options open to his listeners. The result is a corruption of language even more confining: 'fanatical impulsiveness was the mark of a true man, while cautious deliberation was a specious pretext for shirking' (167). As behaviour becomes renamed and reinterpreted the result is catch-22, entrapment for anyone trying to resist the prevailing current opinion; and correspondingly success for the McCarthyist demagogue Cleon whose war economy (complete with its own military-industrial complex) gains unrivalled power.

The second block of chapters on the Peloponnesian War narrates the subjugation of Melos 'in that interval of peace that was known as the cold war' (193 – another cross-period reference) and concludes bleakly with the military defeat and political collapse of Athens. The figure to dominate this section is Alcibiades, whom Heller develops beyond Thucydides' description. If Cleon personified the war cause, Alcibiades represents a self-seeking moralism which Heller portrays through a mock-Platonic dialogue with his teacher Socrates in Chapter 23. Here the roles of teacher and student are reversed and Socrates is reduced to bemused puzzlement by Alcibiades' twists and turns of argument. When taken to task for his extravagance at the Olympic Games he answers:

'That's why I did it. Don't you remember? You used to try to teach me contempt for wealth.'
'Did I fail or did I succeed? It's impossible to say from the example you give . . .'
'I wished to display to the entire Greek world how much wealth I had,' explained Alcibiades, 'and to make clear, by throwing so much of it away, with such open vulgarity, how little I valued it.'
'But when you spoke in the Assembly for your Sicilian war resolution,' said Socrates, 'you maintained that you entered these seven chariots to demonstrate the glory of Athens . . .'
'I was telling a lie they would adore to hear. And they lapped it up like intoxicating wine.' (205).

It is an important motif running through all the chapters on the Peloponnesian War that speeches play a major role in determining action and Alcibiades simply exposes their manipulative nature here. This scene links the Socratic method with historical narrative by presenting Alcibiades as the ultimate cynic. His sheer ingenuity at explanation undermines the difference between materialism and its opposite and reduces all behaviour to amoral tactics. It is therefore consistent that Alcibiades should change sides several times in these wars and appropriate to Heller's general perspective that his cynicism should be so efficient at identifying the true motives of others. When he pinpoints the class interests of the Athenian businessmen and the gullibility of his audience in this quotation he is in effect bringing out another motif of these historical chapters: the pliability and fickleness of the populace. Heller's free-ranging ironies allow only the bleakest of political interpretations to stand unchallenged.

The chapters of *Picture This* dealing with Athenian history are woven into a whole series of references to the two leading figures of the era who attempted a systematic inquiry into the meaning of human behaviour – Aristotle and Plato. Heller contrasts the two philosophers in the following way:

> Plato had his head in the clouds and his thoughts in the heavens . . .
> Aristotle had his feet on the ground and his eyes everywhere.(21)

By transposing Aristophanes' burlesque of Socrates (*The Clouds*) Heller sets up an opposition between theory and realism, abstraction and specifics. It is a totally loaded contrast because Heller draws extensively on Diogenes Laertius' rather sceptical life of Plato, and denies that 'character' a consciousness. We are thus constantly looking *at*, not *from*, Plato and receiving summaries of his works with a clear adverse judgement built into them. From these accounts a figure emerges who is self-mystifying but – even more importantly in a book which interrogates the value of human actions – also a sceptic whose disillusionment with specific regimes leads him to plan out an astonishing system of state dictatorship. His three missions to Sicily to find a philosopher-ruler are presented by Heller as quixotic evidence of his having lost touch with reality, but the long discussion of his *Laws* in Chapter 29 piles example on example of more sinister contradictions ('Denouncing wealth, he gave power to the wealthy': 264). Once Heller turns to Aristotle as a theorist he, too, is subjected to an ironic examination which reveals disparities between stated principles and likely consequences.

If Plato's fate in this novel is to be ridiculed, Aristotle's role is far more complex. Firstly, he is used as a personal witness and therefore commentator on his former master's lessons, on the pompous obscurity of his lectures and on the political implications of his *Laws*. Heller makes Aristotle into a major point-of-view character and also a vocal presence; hence the culmination of the contrast between the two philosophers in a dialogue which destructively feeds Plato's late scepticism back into his earlier works:

> [Plato:]   'In my virtuous communist republic, it will be the role of the individual to do the bidding of the state.'
> [Aristotle:]   'And if people don't agree?'
> 'They will be oppressed, for the good of the state. The Guardians will make them.'
> 'Who will make the Guardians obey?', inquired Aristotle. 'Where is the stronger force to compel them?'
> 'What difference does it make?', said Plato, vexed. 'What people do in this world is of no consequence.'
> 'Then why are you bothering? Why are we talking? Why did you write your *Republic*?' (283).

In this scene Aristotle is used to bring out Plato's vagueness over specifying virtuous rule, the practical difficulty of defining the 'best' citizens, and to restate the traditional objection to *The Republic*, namely who guards the Guardians? Aristotle's insistent questions represent an extension of Heller's narrative voice in that realism leads to an awareness of the presence of self-interest in human action. This passage implicitly draws on the chapters describing the Peloponnesian War to reveal how unrealistic is Plato's assumption, for instance, that any ruler will voluntarily relinquish power. Aristotle is particularly described in his old age, that is, in that period of his life where he has developed a gloom about human behaviour but without retreating into Plato's totalitarian political fantasies. Aristotle's consciousness, however, is extended beyond its biographical limits so that he can comment on the whole span of history, and so that his consciousness can be brought to bear on the twentieth century. Indeed, his expressed alienation from any specific period marks his consciousness as a characteristically modern one. The object which enables this continuity to be established is Rembrandt's portrait and to that we must now turn.

Although *Picture This* alternates between blocks of information dealing with the Netherlands and blocks dealing with classical Greece, the very fact of alternation means that the act of comparison is foregrounded. No single historical period is established as the main one and therefore the possibilities of anachronism are severely limited. In *God Knows* the engagement between modern scepticism and Christian tradition is enacted through stylistic disruptions of the language of the King James Bible. A startlingly modern colloquial idiom supplies the means of undercutting the solemnity of stories centring on King David. In other words anachronism becomes tactical. However, in *Picture This* Heller is constantly moving backwards and forwards in time and reminding us of an inescapably modern viewpoint on the action. Socrates' trances are glossed medically, for instance, to demystify them and to make it clear that he was not a mystic or spiritual leader. Heller's secular description of history scarcely ever mentions religion and when it does religion is always reduced to self-deception, hypocrisy or a mask for commercialism. In *Catch-22* we noted examples of Heller using key words as signals to the reader to transpose the descriptions on to the period of McCarthyism and a similar device is used here. A term like 'gulag' occurs within the description of the rule of the Thirty in Athens to extend comparative links into other historical periods and to imply the recurrence of certain patterns of totalitarianism.

The most striking example of this procedure occurs at the beginning of Chapter 11, whose section title ('Rise of the Dutch Republic') leads us to expect concentration on the Netherlands. Instead Heller outlines the relation between the superpowers Russia and America as a symbiosis fed by war which oddly undermines their apparent political differences:

> the government of each was helpless without the threat from the other . . .
> Peace on earth would mean the end of civilization as we know it. (92)

Parallelism is built into the very structure of this description which uses symmetry and balanced repetition ('It is impossible . . . It is easy . . .') to bring out the mutual dependence screened by the rhetoric of political hostility. It is entirely consistent for Heller to move on to a brief description of the Athenian demagogue Cleon, because here he implicitly draws on the reader's capacity to identify resemblances – specifically with McCarthy's verbal attacks on liberals and Hitler's violent speech technique. If the opening of the chapter collapses together extremes from each end of the political spectrum these analogies extend the comparison

into other historical periods and make a very ironic context indeed
for recounting the Dutch achievement of independence. For Heller
the latter event is implicitly a prelude to the exercise of the only
political principle spelt out in Chapter 11, namely 'the right of the
strong to suppress the weak' (92). This implication is realized in the
chapters which follow as they pile up factual demonstrations that
the Netherlands rapidly established themselves as a major military
power. Such connections give *Picture This* a contemporary reference not immediately apparent. There are nevertheless hints, as in
the opening to Chapter 23: 'From Athens to Syracuse by oar and
sail was just about equivalent to the journey by troopship today
from California to Vietnam, or from Washington, D.C., to the
Beirut airport in Lebanon or to the Persian Gulf' (200). The comparison is obviously political not geographical, and draws a parallel
between the Sicilian expedition in the Peloponnesian War and
American foreign policy in this century. Here and elsewhere Heller
lists examples of military adventurism where the crude purposes of
the expedition are hidden by the catch-phrase 'to protect national
interests'. So, just as Mailer uses the narrative of a bear hunt to
'explain' America's presence in Vietnam, Heller describes Athenian and Dutch foreign policy in such a way that a continuity of
imperialistic design takes shape and extends into American politics
of the 1980s.[21]

Rembrandt's painting of Aristotle functions as an ingeniously
versatile central object linking the fifth century BC with the
seventeenth and twentieth centuries. Heller gives the Aristotle in
the portrait a consciousness which helpfully guides the reader
towards the required connections: 'Aristotle could see similarities
. . . between the Holland of the Dutch Republic . . . and the ancient
Athens that had existed before his birth . . .' (34). Here Heller is
using this figure as a structural convenience. At other points he
uses him as a kind of historical commentator, gloomily denying
that change has brought about an improvement in man's lot; in
other words he functions often as a mask for Heller's own
reflections, his reactions blending easily into the sceptical generalizations described above.

Heller's main use of the painting, however, is as the protagonist
in an 'odyssey' with 'chapters of danger, adventure, mystery, and
treasure, and with comical details of mistaken identity'. This
promise is facetious because he immediately adds 'the details
would be fascinating if we knew what they were' (8)! Nevertheless

narrative interest is not left entirely behind since in the sequel to Rembrandt's death Heller does compose a mock-picaresque account of the painting's movements from Sicily to England and New York. As in all picaresque narratives there is a stress on travel and pure contingency, and Heller even uses Rembrandt's *Homer* as a kind of deuteragonist which suffered the worse fate of being almost destroyed by fire. As he promised, touches of comic relief are supplied by the repeated mis-identifications of the *Aristotle* and hazard comically indicated when Heller lists more wars than the painting could conceivably have escaped. In fact, Heller repeatedly shifts his narrative role in this chapter (32), sometimes speaking as a historian in listing the sales of the painting, sometimes as an art expert and sometimes as a chronicler when he juxtaposes details of the painting's history with contemporary events.[22] Following the 'adventures of a guinea' formula, Heller presents reactions to the painting as glimpses of social values and even sets up a narrative rather like a newsreel where events and his own throw-away asides follow each other in rapid succession. The climax to the chapter comes with the sale by auction of the painting in 1961. This period marks the peak of the portrait's fame and its highest price raised – indeed it becomes a moot point at times whether the painting or its price is the true protagonist here. There is not exactly a happy ending, however, because the crowds tail off and the disgruntled Aristotle is moved into the comparative obscurity of an ordinary gallery in the Metropolitan Museum of Modern Art.

Where Aristotle functions as a commentator Socrates enjoys a position of particular prominence in *Picture This* as the focus of the book's historical scepticism. He personifies a 'satirical dissent' unacceptable to politicians of any persuasion, and is brought to trial perhaps for nothing other than 'reckless levity and ideological noncomformity' (71). Accordingly, Socrates is broadly speaking excluded from Heller's ironies because there are already so many in his actual fate: particularly that he lived unscathed under a dictatorship but was convicted and executed in the very democracy he helped to establish. For Heller he represents a sceptical honesty so scrupulously maintained that it becomes positively reckless, and in that sense Socrates becomes a fixed character against which the other grotesques (Cleon), cynics (Alcibiades) and fashion-mongers are measured. Heller demonstrates at once an awareness of Socrates' textual elusiveness in discussing the problem of there being no writings in existence by the man himself; and also a recognition of his enigmatic character since he seems to fit no category:

> He was not anyone's idea of an intellectual . . .
> Socrates had no school.
> He had no library . . . (87).

Heller suggests that Socrates eludes final summary by listing negative and contradictory qualities typographically separated so that they cannot combine into analytical coherence. The chapters dealing mainly with Socrates draw extensively on Plato's dialogues and assemble a series of excerpts from particular works which change Plato's emphases in a number of ways. Chapter 36, for instance, in recounting Socrates' death predictably draws heavily on *Phaedo* but cuts out Socrates' long discussion with Simmias of the connection between philosophy and preparation for death. This change brings a far greater concentration on the narrative sections of *Phaedo* and correspondingly increases the pathos of Socrates' death. Other chapters carry rather more complex changes.

Chapter 10 presents a collage of glimpses of Socrates culled from the *Protagoras, Republic, Meno, Gorgias* and Diogenes Laertius' life. The initial images give examples of his capacity to throw people into extreme states of frustration or to reduce them to speechlessness. Having established this characteristic, Heller then develops his portrait by using Alcibiades partly as witness, partly as foil. Outlining the latter's physical beauty, social popularity, and sexual promiscuity is essential as a prelude for indicating Socrates' extreme self-control; and essential also to give the reader a context for the former's speech from the *Symposium* which operates as the base-text for the rest of this chapter. Once again we need to note how Heller's selections serve his own purposes.

Plato's *Symposium* describes not so much a dialogue as a series of speeches on the nature of love delivered around the dinner-table of Agathon. It is only when Socrates' turn comes to speak that a question-and-answer sequence of debate is used, and even then only as a prelude to his reporting his own instruction from 'a woman of Mantinea, called Diotima'. Where Socrates' exposition marks the philosophical high point of this work, the dramatic peak undoubtedly comes with the rowdy entrance of Alcibiades. Socrates cringes at an expected attack but Alcibiades' speech actually constitutes a particularly ingenious personal tribute, and a phenomenally coherent one if we consider that he is already drunk and gulps down half a gallon of wine before he begins to speak! One tactic he follows is to develop an analogy between Socrates and Silenus, an uncouth and unattractive old man, but one nevertheless gifted with prophetic powers. And secondly Alcibiades reveals his own helplessness before the mysterious, almost magical impact which Socrates' personality has on him. Let us now see how this sequence appears in Heller's text.

As usual Heller cuts out expository materials and all the speeches preceding Alcibiades' so as to sharpen the contrast between the two men and to allow the very personification of worldliness to pay tribute to his opposite. Indeed, the contrasts accumulate throughout the chapter: youth against age; social status against obscurity; sexual action against spiritual love; and so on. Heller ingeniously pieces together fragments of this speech for new effects, as in the following paragraph where interpolations are marked:

['I must warn you about him,' said Alcibiades, jovial in his cups. 'When Socrates is present, no one else has a chance with anybody who is good-looking.] The Socrates whom you see has a tendency to fall in love with good-looking young men and is always in their society. [See how readily he has found a plausible excuse for getting Agathon beside him]. So I warn you, Agathon, not to be deceived by him. But this is exactly the point. He spends his whole life pretending and playing with people, and it makes no difference to him whether a person is good-looking, nor whether he is rich, nor whether he possesses any of the other advantages that rank high in popular esteem. To him all these things are worthless, and we ourselves are of no account. I may add that I am not the only sufferer this way. He has pretended to be in love with others, too, when in fact he is himself the beloved rather than the lover. Learn from my experience and be on your guard.' (80–1). [23]

The first quoted sentence draws ambiguous attention to Socrates' apparent behaviour in society but Heller then juxtaposes Alcibiades' conclusion to the whole speech ('so I warn you . . .'), making it a specific warning to Agathon against Socrates' social manner. The next short sentence introduces an awkwardness into the sequence by cutting out the Silenus-analogy completely. In the *Symposium* Alcibiades uses this comparison to distinguish between Socrates' outer manner and appearance, and the inner 'treasures' he has discovered. There the 'but' introduces his account of these inner qualities, whereas here it implies a contrast between the warning and what follows. Alcibiades' rhetorical exploitation of the difference between surfaces and depths in Socrates is largely lost in this paragraph which revises the focus of attention on to the social and in so doing suggests that Socrates is a sceptical questioner of accepted values rather than a proponent of new ones. Heller retains, and indeed underlines, the irony that Alcibiades should be phrasing his tribute partly as the complaint of an unrequited lover when he was in fact notorious for his promiscuity with both sexes. The shift in emphasis in the passage quoted is in keeping with the tenor of the chapter as a whole, which repeatedly comes back to Socrates' conflicts with sacrosanct political systems and the social expectations of those around him.

Another example of how Heller modifies Plato can be found in Chapter 35 which consists almost entirely of quotations from *Crito*.[24] In this dialogue, which takes place between Socrates' conviction and his execution, the dramatic urgency of the latter's exchanges with his friend is suspended as the piece shifts into an enquiry about correct civic conduct and it concludes with a lengthy exposition of duty to Socrates by a personification of the Athenian laws. Heller makes a number of changes which have the cumulative effect of reducing Socrates' privileged position. Firstly, the jailer is no longer a mere background presence but now speaks in his own right adding one more voice urging Socrates to escape. Secondly, Heller cuts out most of the theoretical dialogue, reordering quotations so as to retain the issues raised but giving Crito's warnings to Socrates more prominence and therefore more urgency. The laws are articulated in one brief paragraph instead of several pages and this reduction suggests a refusal on Heller's part to recognize the weight of their obligation which would be entirely in keeping with his scathing summary of Plato's *Laws* in Chapter 29 as a blueprint for totalitarianism. Thus, we have far less sense of Socrates as a teacher or sage and a new coda to the chapter even allows Crito to question the other's assumptions:

> 'What of the man', Crito suggested, 'who believes it is right to do wrong?'

'I am not that man'.
'Is it right to disobey a law that is evil?'
'Our laws are not evil.'
'I am asking philosophically.'
'I have no more time for that'.
'I have nothing to say'.
'Leave me then, Crito, to fulfill the will of God and follow whither it leads'. (335)

At the point where Crito speaks here Socrates has just finished laying out his position and has masked its dogmatism by presenting himself as simply responding to an inner voice. Heller then turns Plato's method against itself by having Crito question two of Socrates' cherished assumptions (a harmony between moral value and conduct; and the justness of the laws). Although Crito poses the questions as hypotheses, Socrates answers them with factual statements, in effect refusing to engage in philosophical debate, and then retreats into silence. Just at the point where Heller rejoins Plato's text ('I have nothing to say') Crito's statement now implies impatience or even triumph rather than submission since, just for a second, he has revealed Socrates as a wily and evasive tactician of rhetoric.

One of the major events in *Picture This* is the trial of Socrates and Heller returns to a device he had used in *Catch-22*, namely expanding reference. Socrates' trial and that of an apparently fictional tanner in his jury called Asclepius are referred to several times in the novel, with slightly more details being released on each occasion. This is at once a device for creating suspense and also becomes a way of bringing out an episode's importance. And it is consistent with this particular novel and with Heller's whole *oeuvre* that a key scene should revolve around an abuse of the law. The law, indeed, has figured prominently in the novel as being vulnerable to political expediency, the whims of autocrats, and to the fluctuations in popular fashion. Chapter 29 discusses the ease with which the Athenian oligarchy establishes itself and presents them as the classical forerunners of American industrial barons like Cornelius Vanderbilt, who saw himself as above the law.

Heller ridicules the due process of law by developing two characters – Anytus, one of Socrates' accusers (and ironically a general who earlier escaped his own trial by bribing the jury); and Asclepius, a tanner – into the respective proponent and victim of legal cynicism. Chapter 33 includes a ludicrous 'pre-trial hearing' where Anytus rehearses his charges and Socrates his defence. The former gives yet another twist to the bogus logic we have already seen used by Cleon and Alcibiades, and actually states contradictions which seem to him irrelevant before the grand purpose of preserving the 'system' intact. Thus when Socrates asks whether the Athenian laws allow for unorthodoxy, Anytus answers: 'Of course ... There is full freedom of expression. An unorthodox view can be expressed, provided it is an orthodox unorthodoxy ... One has to be pro-something' (316). Heller takes care to suggest that Socrates' fate was inevitable, given his refusal to compromise his honesty. What comes as much more of a surprise is the trial of Asclepius which, although it happens after Socrates' death chronologically, is inserted into the account of the first trial as a bleakly comic sub-plot. In effect it presents a rerun of the interrogation of the chaplain in *Catch-22* with the same presumption of guilt, the same distortion of the notion of evidence, and the same inducing of guilt in the hapless accused. Heller elaborates the trial out of Socrates' last words, acknowledging a debt of sacrifice to the god of medicine ('I owe a cock to Asclepius') and even suggests that the 'model citizen' dies because his demeanour compares so unfavourably with that of Socrates! In the tanner's hearing we witness a process of inquiry grimly familiar from Heller's earlier works:

> Asclepius began to believe he might indeed be lying.
> But why?
> He wracked his brains ...
> Asclepius ... then unwittingly spoke the words that ensured his indictment. 'The only thing I know is that I know nothing '
> This was practically the same statement of Socrates' a few weeks earlier!
> Yes, it did sound familiar. No, he had never done business with Socrates.
> Why, then, had he either conspired in code with a man who owed nothing or loaned him a chicken? (324).

In the interrogation of the chaplain panic was induced by threats which at that point came to nothing. Here the whole process of accusation, trial and execution works much quicker, the workings of a manic logic leading directly to death. The trial presupposes the least obvious explanations for anything – it is after all based on a pure coincidence of names. The premise that the obvious meaning of Socrates' words cannot be their true meaning leads to the inevitable conclusion of hidden secret significance ('code') and a projection of the illogicality of the prosecution's case on to the accused. Because Asclepius cannot disentangle the contradictions in Anytus' position he finds himself in the catch-22 double-bind. If he denies conspiracy he adds perjury to his already assumed guilt; if he admits guilt he simply accelerates his fate. One of the points about the character of Asclepius is that he is the very opposite of Socrates – inarticulate and obscure. He is in short a representation of the fate of an average citizen at the hands of a corrupt system. By juxtaposing his trial with Socrates' Heller brings out the absurd aspect of the latter without damaging its pathos.

The foregoing discussion has demonstrated how Heller appropriates his source-texts, transforming them into new entities by selection, paraphrase and verbal revision. Direct quotations are used most extensively in the classical sections; the Dutch chapters document themselves thoroughly but use Heller's own words. It would seem then that Heller had joined ranks with those American writers who reproduce the so-called 'nonfiction novel' but here a number of problems arise. The New Journalism and 'fiction of fact' are only more recent manifestations of a long tradition of overlap in American letters between journalism and literature. Recent studies by Shelley Fisher Fishkin and Chris Anderson have demonstrated how writers from Whitman through Dos Passos to Mailer and Tom Wolfe have marshalled a whole series of rhetorical techniques in pursuit of a reportage which is by no means neutral. On the contrary, Anderson insists, 'nonfiction reportage is more than informative: it is an effort to persuade us to attitudes, interpretations, opinions, even actions'.[25] As it happens, in his chosen examples (Mailer, Capote, Wolfe and Didion) language doubles back on itself and reportage fails. In all these cases an attempt is made to engage with *topical* and *contemporary* subjects, and many of the rhetorical devices used by these writers are aiming at an effect of present-ness, of conveying the narrative immediacy of a news item. Now clearly this does not apply to Heller. Again and again he reminds us that he is dealing with chronologically remote materials and their very distance in time from the present allows him to adopt a reflective, ruminative style. A second rarer possibility in American literature seems more relevant, at least to the classical chapters of *Picture This*: the use of extended quotation in the text.

Examples of this procedure could be found in *Paterson* or in Pound's *Jefferson* Cantos. On the latter Stephen Fender has argued that 'the documents are indispensable, not only to an understanding but also to a *reading* of [these works]. The poems quite simply cannot be construed without them'.[26] Fender attributes this use of fragments to a didactic urge in Pound which literally forces the reader to go back to source materials, whereas by contrast sense can be made of Williams' quotations within the poem itself. Similarly, Heller's extended quotations also give perfectly coherent accounts and, as has been shown, combine to suggest a sombre historical continuity of *realpolitik* from the fifth century BC right up to the present. But this would only give a partial explanation of Heller's use of his materials.

If his novel cannot be explained with reference to the New Journalism or the quotation-method of Pound or Williams what contemporary work can shed light on *Picture This*? Julian Barnes' novel *Flaubert's Parrot* (1984) offers us an illuminating comparison. This work, like Heller's, eschews chronological plot and instead presents a fictional meditation on the life of Flaubert. The narrator, named Geoffrey Braithwaite and identified as a doctor (and therefore unambiguously distinguished from the author) is pursuing what is evidently a long-standing fascination with the French novelist and on the way clearly enjoying himself by poking fun at the more sober researches of literary critics. Towards the end of the novel he presents a spoof exam paper to test his reader's reactions. However, the novel genre is notorious for its duplicity and mocking critical solemnity certainly does not amount to mocking scholarship. *Flaubert's Parrot* is actually a learned work which lightly demonstrates an easy familiarity with extraordinarily diverse topics ranging from the colour of nineteenth-century French raspberry jam to the suitability of French hansom cabs for fornication. Barnes' narrator digresses and rambles, mocks his own researches, and uses chapter-titles ('The Train-Spotter's Guide to Flaubert') which humorously underplay his activities as amateurishness. Under his joking lies a problem which comes to the surface again and again: 'How do we seize the past? How do we seize the foreign past? We read, we learn, we ask, we remember, we are humble; and then a casual detail shifts everything'.[27] The eponymous stuffed parrot functions as a comic metonym of the past's elusiveness because by the end of the novel Braithwaite discovers that he has to choose, not between two as he thought, but between 50! The fluidity of Barnes' text now purporting to be a chronology, now a narrative of research, reflects the near-impossibility of achieving a firm sense of the past, and he reserves his most scathing ironies for those writers who ignore this difficulty.

How do these details bear on Heller's novel? A comparable humorous attitude is established on the first page and his sections too carry punning comic meanings ('In Dutch', for instance, that is, in trouble). Barnes embroiders on his subject by having a section narrated by Flaubert's lover, Louise Colet; Heller animates the portrait of Aristotle. Both writers admit the gaps in knowledge of their biographical subjects and use details as a focus for speculation. Both refuse to retell their subject's life chronologically but circle around certain key events and figures. Both are clearly very well researched and refer to biographies as well as raw documentary evidence. Perhaps most interesting of all, both works exist on the borderline between fact and fiction which they have broadened out by implying the promotion of arbitrary inference and literary structuring which go into works of biography and historical record. Barnes refers several times to one of the wiliest literary craftsmen of the century who delights in undermining the reader's sense of reliability in information – Nabokov. Heller discriminates against Xenophon's Memorabilia of Socrates on the grounds that little of it is first-hand, but conversely notes that Plato channels several dialogues through witness-reporters, thereby qualifying their supposed immediacy. And he uses as a main source on the Peloponnesian War Thucydides, who frankly admits that in recording speeches he has adopted a method of making 'the speakers say what, in my opinion, was called for by each situation'.[28] Barnes includes a vast amount of factual data in a fictional frame, whereas Heller places his text comparatively nearer to historical records, especially in chapters which consist almost entirely of quotation. This comparison is not a matter of mere speculation since when it was published (1984, that is, shortly before he started planning his own new work) Heller enthusiastically endorsed *Flaubert's Parrot* as a 'delightful and enriching' book.[29]

Throughout this chapter I have been describing *Picture This* as a novel largely for the sake of convenience but in fact its category is every bit as shifting as that of *Flaubert's Parrot*. At one point Heller will meditate on money; at another he will mimic a chronicler; and at yet another he will condense a Platonic dialogue and then suddenly shift it into burlesque. Barnes at least gives us a fictional narrator to stabilize the text and mediate the historical data, although he is rather contradictory, ostensibly a doctor but with a very well-developed sense of literary method. Heller, on the other hand uses an unnamed narrator with an open identity who can shade easily into the voices of quoted texts. Both Heller and Barnes apply the elusiveness of the past in their comic treatment of biographies, histories and literary criticism. Barnes sportively allows uncertainty to work at his narrator's expense. Heller takes a more sombre tack in showing how the individual is swallowed up by history itself. The ironic coda to *Picture This* presents disparate and antididactic generalizations ('you will learn nothing from history that can be applied') together with a factual contradiction of Socrates' allegedly peaceful death from hemlock. By undermining the plausibility of a key scene in his own book and the authenticity of its central portrait (*Aristotle* may, after all, not be by Rembrandt) Heller denies a final resolving certainty to his own text.

Main Classical Source Materials used in *Picture This*

Diogenes Laertius, life of Plato	Chapters 27, 29
— —, life of Socrates	Chapter 9
Plato, *Apology*	Chapters 9, 33
— —, *Crito*	Chapter 35
— —, *Laws*	Chapter 29
— —, *Phaedo*	Chapter 36
— —, *Symposium*	Chapter 10
Plutarch, life of Alexander	Chapter 30
— —, life of Pericles	Chapters 16, 17
Thucydides, *Peloponnesian War*, Bk. II	Chapters, 15, 16, 17
— —, Bk. III	Chapters 18, 19, 20
— —, Bk. V	Chapter 22
— —, Bk. VI	Chapters 23, 24
— —, Bk. VII	Chapter 24
Xenophon, *Hellenica* II	Chapter 24.

Notes

INTRODUCTION

1. W. J. Weatherby, 'The Joy Catcher', *Guardian*, 20 Nov. 1962, p. 7.
2. James Nagel, *'Catch-22* and Angry Humor: A Study of the Normative Values of Satire', *Studies in American Humor* vol. 1 (1974) p. 102.
3. 'Humor and the Ability to Create It Cannot Be Taught', *US News & World Report*, 12 Nov. 1984, p. 71.
4. 'Joseph Heller Replies', *The Realist* vol. 50 (May 1964) p. 30.
5. 'Howe and Hummel'. MS in Harry Ranson Humanities Research Center, University of Texas at Austin.

CHAPTER 1: THE ROAD TO *CATCH-22*

1. Barbara Gelb, 'Catching Joseph Heller', *New York Times Magazine*, 4 Mar. 1979, p. 51. Many of my biographical details are taken from this article.
2. Deborah Dash Moore, *At Home in America: Second Generation New York Jews* (New York: Columbia University Press, 1981) p. 80.
3. 'South Bank Show' BBC Television, 1984; Philip Roth, *Reading Myself and Others* (Harmondsworth: Penguin, 1985) pp. 125–6.
4. 'South Bank Show'.
5. Moore, p. 98.
6. Peter Lennon, 'Heller's New Gospel', *The Times*, 9 Nov. 1984, p. 10.
7. *New York City* by the Editors of *Look* (Boston: Houghton Mifflin, 1956) p. 279.
8. Leo Rosten, *Under the Boardwalk* (New York: Grove Press, 1970) p. 51.
9. Rosten, *Under the Boardwalk*, p. 6.
10. Charles Ruas, *Conversations with American Writers* (New York: Alfred A. Knopf, 1985) p. 145.
11. On the cover of the 1970 Grove Press edition of the novel.
12. 'Coney Island: The Fun Is Over', *Show* vol. 2 (July 1962) p. 51.
13. Richard Lehan and Jerry Patch, *'Catch-22*: The Making of a Novel', in James Nagel (ed.), *Critical Essays on 'Catch-22'* (Encino and Belmont, Cal.: Dickenson, 1974) pp. 39–40.
14. 'Joseph Heller', in George Plimpton (ed.), *Writers at Work: The 'Paris Review' Interviews 5th Series* (London: Secker & Warburg, 1981) p. 247.
15. *Writers at Work*, p. 233.
16. Ruas, p. 151.
17. *'Catch-22* Revisited', in F. Kiley and W. McDonald (eds), *A 'Catch-22' Casebook* (New York: Thomas Y. Crowell, 1973) p. 321.
18. Letter from Daphne Dorman, 14 Apr. 1986.

19. Dale Gold, 'Portrait of a Man Reading', *Washington Post Book World*, 27 July 1969, p. 2.
20. Letter from Edward J. Bloustein, 30 July 1986.
21. Bernard Oldsey, 'Another Joe from Brooklyn: Heller in Happy Valley', *Town & Gown*, Nov. 1984, p. 26.
22. Josh Greenfeld, '22 was funnier than 14', *Casebook*, p. 252.
23. Paul Krassner, 'An Impolite Interview with Joseph Heller', in *The Best of 'The Realist'* (Philadelphia: Running Press, 1984) p. 78. This interview is also reprinted in the *Casebook*, but in a slightly abbreviated form.
24. Greenfeld, p. 253.
25. Ruas, p. 130.
26. '*Catch-22* Author Now Has to Catch 10', *San Juan Star Magazine*, 19 Apr. 1964, p. 5; 'The Cruelest Taskmaster Of All', *Forbes*, 15 June 1975.
27. Caroline Moorehead, 'Writing novels slowly but with hardly a catch', *The Times*, 17 Oct. 1975, p. 10.
28. Ann Waldron, 'Writing technique can be taught, says Joseph Heller', *Houston Chronicle*, 2 Mar. 1975, p. 2. In connection with his course Baudin published *Edgar Allan Poe and others: representative short stories of the nineteenth century* (1953). It was the stories which Baudin commended that Heller submitted for publication.
29. 'Playboy Interview: Joseph Heller', *Playboy*, vol. 22 (June 1975) p. 68.
30. 'I Don't Love You Anymore', *Story*, vol. 28 (Sept./Oct. 1945) p. 40.
31. In the Brandeis University Heller collection.
32. Letter from Candida Donadio to Whit Burnett, 11 Oct. 1963. Princeton.
33. Letter to Heller from Whit Burnett, 22 Aug. 1946. Princeton.
34. Letter from Heller to Whit Burnett, 22 Nov. 1962. Princeton.
35. James Jones, *The Ice-Cream Headache and Other Stories* (New York: Dell, 1970) p. 1.
36. 'Girl from Greenwich', *Esquire*, vol. 29 (1948) pp. 40–1, 142–3.
37. 'Nothing to be done', *Esquire*, vol. 30 (1948) pp. 73, 129–30.
38. 'A Man Named Flute', *Atlantic Monthly*, vol. 182 (Aug. 1948) pp. 66–70.
39. Ruas, p. 148.
40. 'Bookies, Beware!', *Esquire*, vol. 27 (1947) p. 90.
41. 'Castle of Snow', *Atlantic Monthly*, vol. 101 (Mar. 1948) pp. 52–5.
42. Nelson Algren, 'The Catch', in *Casebook*, p. 4.
43. 'MacAdam's Log', *Gentlemen's Quarterly*, vol. 29 (Dec. 1959) p. 169.

CHAPTER 2: *CATCH-22*

1. In a letter of 1963 to the National Institute of Arts and Letters written in connection with a grant Heller was subsequently awarded (archives of American Academy and Institute of Arts and Letters, New York City).
2. Nelson Algren's review is collected in the *Casebook*. In 1961 Heller's

literary agent was also acting for Thomas Pynchon and sent him a copy of *Catch-22*. The result was a brief but very enthusiastic letter from Pynchon which is among the correspondence in the Heller collection at Brandeis University. Balliett's review is in the *New Yorker*, 9 Dec. 1961, p. 248.

3.   Bob Azurdia, 'The Azurdia Interview: Joseph Heller', BBC Radio Merseyside, 1986.
4.   *Writers at Work*, p. 236; Thomson Prentice, 'Author who was nearly written off', *The Times* 19 Nov. 1985, p. 14a.
5.   James Nagel, 'Two Brief Manuscript Sketches: Heller's *Catch-22*', *Modern Fiction Studies*, vol. 20 (1974) p. 222.
6.   Alden Whitman, 'Something always happens on the way to the office: An interview with Joseph Heller', in M. J. Bruccoli (ed.) *Pages: The World of Books, Writers, and Writing*, vol. 1 (Detroit: Gale, 1976) p. 80.
7.   Richard B. Sale, 'An Interview in New York with Joseph Heller', *Studies in the Novel*, vol. 4 (1972) pp. 63–4.
8.   Vance Ramsey, 'From Here To Absurdity: Heller's *Catch-22*', in *Casebook*, p. 225.
9.   *Catch-22* (London: Jonathan Cape, 1963) p. 70. Subsequent page references in text.
10. Ruas, p. 150.
11. John W. Aldridge, 'The Loony Horror of It All – *Catch-22* Turns 25', *New York Times Book Review*, 26 Sept. 1986, p. 3.
12. Krassner, p. 78.
13. Tony Tanner, *City of Words: A Study of American Fiction in the Mid-Twentieth Century* (London: Jonathan Cape, 1979) p. 77.
14. Within these analogies General Dreedle could be compared with the Queen of Hearts.
15. Gelb, p. 54.
16. Sale, p. 73.
17. Walter Nash, *The Language of Humour* (London: Longman, 1985) p. 110.
18. Krassner, p. 79.
19. For an extended comparison beween the Genesis story and *Catch-22* v. Marcus K. Billson III, 'The Un-Minderbinding of Yossarian: Genesis Inverted in *Catch-22*', *Arizona Quarterly*, vol. 36 (1980) pp. 315–29.
20. 'Joseph Heller in Conversation with Martin Amis', *The New Review*, vol. 2 (1975) no. 20, p. 56.
21. Sale, p. 73.
22. Revised partly for copyright reasons and published separately in *Playboy* (Dec. 1969) and reprinted in the *Casebook* (pp. 309–16). The correspondence relating to this piece is deposited in the Harry Ransom Humanities Research Center, University of Texas at Austin.
23. Martin Gardner (ed.), *The Annotated Alice* (Harmondsworth: Penguin, 1977) p. 263.
24. 'Mel Brooks Meets Joseph Heller,' *Washington Post Book World*, 19

Mar. 1979, F4. Heller states: 'For many of those chapters, particularly the last 30 or 40, there is nothing significant about the
headings'.

25.   Roger H. Smith, 'Review', in J. Nagel, *Critical Essays on 'Catch-22'*,
       p. 31.
26.   Ruas, p. 172.
27.   Lieutenant Scheisskopf is compared to a manic Lear at one point in
       the novel.
28.   Ruas, p. 152.
29.   'Middle-Aged Innocence', *The Nation*, vol. 194, 20 Jan., 1962, pp. 62–3.
30.   'The Heller Cult', in *Casebook*, p. 24.
31.   Krassner, p. 76; Sale, p. 69.
32.   Jesse Ritter, 'Fearful Comedy: *Catch-22* as Avatar of the Social
       Surrealist Novel', in *Casebook*, pp. 73–86.
33.   Jan Solomon, 'The Structure of Joseph Heller's *Catch-22*'; Doug
       Gaukroger, 'Time Structure in *Catch-22*'; in *Casebook*, pp. 122–32 and
       132–44 respectively.
34.   Howard J. Stark, 'The Anatomy of Catch-22', *Casebook*, pp. 145–58;
       James M. McDonald, 'I See Everything Twice! The Structure of
       Joseph Heller's *Catch-22*', in *Casebook*, p. 105; Robert Protherough,
       'The Sanity of *Catch-22*', in *Casebook*, p. 202; Smith, p. 25; Stephen
       W. Potts, *From Here To Absurdity: The Moral Battlefields of Joseph Heller*
       (San Bernardino, Cal.: Borgo Press, 1982) p. 8.
35.   Robert Merrill, *Joseph Heller* (Boston: Twayne, 1987) p. 38.
36.   Paul Ricoeur, 'Narrative Time', *Critical Inquiry*, vol. 7 (1980) p. 171.
37.   C. E. Reilly and Carol Villei, 'An Interview with Joseph Heller',
       Delaware Literary Review, Spring 1975, p. 21.
38.   Robert Merrill rightly cautions against the use of a term like 'flash-
       back' in this context (p. 39).
39.   An excellent discussion of narrative difficulty in this novel is given
       in Peter Brook's *Reading for the Plot. Design and Intention in Narrative*
       (Oxford: Clarendon Press, 1984) chap. 11.
40.   Sale, p. 69.
41.   Merrill, pp. 39, 48–9.
42.   The details in the novel correspond very closely to Heller's 37th
       mission to Avignon (Ken Barnard, 'Interview with Joseph Heller', in
       Casebook, pp. 297–8).
43.   James Nagel, 'The *Catch-22* Note Cards', in James Nagel (ed.),
       Critical Essays on Joseph Heller (Boston: G. K. Hall, 1984) p. 51. This
       article gives unique insights into the composition of the novel.
44.   Sale, p. 74.
45.   Minna Doskow, 'The Night Journey in *Catch-22*', *Critical Essays on
       'Catch-22'*, p. 162.
46.   Sale, p. 66.
47.   Josh Greenfeld, '22 Was Funnier Than 14', in *Casebook*, p. 254.
48.   'Joseph Heller in Conversation with Martin Amis', p. 59.
49.   Whitman, p. 80.
50.   Michael Kustow, 'Joseph Heller' video recording (London: 1CA,
       1985).

51. On these and other devices v. Jean Kennard, 'Joseph Heller: At War with Absurdity', in *Casebook*, pp. 255–69.
52. Gary W. Davis, '*Catch-22* and the Language of Discrutinuity', *Critical Essays on Joseph Heller*, p. 66.
53. Krassner, p. 80.
54. Caroline Gordon and Jeanne Richardson, 'Flies in Their Eyes? A Note on Joseph Heller's *Catch-22*', *Critical Essays on 'Catch-22'*, p. 120.
55. Ruas, p. 159.
56. *Casebook*, p. 295.
57. 'Catch-18', *New World Writing* (New York: New American Library, 1955) p. 208.
58. Krassner, pp. 79–80.
59. *Casebook*, p. 296.
60. Philip Roth, *Reading Myself and Others* (Harmondsworth: Penguin, 1985) p. 12.
61. Moorehead, p. 10.
62. In the course of this speech McCarthy accounted for the current decline in America's world status as follows: 'This must be the product of a great conspiracy, a conspiracy on a scale so immense as to dwarf any previous such venture in the history of man. A conspiracy of infamy so black that, when it is finally exposed, its principles shall be forever deserving of the maledictions of all honest men' (David Brion Davis (ed.), *The Fear of Conspiracy* (Ithaca, New York: Cornell University Press, 1971) p. 307).
63. MS letter, 13 Jan. 1969. Princeton.
64. Jack Anderson and Ronald W. May, *McCarthy: The Man, the Senator, the 'ism'* (Boston: Beacon Press, 1952) pp. 196–7.
65. Murray B. Levin, *Political Hysteria in America* (New York: Basic Books, 1971) p. 150.
66. Gold, p. 2.
67. Franz Kafka, *The Trial* (Harmondsworth: Penguin, 1955) p. 163.
68. Krassner, p. 77.
69. Richard Condon, *The Manchurian Candidate* (London: Michael Joseph, 1978) p. 96.
70. *Playboy* interview, pp. 63–4.
71. For excellent commentary on Milo v. Leon F. Seltzer, 'Milo's "Culpable Innocence"': Absurdity as Moral Insanity in *Catch-22*', *Critical Essays on Joseph Heller*, pp. 74–92.
72. Krassner, p. 77.
73. Elizabeth Sewell, 'The Nonsense System in Lewis Carroll's Work and in Today's World', in Edward Guiliano (ed.), *Lewis Carroll Observed: A Collection of Unpublished Photographs, Drawings, Poetry, and New Essays* (New York: Clarkson N. Potter, 1976) p. 65.

CHAPTER 3: THE PLAYS AND OTHER WRITINGS OF THE 1960S

1. Ruas, p. 149.
2. *Story*, Sept./Oct. 1945, p. 40.

3. Gold, p. 2.
4. Sale, p. 69.
5. Susan Braudy, 'Lauching All The Way To Truth', in *Critical Essays on Joseph Heller*, p. 219.
6. William A. Raidy, 'Meet Joseph Heller: Man Against War', *Long Island Press*, 6 Oct. 1968, p. 34.
7. Robert Brustein, *Making Scenes: A Personal History of the Turbulent Years at Yale, 1966–1979* (New York: Random House, 1981) p. 51.
8. Susan Braudy, ' "C'mon Joe," they would say to him. . .', *The New Journal*, 26 Nov. 1967, p. 7.
9. Israel Shenker, 'Did Heller Bomb On Broadway?' *New York Times*, 29 Dec. 1968, Section 2, p. D3.
10. Moorehead, p. 10.
11. *We Bombed in New Haven* (London: Jonathan Cape, 1969) p. 46. Subsequent page references in text.
12. *Epictetus* (transl. by W. A. Oldfather) vol. 11 (London: Heinemann, 1928) p. 497. I am grateful to my colleague John Pinsent for his help in identifying these quotations.
13. Linda McJ. Micheli, 'In No-Man's Land: The Plays of Joseph Heller' in *Critical Essays on Joseph Heller*, p. 238.
14. Elenore Lester, 'Playwright-in-Anguish', in *Critical Essays on Joseph Heller*, p. 206.
15. *Critical Essays on Joseph Heller*, p. 208.
16. Potts, p. 28.
17. Heller's first draft for the play contained Falstaff's interrogation of the notion of honour in Henry IV Part 1 (Act V.i) (*Critical Essays on Joseph Heller*, p. 220).
18. Gold, p. 2.
19. Potts, p. 27.
20. Shenker, p. D3.
21. George H. Jensen, 'The Theatre and the Publishing House: Joseph Heller's *We Bombed in New Haven*', *Proof* 5 (1977) p. 197.
22. *Playboy* interview, p. 72.
23. Merrill, p. 66.
24. *Critical Essays on Joseph Heller*, p. 240.
25. *Catch-22: A Dramatization* (New York: Delacorte Press, 1973) p. xx.
26. *Catch-22: A Dramatization*, p. xiv.
27. *Playboy* interview, p. 64.
28. Helen Rothhardt, 'That Play Discussed By Author', *Philadelphia Enquirer*, 11 Sept. 1968, p. 51.
29. 'This is Called National Defense', *New York Times*, 24 Nov. 1975, p. 35.
30. 'Letters', *New York Times Magazine*, 12 Mar. 1967, Sect. I, pp. 12, 22.
31. Don Rubin, '*Catch-22* Author Hopes He Won't Bomb in New Haven', *New Haven Register*, 26 Nov. 1967, Sect. 4, p. 1.
32. Shenker, p. D3; cf. Doris Kearns, *Lyndon Johnson and the American Dream* (London: Andre Deutsch, 1976): 'A majority of people believed he regularly lied to them', p. 337.
33. Cecil Woolf and John Bagguley (eds), *Authors Take Sides On Vietnam* (London: Peter Owen, 1967) p. 29.

34. Israel Shenker, 'Joseph Heller Draws Dead Bead on the Politics of Gloom', *New York Times*, 10 Sept. 1968, p. 49.

35. Richard Witkin, 'Antiwar Slate to Oppose Johnson in State Primary', *New York Times*, 21 Sept. 1967, pp. 32–3.

36. Bro. Alexis Gonzales, 'Notes on the Next Novel: An Interview with Joseph Heller', *New Orleans Review*, vol. 2. iii (1971) p. 218.

37. The best account of these revisions has been given by George H. Jensen (v. above note 19).

38. *Critical Essays on Joseph Heller*, p. 206.

39. Sale, p. 71.

40. *Catch-22: A Dramatization*, pp. xii–xiii.

41. *Catch-22: A Dramatization* (London and New York: Samuel French, 1971) p. 6.

42. Merrill, pp. 70–1; *Critical Essays on Joseph Heller*, pp. 235–6.

43. *Playboy* interview, p. 64.

44. *Clevinger's Trial (from 'Catch-22'): A Play in One Act* (London and New York: Samuel French, 1973) p. 6. One significant addition in the dramatisation is an explanation of the allusion in the novel to the boxer Billy Petrolle.

45. Oldsey, p. 30.

46. Al Dinhofer, '*Catch-22* Author Now Has To Catch 10', *San Juan Star Magazine*, 19 Apr. 1964, p. 5.

47. Oldsey, p. 32.

48. 'How I found James Bond, lost my self-respect and almost made $150 000 in my spare time', *Holiday*, vol. 41 (June 1967) p. 123.

49. J. Rawson Lumby (ed.), *Bacon's History Of the Reign of King Henry VII* (Cambridge: Cambridge University Press, 1902) p. 93.

50. 'How I found James Bond', p. 125.

51. Rubin, pp. 1, 7.

52. Gonzales, p. 219.

53. 'On Translating *Catch-22* into a Movie', in *Casebook*, p. 359.

54. *Casebook*, p. 299.

55. 'Irving is everywhere', *Show* vol. 3 (April 1963) p. 104.

56. 'Irving is everywhere', p. 105.

57. 'Irving is everywhere', p. 105.

CHAPTER 4: *SOMETHING HAPPENED*

1. William T. Keough, '*Something Happened* After *Catch-22*', *Philadelphia Evening Bulletin*, 3 Oct. 1974, p. 8. Heller has also given 1964 as the date when he started work on the novel. As with *Catch-22* substantial editorial work was done on Heller's manuscript for *Something Happened* by Bob Gottlieb who reportedly reorganised the last chapter, suggested a new opening, and who found a 'method for organizing the material to give structure' (Israel Shenker, '2nd Heller Book Due 13 Years After First', *New York Times*, 18 Feb. 1974, p. 30). The full extent of these editorial changes has yet to emerge.

2. James Shapiro, 'Work in Progress/Joseph Heller', *Intellectual Digest*, vol. II (1971) p. 6.

3. 'Something Happened' was published in *Esquire* in September 1966; *Something Happened* (London: Jonathan Cape, 1974) p. 427. Subsequent page references in text.

4. Sloan Wilson, *The Man in the Grey Flannel Suit* (London: Reprint Society, 1957) p. 30. In Chapter 3 of this novel when Rath is applying for a new job he is asked to produce a biographical résumé concluding 'the most significant fact about me is. . .' In the event he decides not to play the game and writes that the most significant thing is his job application. In 1955 Heller applied for a job at Simon and Schuster where he was asked to perform the same task. His conclusion to 'the most significant thing about myself' was 'that there *is* no *most* significant thing about myself' (MS, Columbia University). This collection also includes a proposal by Heller for promoting the sales of Dr Smiley Blanton's book *Love or Perish*.

5. William H. Whyte, *The Organization Man* (Harmondsworth: Penguin, 1960) p. 158.

6. Elizabeth Long, *The American Dream and the Popular Novel* (London: Routledge & Kegan Paul, 1985) p. 122.

7. Kurt Vonnegut, '*Something Happened*', in *Critical Essays on Joseph Heller*, p. 95.

8. Ann Waldron, 'Writing technique can be taught, says Joseph Heller', *Houston Chronicle*, 2 Mar. 1975, p. 2.

9. Braudy, ' "C'mon, Joe" ', p. 9; Joseph Heller and Speed Vogel, *No Laughing Matter* (London: Cape, 1986) p. 158.

10. MS letter of June 24, 1955. Columbia.

11. Cf. Nicholas Canaday, 'Joseph Heller: Something Happened to the American Dream', in *Critical Essays on Joseph Heller*, p. 105.

12. Long, p. 121.

13. '*Something Happened*', p. 140. Satirical details such as these make it clear that Slocum is far from being the philistine stereotype described in Emily Stipes Watts' *The Businessman in American Literature* (1982). Astonishingly Watts hardly mentions Heller's fiction in her study.

14. Ernest Becker, *The Denial of Death* (N.Y.: Basic Books, 1973) p. 217.

15. Valerie Singleton, interview with Heller, 'Midweek' BBC Radio 4, 14 May 1980.

16. 'From Sea to Shining Sea, Junk' was published in the *New York Times*, 30 Sept. 1974, p. 37.

17. 'Playboy Interview: Mel Brooks', *Playboy*, Feb. 1975, p. 54. For more details on the Gourmet Club see Chapter 7.

18. James M. Mellard, '*Something Happened*: The Imaginary, the Symbolic, and the Discourse of the family', in *Critical Essays on Joseph Heller*, p. 143.

19. Robert Merrill accordingly suggests (p. 94) that Heller's multifaceted portrait of Slocum demands an excess of detail by the very nature of his method.

20. *Writers at Work*, p. 238.

21. Sale, p. 68.

22. Patricia Merivale, ' "One Endless Round": *Something Happened* and

the Purgatorial Novel', *English Studies in Canada*, vol. 2. iv (1985) pp. 438–49.

23. Fyodor Dostoievsky, *White Nights* (transl. by Constance Garnett) (London: Macmillan, 1950) pp. 57–8.
24. Richard Hauer Costa, 'Notes from a Dark Heller: Bob Slocum and the Underground Man', *Texas Studies in Literature and Language*, vol. 23. ii (Summer 1981) pp. 166–7.
25. Sigmund Freud, *Introductory Lectures on Psychoanalysis* (Harmondsworth: Penguin, 1973) p. 189.
26. Walker Percy, 'The State of the Novel: Dying Art or New Science?' *Michigan Quarterly Review*, vol. 16. iv (1977) pp. 364–5.
27. Philip Roth, *Portnoy's Complaint* (London: Cape, 1969) p. 111.
28. Robert Robinson, 'Thirteen years after *Catch-22* – an interview with Joseph Heller', *The Listener*, 24 Oct. 1972, p. 550.
29. Kenneth Tynan, 'Profiles: Frolics and Detours of a Short Hebrew Man,' *New Yorker*, 30 Oct. 1972, p. 104.
30. *Critical Essays on Joseph Heller*, p. 94.
31. Thomas LeClair, 'Joseph Heller, *Something Happened*, and the Art of Excess,' in *Critical Essays on Joseph Heller*, p. 118.
32. Larry Swindell, 'What Happened to Heller after *Catch-22*?', *Philadelphia Enquirer*, 22 Sept. 1974, G10.
33. Roth, *Reading Myself*, p. 19.
34. *Writers at Work*, p. 242.
35. Joan DelFattore, 'The Dark Stranger in Heller's *Something Happened*,' in *Critical Essays on Joseph Heller*, pp. 128–9.
36. Robinson, p. 550; Singleton interview.
37. Christopher Lasch, *The Culture of Narcissism: American Life in an Age of Diminishing Expectations* (London: Abacus, 1980) p. 38.
38. *The Inferno*, Canto 33.
39. Ruas, p. 159.
40. Frederick R. Karl, *American Fictions 1940–1980* (New York: Harper & Row, 1983) p. 492.
41. *Writers at Work*, p. 237.
42. Lasch, p. 307.
43. Susan Strehle Klemtner, ' "A Permanent Game of Excuses": Determinism in Heller's *Something Happened*', in *Critical Essays on Joseph Heller*, p. 110; George J. Searles, '*Something Happened*: A New Direction for Joseph Heller,' *Critique*, vol. 18. iii (1977) p. 77.
44. 'PW Interviews: Joseph Heller', *Publishers Weekly*, 30 Sept. 1974.
45. Robert Merrill (pp. 87–8) compares Slocum's narrative with that of Jason Compson in *The Sound and the Fury*.
46. LeClair (p. 257 and passim) argues similarly that Slocum's mechanistic search for original causes is doomed to failure. By this argument he is the victim of his own narrow assumptions about reality rather than of Heller's ironies.
47. Amis interview, p. 59.
48. Ruas, p. 160.
49. Stephen A. Shapiro, 'The Ambivalent Animal: Man in the Contemporary British and American Novel', *Centennial Review*, vol. 12 (1968) pp. 1, 2.

50. In *Good as Gold*, Sect. IV, chap 5 a reference is made to the following passage from Becker: 'the foot is the absolute and unmitigated testimonial to our animality, to the incongruity between our proud, rich, lively, infinitely transcendent, free inner spirit and our earthbound body' (p. 237). In his *Paris Review* interview Heller briefly discusses Slocum's attitude of 'denial' towards his brain-damaged child (in *Writers at Work*, p. 141).

51. Lindsey Tucker, 'Entropy and Information Theory in Heller's *Something Happened*', *Contemporary Literature*, vol. 25. iii (1984) pp. 323–40.

52. H. W. Fowler and F. G. Fowler, *The King's English* (Oxford: Clarendon Press, 1958) p. 279.

53. 'Work in Progress', p. 8.

54. Amis interview, p. 56.

55. Reilly and Villei, p. 20.

56. One of the best explanations of Slocum's substitution, transference, etc. is given by James M. Mellard (v. note 18 above).

57. Sale, p. 71.

58. Richard Pearce, 'Enter the Frame' in Raymond Federman (ed.), *Surfiction* (Chicago: Swallow Press, 1975) p. 48.

59. Ruas, p. 161.

CHAPTER 5: *GOOD AS GOLD*

1. Gonzales, p. 219.

2. Malcolm Bradbury, *The Modern American Novel* (Oxford: Oxford University Press, 1984) p. 159.

3. Pearl K. Bell, 'Heller and Malamud, Then and Now', *Commentary*, vol. 67 (1979) p. 72.

4. Singleton interview.

5. *Good as Gold* (London: Cape, 1979) p. 84. Subsequent page references in text.

6. John W. Aldridge, 'The Deceits of Black Humor', in *Critical Essays on Joseph Heller*, p. 162.

7. Charlie Reilly, 'Talking with Joseph Heller', in *Critical Essays on Joseph Heller*, p. 177.

8. *Critical Essays on Joseph Heller*, p. 178.

9. Wayne C. Miller, 'Ethnic Identity as Moral Focus. A Reading of Joseph Heller's *Good as Gold*' in *Critical Essays on Joseph Heller*, p. 184. Robert Merrill also gives a positive reading of Gold's family, arguing that they are depicted realistically (p. 104).

10. Leonard Michaels, 'Bruce Gold's American Experience', in *Critical Essays on Joseph Heller*, pp. 168–9.

11 Potts, p. 55.

12. Melvin J. Friedman, 'Something Jewish Happened: Some Thoughts About Joseph Heller's *Good as Gold*', in *Critical Essays on Joseph Heller*, p. 197.

13. Kustow interview.

14. 'Joseph Heller on America's "Inhuman Callousness"', *U.S. News & World Report*, 4 Sept. 1979, p. 73.
15. Rudith Ruderman, 'Upside-Down in *Good as Gold*: Moishe Kapoyer As Muse,' *Yiddish*, vol. 5. iv (1984) p. 57.
16. Heller quoted in Tynan, p. 104.
17. Nash, p. 120.
18. *Playboy* interview, p. 65.
19. 'Moths at a Dark Bulb', *New York Times*, 24 May 1976, p. 29. At that point Heller was not certain whether the scene would be included in the novel.
20. Helen Thomas, *Dateline: White House* (New York: Macmillan, 1975) p. 130.
21. *Catch-22: A Dramatization* (Delacorte Press) p. xviii.
22. Joseph C. Spear, *Presidents and the Press: The Nixon Legacy* (Cambridge, Mass.: MIT, 1984) p. 75.
23. John Pierson, 'Nixon and the Press', *Wall St. Journal*, 29 Dec. 1969, pp. 1, 14.
24. Moorehead, p. 10.
25. Lennon, p. 10.
26. *Critical Essays on Joseph Heller*, p. 180.
27. Singleton interview.
28. Marvin Kalb and Bernard Kalb, *Kissinger* (London: Hutchinson, 1974).
29. Ruderman, pp. 55, 59.
30. Singleton interview.
31. Chet Flippo, 'Checking in with Joseph Heller', *Rolling Stone*, 16 Apr. 1981, p. 52.
32. Swindell, G10.
33. Quoted in Charles Berryman, 'Heller's Gold', *Chicago Review*, vol. 32. iv (1981) p. 114.
34. 'Mel Brooks Meets Joseph Heller', F4.
35. *Critical Essays on Joseph Heller*, pp. 178–9.
36. 'Mel Brooks Meets Joseph Heller', F4.
37. Flippo, p. 52.
38. Rita Christopher, 'On the train from Wilmington', *Macleans*, vol. 92, 16 Apr. 1979, p. 46.
39. Sam B. Girgus, *The New Covenant: Jewish Writers and the American Idea* (Chapel Hill: University of N. Carolina Press, 1984) p. 20.
40. 'Mel Brooks Meets Joseph Heller', F4.
41. Peter S. Prescott, *Never in Doubt: Critical Essays on American Books, 1972–1985* (New York: Arbor House, 1986) p. 63.

CHAPTER 6: *GOD KNOWS*

1. A. Alvarez, 'Working in the Dark', *New York Review of Books*, 11 Apr. 1985, p. 17; Peter Kemp, 'Biceps baroque', *The Listener*, 22 Nov. 1984, p. 29; Joel Wells, 'A psaltery of one liners', *Commonweal*, vol. 111 (1984) p. 562.

2. Roger Kaplan, 'Heller's Last Gag', *Commentary*, vol. 79 (Feb. 1985) p. 61; Leon Wieseltier, 'Shlock of Recognition', *New Republic*, 29 Oct. 1984, p. 33.

3. Mordecai Richler, 'He Who Laughs Last', *New York Times Book Review*, 23 Sept. 1984, pp. 1, 36.

4. 'South Bank Show'.

5. *Writers at Work*, p. 248.

6. *Casebook*, p. 314.

7. Shenker, 'Joseph Heller Draws Dead Bead', p. 49; Rothbardt, p. 51.

8. Gary Houston, 'Joseph Heller: A novelist who knows he cannot be rushed', *Chicago Sunday Sun-Times*, vol. 111, (1974) p. 1.

9. Sholem Asch, *From Many Countries* (London: Macdonald, 1958) p. ix.

10. *Portnoy's Complaint*, p. 8.

11. Herbert Gold, *Fathers* (London: Secker & Warburg, 1967) p. 232.

12. *Fathers*, pp. 203–4.

13. Philip Toynbee, 'Fathers and Sons', *New Republic*, 17 June 1967, p. 21.

14. Harold Fisch, 'Fathers, Mothers, Sons and Lovers: Jewish and Gentile Patterns in Literature', *Midstream*, vol. 18. iii (1972) p. 40.

15. 'Humor and the Ability', p. 71.

16. *God Knows* (London: Jonathan Cape, 1984) p. 127. Subsequent page references incorporated into text.

17. Richler, p. 36.

18. William Smith, *A Dictionary of the Bible*, vol. 1 (London: John Murray, 1860) p. 411.

19. 'South Bank Show'.

20. Heller comments on the 'almost obscenely erotic' vocabulary of the Song of Songs in Ruas, p. 166.

21. Cathleen Medwick, 'Man bites God', *Vogue*, vol. 174 (Oct. 1984) p. 701.

22. Ruas, p. 167.

23. Otto Rank, *Beyond Psychology* (New York: Dover, 1958) p. 151.

24. 'South Bank Show'.

25. 'South Bank Show'.

26. Ruas, p. 167.

27. 'The Azurdia Interview'. Joe Stein, the author of *Fiddler on the Roof*, is a personal friend of Heller.

28. Clive Sinclair interview with Heller, *Jewish Chronicle*, 16 Nov. 1984, p. 12.

29. Ruas, p. 161.

30. Sholem Asch, *Mary* (New York: Carroll & Graf, 1985) p. 1.

31. Medwick, p. 702.

32. 'Tevye wins a Fortune' is collected in *The Old Country*.

33. Robert Alter, 'Jewish Humor and the Domestication of Myth', in Sarah Blacher Cohen (ed.), *Jewish Wry: Essays on Jewish Humor* (Bloomington: Indiana University Press, 1987) p. 26.

34. Cf. Meredith G. Kline, *The Structure of Biblical Authority* (Grand Rapids, Michigan: Eerdmans, 1972): 'In terms of its edificatory

purpose, covenantal canon may be thought of as the architectural
model for God's sanctuary-residence' (p. 85).

35. Ruas, p. 166.
36. 'Fiction: The personal dimension', in Elizabeth Janeway (ed.), *The Writer's World* (New York: McGraw-Hill, 1969) p. 143.
37. Heller subsequently wove an almost identical comment on Samson into *God Knows*.
38. Merrill, pp. 114, 119.
39. Ian Robinson, *The Survival of English* (Cambridge: Cambridge University Press, 1973) p. 26.
40. Medwick, p. 702.
41. *Writers at Work*, p. 240.
42. Kline, pp. 64, 65, 66.
43. Kline, p. 66.

CHAPTER 7: THE STORY OF AN ILLNESS

1. Ruas, p. 178.
2. *No Laughing Matter* (New York: Putnam; London: Cape, 1986) p. 133. Subsequent page references in text.
3. Dr Jay I. Meltzer, 'Long Island Books', *East Hampton Star*, vol. II, 3 July 1986, pp. 19, 22.
4. William Goldstein, 'Joe and Speed Spend a Summer Day Laughing About *No Laughing Matter*', *Publishers Weekly*, 1 Nov. 1985, p. 33.
5. Norman Cousins, *Anatomy of an Illness as Perceived by the Patient: Reflections on Healing and Regeneration* (New York: Norton, 1979) p. 56.
6. Rob Buckman, 'Images of illness', *The Sunday Times*, 7 Oct. 1986, p. 48.
7. 'Helping a Convalescent Friend (in style)', *New York Times*, 28 July 1982, C16; Goldstein, p. 32.
8. Anthony Burgess, 'With a Lot of Help From His Friends', *New York Times Book Review*, 16 Feb. 1986, p. 8.
9. 'In the Hospital: Crisis and Recovery', *McCalls* (Aug. 1986) p. 86.
10. 'In the Hospital', p. 92.

CHAPTER 8: *PICTURE THIS*

1. 'In the Hospital: Crisis and Recovery,' *McCalls* (August, 1986) pp. 85–92. Heller's article introduces an edited excerpt from *No Laughing Matter* and is followed by short pieces by Speed Vogel and Valerie Humphries
2. 'Oslo: Meet Me at the Cafe', *New York Times* (17 March 1985) VI: pp. 38, 121–2.
3. 'In the Hospital' p.92; 'Heller Unbound', *U.S. News & World Report* (13 October 1986) p. 68.
4. 'Heller Unbound', p. 68

5.   Jakob Rosenberg, *Rembrandt: Life and Work*, revised ed. (London: Phaidon Press, 1964) p. 3.

6.   Gary Schwartz, *Rembrandt: His Life, His Paintings* (New York: Viking Press, 1985) p. 79.

7.   *Picture This* (New York: G. P. Putnam's and London: Macmillan, 1988) pp. 107, 110, 118. Subsequent page references in text.

8.   Simon Schama, *The Embarrassment of Riches* (London: Collins, 1987) p. 165. Heller's other main source on Rembrandt's social context was Paul Zumthor's *Daily Life in Rembrandt's Holland*.

9.   Schwartz pp. 107, 110, 112–16.

10. Schama pp.351–62.

11. John Lothrop Motley, *The Rise of the Dutch Republic* (London: Routledge, 1897) p. 897.

12. C. R. Boxer, *The Dutch Seaborne Empire 1600–1800* (London: Hutchinson, 1977) p.99. The standard study of the Anglo-Dutch wars (v. chapter 14) is Charles Wilson's *Profit and Power* (1957).

13. Aristotle, 'Poetics', translated by Ingram Bywater, in *The Basic Works of Aristotle*, ed. by Richard McKeon (New York: Random House, 1941) p. 1470.

14. Humphry House, *Aristotle's Poetics* (London: Rupert Hart-Davis, 1964) p. 125.

15. Plato, *Phaedrus*, translated by W. C. Helmbold and W. G. Rabinowitz (New York: Bobbs-Merrill, 1956) p. 69.

16. Schwartz p. 170.

17. John Berger, *Ways of Seeing* (Harmondsworth: Penguin, 1976) p. 110.

18. 'Heller Unbound', p. 68.

19. Plutarch (Life of Pericles) suggests that Pericles was responsible for the war because of his grudge against the Megarians. Thucydides spreads the responsibility and declares: 'what made war inevitable was the growth of Athenian power and the fear which this caused in Sparta' (*The Peloponnesian War*, translated by Rex Warner [Harmondsworth: Penguin, 1974] p. 49). Heller follows the latter interpretation explicitly and implicitly by quoting long passages verbatim from Thucydides' account.

20. Heller has expressed his interest in Aristophanes' plays in, for instance, Gold, p. 2.

21. Heller's disgust at the Vietnam War (discussed in Chapter 3) resurfaces here when he sardonically quotes L. B. Johnson's statements of justification.

22. One of Heller's sources of information on the painting was Theodore Rousseau's 'Aristotle Contemplating the Bust of Homer', *Metropolitan Museum of Art Bulletin* 20 (1962) 149–56.

23. This passage puts together quotations from W. Hamilton's translation of *The Symposium* (Harmondsworth: Penguin, 1959) pp. 102, 103, 111.

24. The main translation of *Crito* used for this chapter is Hugh Tredennick's from his edition of *The Last Days of Socrates* (Harmondsworth: Penguin, 1964).

25. Chris Anderson, *Style as Argument: Contemporary American Nonfiction*

(Carbondale: Southern Illinois University Press, 1987) p. 2; Shelley Fisher Fishkin, *From Fact to Fiction: Journalism and Imaginative Writing in America* (Baltimore: Johns Hopkins University Press, 1985).

26. Stephen Fender, 'Ezra Pound and the Words Off the Page; Historical Allusions in Some American Long Poems', *Yearbook of English Studies* 8 (1978) 105.

27. Julian Barnes, *Flaubert's Parrot* (London: Pan, 1985) p. 90. I am grateful to Brian Nellist for drawing this novel to my attention.

28. Thucydides, p. 47

29. Another recent novel which Heller has also endorsed is George Mandels' narrative of sexual and civic violence in the Florida swamps, *Crocodile Blood* (1985).

Bibliography

WORKS BY HELLER (*CHRONOLOGICALLY LISTED*)

Books

Catch-22, 1961.
We Bombed in New Haven, 1968.
Catch-22: A Dramatization, 1971 (acting edition).
Catch-22: A Dramatization, 1973.
Clevinger's Trial (from 'Catch-22'): A Play in One Act, 1973.
Something Happened, 1974.
Good as Gold, 1979.
God Knows, 1984.
No Laughing Matter, 1986 (with Speed Vogel).
Picture This, 1988.

Stories

'I Don't Love You Any More', *Story*, vol. 27 (Sept.–Oct. 1945) pp. 40–4.
'Castle of Snow', *Atlantic Monthly*, vol. 171 (Mar. 1948) pp. 52–5.
'Girl from Greenwich', *Esquire*, vol. 29 (June 1948) pp. 40–1, 142–3.
'A Man Called Flute', *Atlantic Monthly*, vol. 172 (Aug. 1948) pp. 66–70.
'Nothing to Be Done', *Esquire*, vol. 30 (Aug. 1948) pp. 73, 129–30.
'McAdam's Log', *Gentlemen's Quarterly*, vol. 29 (Dec. 1959) pp. 112, 166–76, 178.
'World Full of Great Cities', in *Nelson Algren's Own Book of Lonesome Monsters* (New York: Lancer Books, 1962) pp. 7–19.

Excerpts, Articles, etc.

'Bookies, Beware!', *Esquire*, vol. 27 (May 1947) p. 98.
'Catch-18', *New World Writing*, vol. 7 (Apr. 1955) pp. 204–14.
'Middle-Aged Innocence', *The Nation*, vol. 194 (20 Jan. 1962) pp. 62–3.
'Coney Island: The Fun Is Over', *Show*, vol. 2 (July 1962) pp. 50–4, 102–3.
'Too Timid to Damn, Too Stingy to Applaud', *New Republic*, vol. 147 (30 July 1962) pp. 23–4, 26.
'Irving Is Everywhere', *Show*, vol. 3 (Apr. 1963) pp. 104–5, 126–7.
'Something Happened', *Esquire*, vol. 66 (Sept. 1966) pp. 136–41, 212–13.
'Letters', *New York Times Magazine* (12 Mar. 1967) Sect. I, pp. 12, 22.
'Catch-22 Revisited', *Holiday*, vol. 41 (Apr. 1967) pp. 44–61, 130, 141–2, 145 (reprinted in *Casebook*).
'How I Found James Bond, Lost My Self-Respect, and Almost Made $150 000 in My Spare Time', *Holiday*, vol. 41 (June 1967) pp. 123–5, 128, 130.

'Love, Dad', *Playboy* (Dec. 1969) pp. 181–2, 348 (reprinted in *A 'Catch-22' Casebook*).
'On Translating *Catch-22* into a Movie', in *A 'Catch-22' Casebook*, pp. 346–2.
'From Sea to Shining Sea, Junk', *New York Times*, 30 Sept. 1974, p. 35.
'This Is Called National Defense', *New York Times*, 24 Nov. 1975, p. 35.
'Moths at a Dark Bulb', *New York Times*, 24 May 1976, p. 29.
'Joseph Heller on America's "Inhuman Callousness",' *US News & World Report*, 4 Sept. 1979, p. 73.
'Humor and the Ability to Create It Cannot Be Taught,' *US News & World Report*, 12 Nov. 1984, p. 71.
'Oslo: Meet Me at the Cafe', *New York Times*, 17 Mar. 1985, VI: pp. 38, 121–2.
'Joseph Heller: The Road Back', *New York Times Magazine*, 12 Jan. 1986, pp. 30, 34, 36–7, 50, 52.
'In the Hospital: Crisis and Recovery', *McCalls* (Aug. 1986) pp. 85–92 (with Speed Vogel and Valerie Humphries).

WORKS ABOUT HELLER

Interviews

____ 'Fiction: The Personal Dimension', in *The Writer's World* (New York: McGraw-Hill, 1969) pp. 137–74.
____ 'Heller, in Sweden, Says Why He Likes Living in New York,' *New York Times*, 9 Nov. 1974, p. 22.
____ 'Joseph Heller in Conversation with Martin Amis,' *The New Review*, vol. 2. xx (1975) pp. 55–6, 58–9.
____ 'Mel Brooks Meets Joseph Heller', *Washington Post Book World*, 19 Mar. 1979, F1, 4.
____ 'So They Say: Guest Editors Interview Six Creative People,' *Mademoiselle*, vol. 57 (1963) pp. 234–5.
Bannon, Barbara A., 'PW Interviews; Joseph Heller,' *Publishers Weekly*, 30 Sept. 1974, p. 6.
Bragg, Melvyn, 'South Bank Show: Joseph Heller', BBC Television, 1984.
Braudy, Susan, ' "C'mon, Joe," they would say to him. . .', *The New Journal*, 26 Nov. 1967, pp. 7, 9–10.
Charles, Gerda, 'Catch 22 minus seven,' *Jewish Chronicle*, 6 June 1980, p. 10.
Flippo, Chet, 'Checking in with Joseph Heller,' *Rolling Stone*, 16 Apr. 1981, pp. 50–2, 57, 59–60.
Gold, Dale, 'Portrait of a Man Reading', *Washington Post Book World*, 27 July 1969, p. 2.
Gonzales, Bro. Alexis, 'Notes on the Next Novel: An Interview with Joseph Heller,' *New Orleans Review*, vol. 2. iii (1971) pp. 216–19.
Goodman, Walter, 'Heller Talks of Illness And King David Book,' *New York Times*, 24 Sept. 1984, C13.
Keough, William T., 'Something Happened After Catch-22,' *Philadelphia Evening Bulletin*, 3 Oct. 1974, pp. 8, 11.

Krassner, Paul, 'An Impolite Interview with Joseph Heller', in *The Best of The Realist'* (Philadelphia: Running Press, 1984) pp. 75–81 (reprinted in *Casebook*).

Kustow, Michael, 'Joseph Heller', video recording (London: ICA, 1985).

Lennon, Peter, 'Heller's New Gospel', *The Times*, 9 Nov. 1984, p. 10.

McFadden, Ian, 'Peddling Novels,' *The Times Educational Supplement (Scotland)*, 11 July 1980, p. 72.

Merrill, Sam, '*Playboy* Interview: Joseph Heller,' *Playboy* (June 1975) pp. 59–61, 64–6, 68, 70, 72–4, 76.

Moorehead, Caroline, 'Writing novels slowly but with hardly a catch,' *The Times*, 17 Oct. 1975, p. 10.

Plimpton, George (ed.), *Writers at Work: The 'Paris Review' Interviews 5th Series* (London: Secker & Warburg, 1981).

Raidy, William A., 'Meet Joseph Heller: Man Against War', *Long Island Press*, 6 Oct. 1968, p. 34.

Reilly, C. E., and Carol Villei, 'An Interview with Joseph Heller,' *Delaware Literary Review* (Spring 1975) pp. 19–21.

Robinson, Robert, 'Thirteen years after *Catch-22* – an interview with Joseph Heller,' *The Listener*, 24 Oct. 1972, p. 550.

Rothbardt, Helen, 'First Play Discussed by Author,' *Philadelphia Enquirer*, 11 Sept. 1968, p. 51.

Ruas, Charles, *Conversations with American Writers* (New York: Alfred A. Knopf, 1985).

Rubin, Don, '*Catch-22* Author Hopes He Won't Bomb in New Haven,' *New Haven Register*, 26 Nov. 1967, Section IV, pp. 1, 7.

Sale, Roger B., 'An Interview in New York with Joseph Heller,' *Studies in the Novel*, vol. 4 (1972) pp. 63–74.

Schnedler, Jack, '*Catch-22*'s Joe Heller: He's back after 13 years. . .,' *Chicago Daily News*, 5–6 Oct. 1974, p. 2.

Shapiro, James, 'Work in Progress/Joseph Heller,' *Intellectual Digest*, vol. II (1971) pp. 6, 8, 10–11.

Shenker, Israel, 'Did Heller Bomb on Broadway?' *New York Times*, 29 Dec. 1968, Section 2, D1, 3.

—— 'Joseph Heller Draws Dead Bead on the Politics of Gloom,' *New York Times*, 10 Sept. 1968, p. 49.

Sinclair, Clive, interview with Joseph Heller, *Jewish Chronicle*, 16 Nov. 1984, p. 12.

Singleton, Valerie, 'Midweek', BBC Radio 4, 14 May 1980.

Strafford, Peter, 'Mr. Heller catches the spirit of a generation,' *The Times*, 19 Oct. 1974, p. 12.

Swindell, Larry, 'What Happened to Heller after *Catch-22*?' *Philadelphia Enquirer*, 22 Sept. 1974, G1, 10.

Thorne, Creath, 'Joseph Heller: An Interview,' *Chicago Maroon Literary Review* vol. 3. i (3 Dec. 1974) pp. 1, 8.

Waldron, Ann, 'Writing technique can be taught, says Joseph Heller,' *Houston Chronicle*, 2 Mar. 1975, p. 2.

Weatherby, W. J., 'The Joy Catcher', *Guardian*, 20 Nov. 1962, p. 7.

Whitman, Alden, 'Something always happens on the way to the office: An interview with Joseph Heller,' in Bruccoli M. J. (ed.), *Pages: The*

World of Books, Writers, and Writing, vol. 1 (Detroit: Gale, 1976) pp. 74–81.

Criticism

_____ 'Heller Unbound,' *US News & World Report*, 13 Oct. 1986, p. 68.

_____ 'Pre-*Catch-22* Heller,' *New York Times*, 3 May, 1979, C16.

Aldridge, James W., 'The Loony Horror of It All — *Catch-22* Turns 25,' *New York Times Book Review*, 26 Sept. 1986, pp. 3, 55.

Alvarez, A., 'Working in the Dark,' *New York Review of Books*, 11 Apr. 1985, pp. 16–17.

Balliett, Whitney, review of *Catch-22*, *New Yorker*, 9 Dec. 1961, p. 248.

Bell, Pearl K., 'Heller and Malamud, Then and Now,' *Commentary*, vol. 67 (June 1979) pp. 71–5.

Bernard, Bina, 'The Author of *Catch-22* Brings Forth Another Novel,' *People*, 7 Oct. 1979, pp. 48–9.

Berryman, Charles, 'Heller's Gold,' *Chicago Review*, vol. 32. iv (1981) pp. 108–18.

Billson, Marcus K., III, 'The Un-Minderbinding of Yossarian: Genesis Inverted in *Catch-22*,' *Arizona Quarterly*, vol. 36 (1980) pp. 315–29.

Buckman, Rob, 'Images of Illness,' *The Sunday Times*, 7 Oct. 1986, p. 48.

Burgess, Anthony, 'With a Lot of Help From His Friends,' *New York Times Book Review*, 16 Feb. 1986, p. 8.

Christopher, Rita, 'On the train from Wilmington,' *Macleans*, vol. 92 (16 April 1979) p. 46.

Costa, Richard Hauer, 'Notes from a Dark Heller: Bob Slocum and Underground Man,' *Texas Studies in Literature and Language*, vol. 23. ii (Summer 1981) pp. 159–82.

Dinhofer, Al, '*Catch-22* Author Now Has To Catch 10', *San Juan Star Magazine*, 19 Apr. 1964, p. 5.

Gelb, Barbara, 'Catching Joseph Heller', *New York Times Magazine*, 4 Mar. 1979, pp. 14–16, 42, 44, 46, 48, 51–2, 54–5.

Goldstein, William, 'Joe and Speed Spend a Summer Day Laughing About *No Laughing Matter*', *Publishers Weekly*, 1 Nov. 1985, pp. 32–3.

Houston, Gary, 'Joseph Heller: A novelist who knows he cannot be rushed,' *Chicago Sunday Sun-Times*, 6 Oct. 1974, pp. 1, 8.

Jensen, George H., 'The Theatre and the Publishing House: Joseph Heller's *We Bombed in New Haven*', *Proof*, vol. 5 (1977) pp. 183–216.

Kaplan, Roger, 'Heller's Last Gag', *Commentary*, vol. 79 (February 1985) pp. 59–61.

Keegan, Brenda M., *Joseph Heller: A Reference Guide* (Boston: G. K. Hall, 1978).

Kemp, Peter, 'Biceps baroque,' *The Listener*, 22 Nov. 1984, p. 29.

Kiley, Frederick and Walter McDonald (eds), *A 'Catch-22' Casebook* (New York: Crowell, 1973).

Medwick, Cathleen, 'Man bites God,' *Vogue*, vol. 174 (October 1984) pp. 637, 701–2.

Meltzer, Dr Jay I., 'Long Island Books,' *East Hampton Star*, vol. II (3 July 1986) pp. 22, 19.

Merivale, Patricia, ' "One Endless Round": *Something Happened* and the Purgatorial Novel,' *English Studies in Canada*, vol. 2. iv (1985) pp. 438–49.

Merrill, Robert, *Joseph Heller* (Boston: Twayne, 1987).

Nagel, James, '*Catch-22* and Angry Humor: A Study of the Normative Values of Satire,' *Studies in American Humor*, vol. 1 (1974) pp. 99–106.

—— (ed.), *Critical Essays on 'Catch-22'* (Encino: Dickenson, 1974).

—— (ed.), *Critical Essays on Joseph Heller* (Boston: G. K. Hall, 1984).

—— 'Joseph Heller', in Martine, James J. (ed.), *Contemporary Authors Bibliographical Series: American Novelists*, vol. I (Detroit: Gale, 1986) pp. 193–218.

—— 'Two Brief Manuscript Sketches: Heller's *Catch-22*,' *Modern Fiction Studies*, vol. 20 (1974) pp. 221–4.

Oldsey, Bernard, 'Another Joe from Brooklyn: Heller in Happy Valley', *Town & Gown* (Nov. 1984) pp. 24–6, 28, 30, 32.

Potts, Stephen W., *From Here to Absurdity: The Moral Battlefields of Joseph Heller* (San Bernardino, Cal.: Borgo Press, 1982).

Prentice, Thomson, 'Author who was nearly written off,' *The Times*, 19 Nov. 1985, p. 14.

Richler, Mordecai, 'He Who Laughs Last,' *New York Times Book Review*, 23 Sept. 1984, pp. 1, 36.

Ruderman, 'Upside-Down in *Good as Gold*: Moishe Kapoyer as Muse,' *Yiddish*, vol. 5. iv (1984) pp. 55–63.

Scotto, Robert M. (ed.), '*Catch-22*': *A Critical Edition* (New York: Delta, 1973).

Searles, George J., 'Joseph Heller', in Walden, Daniel (ed.), *Twentieth-Century American-Jewish Fiction Writers*, Dictionary of Literary Biography, vol. 28 (Detroit: Gale, 1984) pp. 101–7.

—— '*Something Happened*: A New Direction for Joseph Heller,' *Critique*, vol. 18. iii (1977) pp. 74–82.

Shenker, Israel, '2nd Heller Book Due 13 Years After First,' *New York Times*, 18 Feb. 1974, Section I, p. 30.

Tucker, Lindsay, 'Entropy and Information Theory in Heller's *Something Happened*', *Contemporary Literature*, vol. 25. iii (1984) pp. 323–40.

Weixlmann, Joseph, 'A Bibliography of Joseph Heller's *Catch-22*,' *Bulletin of Bibliography*, vol. 31 (1974) pp. 32–7.

Wells, Joel, 'A psaltery of one liners', *Commonweal*, vol. 111 (19 October 1984) pp. 561–2.

Wieseltier, Leon, 'Schlock of Recognition,' *New Republic*, 29 Oct. 1984, pp. 31–3.

OTHER MATERIAL CONSULTED

—— '*Playboy* Interview: Mel Brooks', *Playboy* (Feb. 1975) pp. 47–9, 52–6, 60–6, 68.

Aleichem, Sholom, *The Old Country* (London: Andre Deutsch, 1958).

Anderson, Chris, *Style as Argument: Contemporary American Nonfiction* (Carbondale: Southern Illinois University Press, 1987).

Anderson, Jack and Ronald W. May, *McCarthy: The Man, the Senator, the 'ism'* (Boston: Beacon Press, 1952).

Asch, Sholem, *From Many Countries* (London: Macdonald, 1958).

—— *Mary* (New York: Carroll & Graf, 1985).

Barnes, Julian, *Flaubert's Parrot* (London: Pan, 1985).
Becker, Ernest, *The Denial of Death* (New York: Basic Books, 1973).
Berger, John, *Ways of Seeing* (Harmondsworth: Penguin, 1976).
Bloom, Harold, *The Anxiety of Influence* (New York: Oxford University Press, 1973).
Boxer, C. R., *The Dutch Seaborn Empire 1600–1800* (London: Hutchinson, 1977).
Bradbury, Malcolm, *The Modern American Novel* (Oxford University Press, 1984).
Brooks, Peter, *Reading for the Plot. Design and Intention in Narrative* (Oxford: Clarendon Press, 1984).
Brustein, Robert, *Making Scenes: A Personal History of the Turbulent Years at Yale, 1966–1979* (New York: Random House, 1981).
Cohen, Sarah Blacher (ed.), *Jewish Wry: Essays on Jewish Humor* (Bloomington: Indiana University Press, 1987).
Condon, Richard, *The Manchurian Candidate* (London: Michael Joseph, 1978).
Cousins, Norman, *Anatomy of an Illness as Perceived by the Patient: Reflections on Healing and Regeneration* (New York: Norton, 1979).
Davis, David Brion (ed.), *The Fear of Conspiracy* (Ithaca, New York: Cornell University Press, 1971).
Dostoievsky, Fyodor, *White Nights* (trans. by Constance Garnett) (London: Macmillan, 1950).
Federman, Raymond (ed.), *Surfiction* (Chicago: Swallow Press, 1975).
Fender, Stephen, 'Ezra Pound and the Words Off the Page: Historical Allusions in Some American Long Poems', *Yearbook of English Studies* 8 (1978), pp. 95–108.
Fisch, Harold, 'Fathers, Mothers, Sons and Lovers. Jewish and Gentile Patterns in Literature', *Midstream*, vol. 18. iii (March 1972) pp. 37–45.
Fishkin, Shelley Fisher, *From Fact to Fiction: Journalism and Imaginative Writing in America* (Baltimore: Johns Hopkins University Press, 1985).
Fowler, H. W. and F. G., *The King's English* (Oxford: Clarendon Press, 1958).
Freud, Sigmund, *Introductory Lectures on Psychoanalysis* (Harmondsworth: Penguin, 1973).
Gardner, Martin (ed.), *The Annotated Alice* (Harmondsworth: Penguin, 1977).
Girgus, Sam B., *The New Covenant. Jewish Writers and the American Idea* (Chapel Hill: University of North Carolina Press, 1984).
Giuliano, Edward (ed.), *Lewis Carroll Observed: A Collection of Unpublished Photographs, Drawings, Poetry, and New Essays* (New York: Clarkson N. Potter, 1976).
Gold, Herbert, *Fathers* (London: Secker & Warburg, 1967).
House, Humphry, *Aristotle's Poetics* (London: Rupert Hart-Davis, 1964).
Jones, James, *The Ice-Cream Headache and Other Stories* (New York: Dell, 1970).
Kafka, Franz, *The Trial* (Harmondsworth: Penguin, 1955).
Kalb, Marvin and Bernard, *Kissinger* (London: Hutchinson, 1974).
Karl, Frederick R., *American Fictions 1940–1980* (New York: Harper & Row, 1983).

Kearns, Doris, *Lyndon Johnson and the American Dream* (London: André Deutsch, 1976).
Kline, Meredith G., *The Structure of Biblical Authority* (Grand Rapids, Michigan: Eerdmans, 1972).
Lasch, Christopher, *The Culture of Narcissism: American Life in an Age of Diminishing Expectations* (London: Abacus, 1980).
Levin, Murray B., *Political Hysteria in America* (New York: Basic Books, 1971).
Long, Elizabeth, *The American Dream and the Popular Novel* (London: Routledge & Kegan Paul, 1985).
Look, editors of, *New York City* (Boston: Houghton Mifflin, 1956).
Lumby, J. Rawson (ed.), *Bacon's History of the Reign of King Henry VII* (Cambridge: Cambridge University Press, 1902).
McKeon, Richard (ed.), *The Basic Works of Aristotle* (New York: Random House, 1941).
Moore, Deborah Dash, *At Home in America: Second Generation New York Jews* (New York: Columbia University Press, 1981).
Nash, Walter, *The Language of Humour* (London: Longman, 1985).
Oldfather, W. A. (trans.), *Epictetus* (London: Heinemann, 1928).
Percy, Walker, 'The State of the Novel: Dying Art or New Science?' *Michigan Quarterly Review*, vol. 16. iv (1977) pp. 359–73.
Pierson, John, 'Nixon and the Press', *Wall St. Journal*, 29 Dec. 1969, pp. 1, 14.
Plato, *Phaedrus*, trans. W. C. Helmbold and W. G. Rabinowitz (New York: Bobbs–Merrill, 1956).
Plato, *The Last Days of Socrates*, trans. Hugh Tredennick (Harmondsworth: Penguin, 1964).
Plato, *The Symposium*, trans. W. Hamilton (Harmondsworth: Penguin, 1959).
Prescott, Peter S., *Never in Doubt: Critical Essays on American Books, 1972–1985* (New York: Arbor House, 1986).
Rank, Otto, *Beyond Psychology* (New York: Dover, 1958).
Ricoeur, Paul, 'Narrative Time', *Critical Inquiry*, vol. 7 (1980) pp. 169–90.
Robinson, Ian, *The Survival of English* (Cambridge University Press, 1973).
Rosenberg, Jakob, *Rembrandt: Life and Work*, rev. ed. (London: Phaidon Press, 1964).
Rosten, Leo, *Under the Boardwalk* (New York: Grove Press, 1970).
Roth, Philip, *Portnoy's Complaint* (London: Cape, 1969).
—— *Reading Myself and Others* (Harmondsworth, Penguin, 1985).
Rousseau, Theodore 'Adriano Contemplating the Bust of Homer', *Metropolitan Museum of Art Bulletin* 20 (1962) pp. 149–56.
Schama, Simon, *The Embarrassment of Riches* (London: Collins, 1987).
Schwartz, Gary, *Rembrandt: His Life, His Paintings* (New York: Viking Press, 1985).
Shapiro, Stephen A., 'The Ambivalent Animal: Man in the Contemporary British and American Novel', *Centennial Review*, vol. 12 (1968) pp. 1–22.
Siegel, Larry, '*Playboy* Interview: Mel Brooks,' *Playboy* (Oct. 1966) pp. 71–2, 76, 78, 80.
Smith, William, *A Dictionary of the Bible* (London: John Murray, 1860).

Spear, Joseph C., *Presidents and the Press: The Nixon Legacy* (Cambridge, Mass.: MIT, 1984).

Tanner, Tony, *City of Words: A Study of American Fiction in the Mid-Twentieth Century* (London: Cape, 1979).

Thomas, Helen, *Dateline: White House* (New York: Macmillan, 1975).

Thucydides, *The Peloponnesian War*, trans. Rex Warner (Harmondsworth: Penguin, 1974).

Toynbee, Philip, 'Fathers and Sons,' *New Republic*, 17 June 1967, pp. 21–2.

Tynan, Kenneth, 'Profiles: Frolics and Detours of a Short Hebrew Man,' *New Yorker*, 30 Oct. 1972, pp. 46–50, 53–4, 56, 58, 60, 65–6, 68, 73–4, 76–80, 82, 87–8, 90–4, 96, 101–2, 104–10, 112, 114–16, 119–30.

Vogel, Speed, 'Helping a Convalescent Friend (in Style),' *New York Times*, 28 July 1982, C16.

Watts, Emily Stipes, *The Businessman in American Literature* (Athens, Ga.: University of Georgia Press, 1982).

Whyte, William H., *The Organization Man* (Harmondsworth: Penguin, 1960).

Wilson, Sloan, *The Man in the Grey Flannel Suit* (London: Reprint Society, 1957).

Witkin, Richard, 'Antiwar Slate to Oppose Johnson in State Primary,' *New York Times*, 21 Sept. 1967, Section I, pp. 32–3.

Woolf, Cecil and John Bagguley (eds), *Authors Take Sides on Vietnam* (London: Peter Owen, 1967).

Yacowar, Maurice, *The Comic Art of Mel Brooks* (London: W.H. Allen, 1982).

Index

242 *Index*